This book contains illuminating remarks and a nove..
perspective on an important and widely discussed classic.
And it has a special authority, being the work of one of
the author's best students and closest friends.
William Brenner, Old Dominion University, Norfolk, Virgina

This book contains two remarkable and original
contributions by Rush Rhees and D. Z. Phillips to the
burgeoning scholarship on Wittgenstein's On Certainty.
I recommend it strongly.
Avrum Stroll, University of California, San Diego

You must bear in mind that the language-game is so to say something unpredictable. I mean: it is not based on grounds. It is not reasonable (or unreasonable).

It is there – like our life.

Wittgenstein's *On Certainty*

There – Like Our Life

Rush Rhees

Edited by D. Z. Phillips

Blackwell
Publishing

© 2003, 2005 by D. Z. Phillips

BLACKWELL PUBLISHING
350 Main Street, Malden, MA 02148-5020, USA
9600 Garsington Road, Oxford OX4 2DQ, UK
550 Swanston Street, Carlton, Victoria 3053, Australia

The right of Rush Rhees to be identified as the Author of this Work has been asserted
in accordance with the UK Copyright, Designs, and Patents Act 1988.

First published 2003
First published in paperback 2005 by Blackwell Publishing Ltd

1 2005

Library of Congress Cataloging-in-Publication Data

Rhees, Rush.
    Wittgenstein's On certainty : there – like our life / Rush Rhees ; edited by
D.Z. Phillips.
        p. cm.
    Includes bibliographical references and index.
ISBN 1-40510-579-8 (alk. paper) — ISBN 1-4051-3424-0 (pbk. : alk paper)
        1. Wittgenstein, Ludwig, 1889–1951. über Gewissheit. 2. Certainty.
    I. Phillips, D.Z. (Dewi Zephaniah) II. Title.

    B3376.W563 U3 2002
    121'.63—dc21

                                                        2002074366

ISBN-13: 978-1-4051-0579-8 (alk. paper) — ISBN-13: 978-1-4051-3424-8 (pbk. : alk paper)

A catalogue record for this title is available from the British Library.

Set in 10 on 12.5 pt Galliard
by Ace Filmsetting Ltd, Frome, Somerset
Printed and bound in the United Kingdom
by TJ International, Padstow, Cornwall

The publisher's policy is to use permanent paper from mills that operate a sustainable
forestry policy, and which has been manufactured from pulp processed using acid-free and
elementary chlorine-free practices. Furthermore, the publisher ensures that the text paper
and cover board used have met acceptable environmental accreditation standards.

For further information on
Blackwell Publishing, visit our website:
www.blackwellpublishing.com

CONTENTS

CONTENTS

PREFACE

The first thing to be said of the work presented here is that it has been compiled, in the main, from notes. The notes come from two sources: those handed out by Rush Rhees during the seminars he gave on *On Certainty* in the 1970 Lent and Summer Terms at the University College of Swansea, as it was then called, and the notes I took on those occasions. The sources of the other material I have included are given in footnotes. Apart from Rhees's letter to Norman Malcolm (chapter 15), I am responsible for the titles of the chapters. I am also responsible for the title of the book, and for the divisions in the text.

The second thing to be said of the present work is that in the unlikely event of Rhees ever having published any of his notes, I am sure that the work would have taken a very different form.

These two observations bring me to the form which the present work does take. If I am asked why the notes should be published at all, my answer is easy: I think Rhees is the most perceptive reader of Wittgenstein's work, the one who sees more deeply than anyone else, in my opinion, the *connections* between different aspects of Wittgenstein's work. Rhees saw such connections in philosophy generally. It was not for him a collection of loosely knit specialisms, but a continuous enquiry into human discourse which, for Rhees, as for Wittgenstein, meant addressing the central question: What does it mean to say something? Rhees's insistence on the continuity in the *problems* Wittgenstein addressed, from his earliest to his last work, is another instance of stressing these connections, and is one of the valuable aspects of the present work.

My opinion of the value of Rhees's observations did not, in itself, solve the problem of organizing the notes at my disposal. In this matter, I have benefited from the remarks of the anonymous readers of the two publishers to whom the work was submitted. As usual, with Rhees, reactions varied from the unimpressed and slightly indignant, to the warmly receptive. The effect on me was to think the former too severe, and the latter too kind, but, in different ways, I learned from them all. For example, from the bewildered reader who said: while it would indeed be a novel and original thesis to claim that *On Certainty* was a work in logic, and that here, too, Wittgenstein is concerned with what it means to say something, there is not the slightest indication that this is so, as shown by the absence of discussions of syntax and grammar – I was given a renewed determination to show that the claims about logic and discourse are well-founded in *On Certainty*. On the other hand, I realized, later, that I could not do this without a radical reorganizing of the text. More sympathetic readers, while complaining of some repetition in the text, simply requested that, in my introduction, I should relate Rhees's emphases more explicitly to other views of *On Certainty* propounded by contemporary philosophers. I have met their request by replacing my introduction with an afterword, in which I decided that the best service I could do for the reader would be to highlight the controversial issues, in reading *On Certainty*, where Rhees differs from some other readers. In this way, hopefully, readers will be helped to reflect on these differences for themselves and carry the discussion forward. Despite my preference, however, some readers may be helped by reading the afterword first.

The sympathetic readers were too kind, however, in not calling for a more radical revision of the text, and I now find it hard to believe that I thought the version I submitted to them was acceptable. So a word of explanation is necessary.

In my first attempt at organizing the notes, I simply divided the work into two parts consisting of Rhees's notes and my own. This not only created a considerable overlap in topics, but failed to establish sufficient textual continuity. I am grateful to an early anonymous reader for getting me to see this.

In my second attempt at organizing the notes, I concentrated on a fact that I still think is very important, namely, Rhees's insistence that Wittgenstein's interest in the issues discussed in *On Certainty* did not constitute for him a new topic, the product of discussions of G. E. Moore with Norman Malcolm in 1949. Rhees insists that the questions Wittgenstein discusses are different from Moore's interests, and go back as far as 1930. I thought it a good idea, therefore, given the care Rhees took to establish this fact, to divide the work in a new way. The first half would discuss the philosophical background to *On Certainty*, namely, the discussions which lead, quite naturally, to the new issues discussed in it. The second half would then concentrate on discussions of *On Certainty* itself. Instead of keeping Rhees's notes separate from mine, I would now intersperse them in the new divisions, while still respecting the separate identity of each seminar. This was the form of my penultimate submission of the work. All that was needed, after that, I thought, was the revision of the introduction.

The question of repetition, however, continued to bother me. It was not unconnected, I believe, with my varying reactions to reading the newly constructed first half, liking it on some readings, and disliking it strongly on others. I could not help noticing that my dislike centred on my own notes, rather than those of Rhees. It took me some time to realize why. Unlike the handouts, which were self-contained and could be read at leisure, Rhees, in teaching, came back to the same points again and again from different angles. Hence the repetition in my notes. I saw that what was needed to present the background to *On Certainty* was to extract the different themes to which Rhees returned in his seminars. This is what I have tried to do in the first half of the present work. I have, therefore, made free use of my notes over the two terms, combining elements of seminars which contributed to a common theme. I hoped the result created the continuity in Wittgenstein's philosophical concerns that Rhees wanted to bring out. That result was finally improved by further useful suggestions from Blackwell's anonymous reader.

There is one piece of repetition which I have not attempted to rectify. This is the number of times it is said that Wittgenstein is concerned with what he called 'the peculiar role' played by certain empirical propositions in our discourse. I have left this unchanged simply because Rhees insists that, from first to last, this is the main theme of *On Certainty*.

I want to express my gratitude to some people other than the anonymous readers, before concluding this preface. My thanks to Timothy Tessin and Mario von der Ruhr are indicated in the text, but I am also grateful to the latter for help with proofreading the typescript. I am also grateful to Helen Baldwin, Secretary to the Department of Philosophy, for coping, with her usual efficiency, with my handwritten text in preparing the manuscript for publication.

I also want to express my gratitude to those publishers who have made it possible for me to present Rush Rhees's philosophical work to a wider audience. Two further works are under consideration at the moment: *In Dialogue with the Presocratics* and *Plato and Dialectic*. The first two works to be published were *On Religion and Philosophy* (Cambridge University Press, 1997) and *Wittgenstein and the Possibility of Discourse* (Cambridge University Press, 1998). A biographical sketch of Rhees appears in both works. These were followed by *Moral Questions* (Macmillan and St Martin's Press, 1999) and *Discussions of Simone Weil* (State University of New York Press, 1999).

I gratefully acknowledge the financial support provided by the A. E. Heath Memorial Fund at Swansea for the typing of the manuscript. It was also this fund, set up as the result of a generous gift by Mrs Heath and subscriptions by friends, in memory of A. E. Heath, Foundation Professor of Philosophy at Swansea (1925–52), which enabled the Department of Philosophy to purchase Rhees's papers after his death. The Rush Rhees Archive consists of 16,000 pages of manuscript of various kinds. Rhees, who published little during his lifetime, wrote for himself, friends and acquaintances, almost every day.

With respect to the present essay on *On Certainty*, I am deeply appreciative for the faith shown in the work by Jeff Dean of Blackwell. Over the six years I have worked on it, off and on, I think my own understanding of *On Certainty* has deepened. My hope is that, either through agreement or disagreement, this will also be the experience of readers of Rhees's discussions.

D. Z. Phillips
Swansea/Claremont

Part I
THE PHILOSOPHICAL BACKGROUND TO *ON CERTAINTY*

1

ON CERTAINTY: A NEW TOPIC?

In the last months of his life, Wittgenstein was interested in certain propositions which had been discussed by G. E. Moore. Wittgenstein's notes make up the work now called *On Certainty*. The title is not an altogether happy one. 'Certainty' is no more prominent a theme than 'knowledge', 'mistake' or 'what it is to say anything at all'.

The reference to Moore's propositions can give, and has given, readers the impression that Wittgenstein's work is devoted to a polemic against Moore's writings. This is a mistake. Wittgenstein quotes several propositions which Moore had selected and spoken about, returns to them repeatedly, as he does to other, additional, propositions, because he thinks they play a curious role in our speaking and thinking. An investigation of this role (and that is what the remarks from the beginning to the end of this book are) leads to a better understanding of human language, thought and language-games (and because of that, of science and logic, for example). Moore does not go into these questions. The propositions from Moore stand at the centre of Wittgenstein's investigations, but something different interests him. That aspect of the propositions which so impressed Wittgenstein, Moore did not notice or find very interesting. (Which is not surprising. The seeds bore fruit for Wittgenstein because they fell into the soil of his other thoughts and interests.)

Adapted, in the main, from a letter by Rhees to G. E. M. Anscombe and G. H. von Wright, dated 18 June 1969, commenting on an earlier draft of their preface to *On Certainty*, and from scattered notes in German by Rhees in the late 1960s from which Timothy Tessin extracted and translated relevant passages.

Wittgenstein quotes these propositions (a) from Moore's essay 'A Defence of Common Sense' (1925); (b) from Moore's lecture 'Proof of the External World' (1939); and (c) from Norman Malcolm's accounts of philosophical discussions with Moore.

(a) Moore lists a series of propositions which he 'knows with certainty'. Such as: that a living body now exists 'which is *my* body'; that this body was born at a definite time in the past; that since his birth he was continuously on the Earth's surface or not far from the Earth's surface; that the Earth existed many years before his birth ... and still others.

(b) Moore says: 'I can prove now, for instance, that two human hands exist. How? By holding up my two hands, and saying, as I make a certain gesture with the right hand, "Here is one hand", and adding, as I make a certain gesture with the left, "and here is another".'[1]

(c) When Malcolm lived for a time with Moore, they used to sit in the garden and discuss philosophical questions. Moore would point to a tree repeatedly and say: 'I know that that is a tree'. Wittgenstein refers to this in *On Certainty*:

> I am sitting with a philosopher in the garden; he says again and again 'I know that that's a tree', pointing to a tree that is near us. Someone else arrives and observes this, and I tell him: 'This fellow isn't insane. We are only doing philosophy.' (467)

Wittgenstein had conversations with Malcolm on a visit to the United States in 1949, including discussions of Moore's 'Defence of Common Sense' (see Malcolm's *Knowledge and Certainty*). A case may be made for saying that Malcolm aroused his interest and that *On Certainty* gives us what Wittgenstein wrote on this topic from that time until his death. This suggests that this is not the sort of discussion that Wittgenstein had had before; or that he had not written on, or discussed, these questions in these ways before. I think this is very misleading. And it may prevent people from recognizing the constant connections between these remarks and his earlier discussions. There are parallels going back at least to 1930, to the time when he began to be dissatisfied with the ways in which people spoke of 'logische Möglichkeit' and 'logisch unmöglich' (logical possibility and logical impossibility). These are examples, not just analogies.[2]

Wittgenstein used to speak of Moore's 'Defence of Common Sense' again and again, years before that visit to Malcolm. In one of his discussions in which he spoke of it, he said he had told Moore he thought this was his best article, and Moore had replied that he also thought it was. And he used to speak of the queer character of Moore's 'obviously true' propositions.

I am not questioning the point that his 1949 discussions with Malcolm about Moore's 'defence of common sense' interested him, particularly at the period he was writing the notes in *On Certainty*. My point is rather that his 1949 conversations with Malcolm stimulated Wittgenstein to take up thoughts which were not new to him, and to develop them further. These thoughts were already present in some remarks in Wittgenstein's lectures in Cambridge in the Lent and Summer Terms of the session 1937–8.

Consider the following remarks in Wittgenstein's *Investigations*.

> It is possible to imagine a case in which I *could* find out that I had two hands. Normally, however, I *cannot* do so. 'But all you need is to hold them up before your eyes!' – If I am *now* in doubt whether I have two hands, I need not believe my eyes either. (I might just as well ask a friend.)
>
> With this is connected the fact that, for instance, the proposition 'The Earth has existed for millions of years' makes clearer sense than 'The Earth has existed in the last five minutes'. For I should ask anyone who asserted the latter: 'What observations does this proposition refer to; and what observations would count against it?' – whereas I know what ideas and observations the former proposition goes with.

I know, of course, that there is much more than this in *On Certainty*. But it is not a development which began in 1949.

[In their published preface to *On Certainty*, G. E. M. Anscombe and G. H. von Wright write: 'Malcolm acted as a goad to his interest in Moore's "defence of common sense"', and the propositions he discussed there, but also that 'Wittgenstein had long been interested in these'. The following chapters show how that interest is connected with wider issues and wider developments in Wittgenstein's earlier and later thought.][3]

2

SAYING AND DESCRIBING

Wittgenstein's earliest and last concern was: what does it mean to say something? For Wittgenstein, the earliest asking of this question took the form: what is a proposition? Plato in the *Sophist* speaks of conditions for the possibility of discourse. He was concerned with the distinction between philosophy and sophistry, between genuine discourse and sham discourse. Not showing *how* the distinction is to be made, but *that* there is one to make. There are dangers in this way of speaking. If you speak of 'conditions', of genuine and sham discourse, it may seem as though you could find some sort of measure or criterion by which what is really language can be distinguished from what is not, although it appears at first as if it were.

What is to rule out a sentence whose surface grammar is correct as nonsense? Unless you have a general criterion doesn't anything go? In his earlier work, as Wittgenstein characterized it later, he recognized that there is a great deal of ambiguity and imperfection in colloquial speech. He then searched for the 'pure article'. He was interested in the question of what makes language into language:

'But still, it isn't a game, if there is some vagueness *in the rules*'. – But *does* this prevent its being a game? – 'Perhaps you'll call it a game, but at any rate it certainly isn't a perfect game.' This means: it has impurities, and what I am interested in at present is the pure article. – But I want to say: we misunderstand the role of the ideal in our language. That is to say: we too should call it a game, only we are dazzled by the ideal and therefore fail to see the actual use of the word 'game' clearly. (*Investigations* I: 100)

So this is one of the dangers we may fall into in recognizing Plato's distinction between genuine and sham discourse. Sham discourse for Wittgenstein would include metaphysics – we seem to be asking or saying something when we are not.

In the *Tractatus* it seems as though he were trying to discover, by logical analysis, certain principles on which the intelligibility of language depends. He wanted to find the general form of the proposition. What is the difference between saying something and making a noise or a mark on paper? At the time of the *Tractatus* he thought that if it is 'saying something', it must have something in common with all other cases of saying something. If you admit ambiguity, all seems lost. We don't have to learn sentences. If we understand words and syntax then we understand the sentence. That assumes that words in their syntax do say something.

Wittgenstein argued in the *Tractatus* that there are elementary propositions and that we can show their relation to each other. In all this there does seem to be an attempt to show what the intelligibility of what is said depends on.

One of the curious things about the *Tractatus* was that he wanted to say that certain combinations of symbols not only *didn't* have sense, but *couldn't* have sense. This was a position which he gave up later. From the early 1930s on he didn't try to discover something in the way words in a proposition are put together, which would show how they could have sense or not. In the *Tractatus* he said that certain propositions haven't any meaning because we haven't given them any, but there were some propositions which couldn't have meaning.

At one stage, fairly soon after the *Tractatus*, Wittgenstein held that if a proposition is a genuine proposition its meaning can be brought out by logical analysis. The use of analysis differed from the *Tractatus* period. He thought of it as showing the relation between any proposition and the sense-data in terms of which the meaning of any proposition can in some way be analysed. Certain data are heard, felt, seen, etc., and the possibility of analysing more complex expressions, and the possibility of there being meaning in them, depends on showing their relation to those immediately experienced data.[1] The Logical Positivists said that the meaning of a proposition is its method of verification.

The idea was that 'the given', say, a red patch, is simply seen. We don't have to ask what it means. The whole analysis ends with what is seen, as though the notion of 'seeing' were itself simply given, and not open to further analysis. This is what Wittgenstein is countering in the later discussions in the *Investigations*. Compare what he says about related concepts – seeing, experiencing, etc.

7

Wittgenstein wants to reject this way of speaking, the view that there must be primary data on which all else depends (Russell's ultimate furniture of the world, Quine's ontology – 'what there is'); that on which the possibility of discourse depends.

If the idea of 'seeing' is not as unitary or simple as analysis in terms of sense-data suggests – if the concept of seeing itself stands in need of conceptual analysis – it does not have the unquestioned character that seems to qualify it as the basis for all analysis.

But the matter goes further. A long time before writing Part Two of the *Investigations* Wittgenstein had begun to question the assumption that there must be one way to distinguish language from what is not language. The notion of 'saying something' is not a single notion, but a family of notions, and the same is true of language itself. The question 'What makes language possible?' hasn't much meaning for Wittgenstein.

If one says that language doesn't always mean the same thing, it isn't simply that there are different styles and different grammars – that French is more idiomatic than German – but that *what you mean by speaking of it as language is different in the one case from the others.* This is what Wittgenstein is trying to work through by his conceptual analysis and his ideas of games and families.

In the notes he was writing for the 1930 'Preface', he says of the *Tractatus* (he does not use that title) that it gave too much the appearance of a scientific work, suggesting that it was making or stating *discoveries*. He said this went with a false view of logical analysis he had held at the time.

> In my earlier book the solution of the problems is not presented in a sufficiently common-or-garden way; it makes it seem as though discoveries were needed in order to solve our problems; and not enough has been done to bring everything into the form of the grammatically obvious in ordinary ways of speaking. Everything gives too much the appearance of discoveries.

He made other remarks on these lines again and again. He thought it very important; he was constantly revising what he had written in this sense; and he knew (and said) that the greatest difficulty was to state everything in common-or-garden language (the Austrian 'hausbacken' is literally, 'home-baked') and *at the same time* to achieve and preserve exactitude, and avoid woolliness. Russell, for instance, could not see that Wittgenstein *was* preserving exactitude, or even that he was trying to. So he said that in later life Wittgenstein grew tired of hard thinking and invented a method to make it unnecessary. Although Wittgenstein sent Russell a copy of the *Blue Book*, I doubt if Russell ever read more than the first few pages, if that.

People like Quine, for instance – whom Russell admires – think that the use of special terms and symbolism is indispensable in philosophy, and that it 'yields new insights' which could not be reached if we just kept to ordinary home-baked expressions. Wittgenstein's opposition to this sort of view is not just an aesthetic one. It goes with his whole investigation of, and discussion of, the difference between sense and nonsense; of meaning, of insight, of the relation of thought and reality. He went into these questions more deeply and more persistently than Russell ever did, and, I suspect, Quine.

Discussing questions in a 'common-or-garden' way is connected with the 'revolution' in the way of discussing philosophical problems which Wittgenstein was introducing. The phrase 'revolution in philosophy' (not Wittgenstein's, I think) is likely to be misleading too. For Wittgenstein used to say and repeat that he was discussing the same problems that Plato discussed. We cannot say: 'It is a pity that Wittgenstein could not have presented his ideas in something more nearly the accepted philosophical style, more in the style of Ayer or Quine.' *That would not have been a presentation of his philosophical views.* The point is partly that he was bringing out – from many angles, coming back to the question again and again – the connection of these questions: the questions Plato was discussing, with our understanding and thinking altogether. And I would add: with our *lives* altogether. Cf: 'to imagine a language is to imagine a form of life' – and, more important, *Investigations* II: xii, p. 230. If Russell and others want to talk of 'the *cult*' of ordinary language – well, so it seems to them, I suppose. But Wittgenstein had *very* deep reasons for what he was doing.[2]

By *On Certainty* Wittgenstein is pretty far from any attempt to show what the intelligibility of what is said depends on. He has given up the idea of a general form of the proposition, or of a general structure of language. If we ask what it is to say something, or how a set of sounds is distinct from gibberish, no single answer is given, unless we take as a single answer that it must play a part in a language-game. This latter expression is far vaguer than the expression 'general form of the proposition'. It may be determinate enough in certain cases: a meeting to clinch a business deal is very different from a meeting of people to relate the latest gossip. So what we call a language-game is extremely varied. The notion of a language-game is not closed. No definite limit about what you would count in it. So if you do take the above as a single answer, it does not tell you how to fit it to any particular case so far.

Language-games *are* different. Haggling over prices in the market-place, discussion of a report in physics, discussion of how the scrum-half should have played. *What you would mean by playing a role would differ greatly.* So 'proposition' or 'sentence' doesn't have one meaning. *Whether* it plays a role is not determined by what combination of sounds or marks are logically possible, but by whether uttering that sound or making that set of marks makes any difference to what people say and whether it brings any response.

On a superficial level this may seem like a quasi-sociological or a quasi-psychological report. This may be reinforced by what Wittgenstein says repeatedly about not giving an explanation or justification – not wanting to discover something we didn't know before. So isn't it like sociology – a description of the natural practice?

Wittgenstein's use of 'description' here is puzzling. It isn't like describing the habits and customs of a particular tribe. It isn't like describing a conversation. If a man is gifted he can describe a conversation in a gripping or humorous manner. So far that isn't sociology: it is reporting. In the English counties they speak in a certain way, and this could be compared and contrasted with the way they speak on Tyneside or in Somerset. This might be part of a sociological investigation of some sort. It wouldn't be the sort of thing that would be called a philosophical account of language. Sometimes, Wittgenstein is as concerned to describe possible ways of talking as he is to describe actual ones. His interest is not to formulate laws about the behaviour of people, but to consider different possibilities in what we would call language or speaking. His interest is still in the question of what speaking or saying something is. But now he wouldn't say 'It must be of the form so-and-so'.

In the remarks in *On Certainty* he uses 'logic' as equivalent to philosophy. He makes such statements as that the description of a language-game belongs to logic. It looks as if logic is now a set of descriptions. But if one thinks of descriptions of conversations like John Morgan's or Margaret Mead's, that is not what he calls logic. As we have seen in 'A Defence of Common Sense', Moore enumerates a number of propositions which he says that he knows, with certainty, to be true. Wittgenstein gives no such list of things that can be known. What interests him is the peculiar role these propositions play. He is investigating what we do with these propositions. The investigation becomes a concern of logic in asking these questions; in asking what the possibility of going on speaking depends on.

3

CONCEPT-FORMATION

In *On Certainty* Wittgenstein is interested in the role played in our lives by the propositions which, Moore says, we do not question. Someone may say that it is difficult to see how these propositions which constitute the ground that we have our feet on, account for the grammatical forms that we do use. Wittgenstein doesn't pretend that they do. What needs emphasizing is that when we consider the roles of these propositions it seems that we have to start with our feet on the ground. We have to learn the language in use. You start with certain matters of fact. Without that, language could not be carried on at all. But this doesn't do much to tell us why the language has the form it does.

There is an important passage in the *Investigations* which is closely related to these issues. I am referring to sub-section xii of Part Two:

> If the formation of concepts can be explained by facts of nature, should we not be interested, not in grammar, but rather in that in nature which is the basis of grammar? – Our interest certainly includes the correspondence between concepts and very general facts of nature. (Such facts as mostly do not strike us because of their generality.) But our interest does not fall back upon these possible causes of the formation of concepts; we are not doing natural science; nor yet natural history – since we can invent fictitious natural history for our purposes.
>
> I am not saying: if such-and-such facts of nature were different, people would have different concepts (in the sense of a hypothesis). But: if anyone believes that certain concepts are absolutely the correct ones, and that having different ones would mean not realizing something that we realize – then let him imagine certain very general facts of nature to be different from what we are used to, and the formation of concepts different from the usual ones will become intelligible to him.

> Compare a concept with a style of painting. For is even our style of paint-
> ing arbitrary? Can we choose one at pleasure? (The Egyptian, for instance.)
> Is it a mere question of pleasing and ugly?

Can the formation of concepts be explained by the facts of nature? Wittgenstein would not be ready himself to say that they could be explained by facts of nature. He is not saying: given different facts of nature then you will have these different concepts. It is not like Newton's definition of a body: must have a definite size, shape, etc. (cf. Locke's primary qualities). Suppose we talk in a different way. He says that if you can imagine that certain facts of nature were different, you could imagine how the formation of concepts could be different. So it seems as if the formation of concepts is at the separate pole from the notion of empirical propositions which you can't doubt.

For example, Wittgenstein talks of measuring the length of rods. It may be said that our methods of measurement, and the possibility of calling it 'measurement' at all, depends on the fact that the instruments we employ are rigid. They don't change their shapes. The grocer takes it for granted that he can weigh a piece of cheese. If it were to diminish or expand suddenly – Well?

But there is an institution of weighing. It might have been a game. It is called 'weighing' because it is connected with prices and other things we do. It isn't placing the rod on the table which makes it 'measuring'. You might do that and it is not measuring. It depends on the institution. (There is no sharp boundary between what is and what is not an institution.)

'But measurement *depends* on the behaviour of rods, etc. ...' But what does 'depend on' mean? Would it be impossible to measure if rods were not rigid? Could we weigh cheese if rods suddenly diminished or expanded? No, but we might still go on doing with them what we do. We might get results that we now call crazy, but we could go on. (If we're British we probably would!)

More radically, imagine a nuclear war in which all countries where science is practised are annihilated, or serious brain damage is caused so that no one remembers science. The people consult oracles (*OC:* 608). The presence of scientific thinking (the law of induction, conducting experiments and drawing conclusions from them) is one of the principal features of what we would call 'our way of speaking' and it distinguishes it from others. This does rest on the existence of a body of scientific teaching and of certain practices or methods of investigation. They aren't justified or doubted. But, now, after the changes, people consult oracles. Wittgenstein considers a likely reaction:

12

'But is there no objective truth? Isn't it true or false, that someone has been on the moon?' If we are thinking within our system, then it is certain that no one has ever been on the moon. Not merely is nothing of the sort ever seriously reported to us by reasonable people, but our whole system of physics forbids us to believe it. For this demands answers to the questions 'How did he overcome the force of gravity?' 'How would he live without an atmosphere?' and a thousand others which could not be answered. But suppose that instead of all these answers we met the reply: 'We don't know *how* one gets to the moon, but those who get there know at once that they are there; and even you can't explain everything.' We should feel ourselves intellectually very distant from someone who said this. (*OC:* 108)

Now you could answer these questions, but the important point is the last answer in the paragraph. 'We don't know *how* one gets to the moon, but those who get there know at once that they are there; and even you can't explain everything.' We feel intellectually distant from someone who would give *that* answer. We want to ask certain questions, and if someone says that they aren't relevant, we find it hard to see what 'relevance' could mean. In other cases you can imagine the sort of differences challenging what we take for granted would make.

Wittgenstein said in conversation (with me), but soon retracted it, that the propositions he was interested in are self-evident. He meant, not simply propositions in geometry, but propositions such as 'There can't be a reddish-green'. We might say that the latter is not self-evident since people have questioned it. Blue-red-green-yellow are named by people who write about colours as primary colours, and they treat other colours as 'mixed colours'. (There are objections to this way of talking since it suggests 'components'. This is all right for the points, but not for the colour of the points.) It is better to speak of 'intermediate colours'. Some who talk of 'pure' colours say that no one has ever seen them! They argue over how many primary colours there are. Some say 'yellow' is not a primary colour, but a mixture of blue and green.

None of these is an empirical proposition. Neither is 'Blue is darker than yellow'. They are part of our grammar of colours. Many have said, 'The same spot cannot be red and green', meaning 'reddish-green', but say, 'We can say it is red and yellow', meaning it is orange. Wittgenstein would call the phrase 'There can't be a reddish-green' a concept-forming phrase since it helps to fix our conception of 'red' and 'green'. Suppose someone says, 'Have you looked far enough?' Nonsense. There is no more chance of finding that than there is of finding a round square. Some have said that 'olive-green' counts, but others rule it out.

13

The clearest examples of concept-formation are in mathematics. Suppose that you prove that you can't trisect an angle with ruler and compass. Suppose you say that you can't construct a heptagon – a building with seven sides doesn't count. You are fixing conceptions in geometry. You can divide an angle into three parts, but that isn't trisection in geometry. But you can find examples of concept-formation in other contexts, too, for example, in the legal sphere in conceptions of property, etc. What if someone says that a poet is original because he wrote a sonnet with sixteen lines?

We might ask how far this business of concept-formation is arbitrary. Is mathematics arbitrary, like a game? Like the game of chess? (Frege: people didn't distinguish between the game and the theory of chess. *Given* the game, the theory isn't arbitrary.) If we said mathematics has no connection with 'application' then we might wonder how, if it has no connection with what goes on in physics, etc., it ever got going. Those revolted at the idea of mathematics as a game, suggested that mathematics refers to facts. Wittgenstein discusses this in his *Remarks on the Foundation of Mathematics*.

Multiplication is not an experiment. All right. But what is a fact? Doesn't mathematics enter into the character of what you call a fact? Mathematics determines the form of the kinds of questions you ask in physics. How many vibrations in a sound? Thus it gets its meaning from mathematics – 'How many?' Whenever you're applying the physical sciences, mathematics enters what you call 'the facts'; the sorts of things you look for are determined by mathematics. So mathematics is an important concept-forming activity.

> 'If calculation is to be practical, then it must uncover facts. And only experiment can do that.'
>
> But what things are 'facts'? Do you believe that you can show what fact is meant by, e.g., pointing to it with your finger? Does that of itself clarify the part played by 'establishing' a fact? – Suppose it takes mathematics to define the *character* of what you are calling a 'fact'!
>
> 'It is interesting to know *how many* variations this note has! But it took arithmetic to teach you this question. It taught you to see this kind of fact.'[1]

In *On Certainty* Wittgenstein is exploring the role played by the kind of empirical propositions mentioned by Moore. There is an important difference between the role of concept-formation in mathematics, and the way that seems to determine the way we speak, on the one hand, and, on the other hand, the role played by these empirical propositions. It seems that the latter play a very different role. Consider the following in *On Certainty.*

14

What sort of proposition is: 'What could a mistake here be like!'? It would have to be a logical proposition. But it is a logic that is not used, because what it tells us is not taught by means of propositions. – It is a logical proposition; for it does describe the conceptual (linguistic) situation. (*OC:* 51)

This situation is thus not the same for a proposition like 'At this distance from the sun there is a planet' and 'Here is a hand' (namely my own hand). The second can't be called a hypothesis. But there isn't a sharp boundary line between them. (*OC:* 52)

But the difference is not a difference in degree:

For it is not true that a mistake merely gets more and more improbable as we pass from the planet to my own hand. No: at some point it has ceased to be conceivable.

This is already suggested by the following: if it were not so, it would also be conceivable that we should be wrong in *every* statement about physical objects; that any we ever make are mistaken. (*OC:* 54)

When one says: 'Perhaps this planet doesn't exist and the light-phenomenon arises in some other way', then after all one needs an example of an object which does exist. This doesn't exist – as *for example* does ...

Or are we to say that *certainty* is merely a constructed point which some things approximate more, some less closely? No. Doubt gradually loses its sense. This language-game just *is* like that.

And everything descriptive of a language-game is part of logic. (*OC:* 56)

15

4

'SEEING' AND 'THINKING'

In section 2 we said that

> fairly soon after the *Tractatus*, Wittgenstein held that if a proposition is a
> genuine proposition its meaning can be brought out by logical analysis ...
> He thought of it as showing the relation between any proposition and the
> sense-data in terms of which the meaning of any proposition can in some
> sense be analysed. Certain data are heard, felt, seen, etc., and the possibility
> of analysing more complex expressions, and the possibility of there being
> meaning in them, depends on showing their relation to these immediately
> experienced data. The Logical Positivists said that the meaning of a proposi-
> tion is its method of verification. The idea was that 'the given', say, a red
> patch, is simply seen. We don't have to ask what it means. The whole analysis
> ends with what is seen, as though the notion of 'seeing' were itself simply
> given, and not open to further analysis. (See p. 7)

Why did people emphasize primary data? They, like Russell and
Wittgenstein, were interested in showing *definitely* that the propositions
under analysis are verified. In immediate experience it was thought one
had a verification which left no question open.

Carnap and Ayer used to speak of observation statements in a physicalist
sense as 'pure reporting' of what you see – as if 'what you see' is
unproblematic. Compare the attempt to define 'physical object'. Russell
attempted this in terms of his 'logical constructions'. A table is a logical
construction out of sense-data. G. E. Moore put it by saying that to know
what is meant by a table we get down to pointing and saying, 'That's a
table'. The difficulty Moore was interested in was what 'that' refers to. The

answer is that it refers to the sense-datum and yet we are not saying of the sense-data, 'That's a stone' or 'That's a table'. The realities are the sense-data. Russell also speaks of tables and stones as 'logical fictions'.

Behind this way of speaking is the suggestion that what is really seen is the sense-datum, and that the physical object is not seen in that sense at all. This is the kind of thing that Wittgenstein is questioning. He is pointing out that 'empirical proposition' is more ragged than you might have thought at first. And this is connected with the fact that this is equally true of the notion of 'seeing'.

Wittgenstein discusses these issues in section xi of Part Two of the *Investigations* which, if it were to have a title, could be called 'Seeing and Thinking'. We stated the problem for any simple appeal to 'what is seen' in the following words in section 2: 'If the idea of "seeing" is not as unitary or simple as analysis in terms of sense-data suggests – if the concept of seeing itself stands in need of conceptual analysis – it does not have the unquestioned character that seems to qualify it as the basis for all analysis' (p. 8). It is the need for further analysis that Wittgenstein illustrates with telling examples in this section of the *Investigations*.

In section xi of Part Two of the *Investigations,* one of Wittgenstein's main points is that if you want to make a comparison between what is said, and what is merely seen, felt or touched, this is odd, because the idea of what is *merely* seen would have a very limited application. It leaves out the notion of seeing something as something. It looks at first sight like a comparison of say a house agent's description of what you see. Here you can compare the account with visual data. But, then, you move to compare *anything* said with purely visual data. How can we compare our agreements and disagreements in use with 'what is there'? This is connected with the difficulty in the *Tractatus* of 'simply seeing' that elementary propositions do or do not hold. The difficulty is that what constitutes agreement or disagreement is not simply given. Similar difficulties are involved in our use of the term 'description'. Nothing counts as 'the one and only fundamental description'. Similar issues are involved in the discussion of the distinction between correct and incorrect description. What is it that decides that? Consider the following:

Two uses of the word 'see'.
The one: 'What do you see there?' – 'I see *this* (and then a description, a drawing, a copy). The other: 'I see a likeness between these two faces' – let the man I tell this to be seeing the faces as clearly as I do myself.'
The importance of this is the difference of category between the two 'objects' of sight.
The one man might make an accurate drawing of the two faces, and the other notice in the drawing the likeness which the former did not see.[1]

17

These differences between the uses of 'see' is not an ambiguity as is the case between 'river bank' and 'Bank of England'. The two uses of 'see' are clearly related. He calls the second 'noticing an aspect'.

For the positivists, all this came under 'pure observation'! The difficulty is that they assume that all this is perfectly simple, but what is to be included? You may report what you see, describe what you see, but the same variety will come into the description.

> The concept of 'seeing' makes a tangled impression. Well, it is tangled – I look at the landscape, my gaze ranges over it, I see all sorts of distinct and indistinct movement; *this* impresses itself sharply on me, *that* is quite hazy. After all, how completely ragged what we see can appear! And now look at all that can be meant by 'description of what is seen'. – But this just is what is called description of what is seen. There is not *one genuine* proper case of such description – the rest being just vague, something which awaits clarification, or which must just be swept aside as rubbish.[2]

We may want to say, 'Language tells us about things', but there are problems here. Pointing – 'That's the thing', or 'It will happen in such-and-such a way, and it did'. What is this correspondence? What is it about words which enabled me to do this?

Wittgenstein asks in Part Two of the *Investigations*, What makes my image of him an image of *him*? The mental image is pretty vague. In so far as it is a physical image it could apply to many, but, no, it is an image of *him*. In one place he says that this sums up the problem of the representational character of language.

I want to relate this to the notion of 'seeing different aspects'. How is seeing different aspects of a picture linked with philosophical logic? How can such details be related to any of the central questions of philosophy? Wittgenstein says:

> F. P. Ramsey once emphasized in conversation with me that logic was a 'normative science'. I do not know exactly what he had in mind, but it was doubtless closely related to what only dawned on me later: namely, that in philosophy we often *compare* the use of words with games and calculi which have fixed rules, but cannot say that someone who is using language *must* be playing such a game. – But if you say that our languages only *approximate* to such calculi you are standing on the very brink of a misunderstanding. For then it may look as if what we were talking about were an *ideal* language. As if our logic were, so to speak, a logic for a vacuum. – Whereas logic does not treat of language – or of thought – in the sense in which a natural science treats of a natural phenomenon, and the most that can be said is that we *construct* ideal languages. But

18

here the word 'ideal' is liable to mislead, for it sounds as if these languages were better, more perfect, than our everyday language; and as if it took the logician to show people at last what a proper sentence looked like.

All this, however, can only appear in the right light when one has attained greater clarity about the concepts of understanding, meaning, and thinking. For it will then also become clear what can lead us (and did lead me) to think that if anyone utters a sentence and *means* or *understands* it he is operating a calculus according to definite rules.[3]

All I am trying to show is that Wittgenstein's discussion of 'seeing different aspects' is part of his discussion of language and understanding. Differences between terms are emphasized – understanding an explanation in physics is different from understanding a poem, and 'explaining' would be different in each context. Now that he has deserted anything like ultimate meanings or constituents, to ask whether something is a proposition is to ask whether it has a role in a language-game. It will not have the same sense in one language-game as in another. But, now, what happens to the charge that, as a result, anything goes? That conclusion simply does not follow. The following needs to be emphasized:

> 'If a proposition too is conceived as a picture of a possible state of affairs and is said to show the possibility of the state of affairs, still the most that the proposition can do is what a painting or relief or film does: and so it can at any rate not set forth what is not the case. So does it depend wholly on our grammar what will be called (logically) possible and what not, – i.e. what the grammar permits?' – But surely that is arbitrary! – Is it arbitrary? – It is not every sentence-like formation that we know how to do something with, not every technique has an application in our life; and when we are tempted in philosophy to count some quite useless thing as a proposition, that is often because we have not considered its application sufficiently.[4]

This may seem vague when compared with the aspiration of showing definitely that the propositions under analysis are verified by an immediate experience which left no question open. All right, but this does not prevent us from recognizing that certain apparent propositions have no application, and in recognizing others as ones we do agree with. This is what Wittgenstein discusses further in *On Certainty*, but here in the *Investigations*, too, he says:

> Our mistake is to look for an explanation where we ought to look at what happens as a 'proto-phenomenon'. That is, where we ought to have said: *this language-game is played.*

19

The question is not one of explaining a language-game by means of our experiences, but of noting a language-game.[5]

But the language-games we need to note differ from each other in many ways. It is important in elementary mathematics that people do agree on the results they get. Without this you wouldn't have a conception of a correct result, but this does not mean that 'correct' *means* 'the results everyone gets'.

> Of course, in one sense mathematics is a branch of knowledge, – but still it is also an *activity*. And 'false moves' can only exist as the exception. For if what we now call by that name became the rule, the game in which they were false moves would have been abrogated.
> 'We all learn the same multiplication table.' This might, no doubt, be a remark about the teaching of arithmetic in our schools, – but also an observation about the concept of the multiplication table. ('In a horse-race the horses generally run as fast as they can.')[6]

Compare colours:

> Does it make sense to say that people generally agree in their judgements of colour? What would it be like for them not to? – One man would say a flower was red which another called blue, and so on. – But what right should we have to call these people's words 'red' and 'blue' *our* 'colour-words'?
> How would they learn to use these words? And is the language-game which they learn still such as we call the use of 'names of colour'? There are evidently differences of degree here.[7]

'The agreement in colour judgements' – is that an empirical or a grammatical remark? It is not like: 'Most people prefer this kind of wine', where we can imagine the contrary. If we didn't agree about colours we couldn't speak of judgements of colour at all. You can't learn the colour word as an individual as though the agreement were one you could check directly, like seeing one's hand in contact with a chair.

Agreement in judgements in mathematics and in colours makes results possible in these two contexts:

> 'But mathematical truth is independent of whether human beings know it or not!' – Certainly, the propositions 'Human beings believe that twice two is four' and 'Twice two is four' do not mean the same. The latter is a mathematical proposition; the other, if it make sense at all, may perhaps mean: human beings have *arrived* at the mathematical proposition. The two propo-

sitions have entirely different *uses*. – But what would *this* mean: 'Even though everybody believed that twice two was five it would still be four'? For what would it be like for everybody to believe that? – Well, I could imagine, for instance, that people had a different calculus, or a technique which we should not call 'calculating'. But would it be *wrong*?[8]

About half way through sub-section xi of Part Two of the *Investigations* Wittgenstein introduces the term *aspect-blindness* (p. 213), by analogy with colour-blindness or tone deafness. Some will hear a melody, but others don't. Some see colour distinctions, and others don't. He wants to emphasize or ask whether there might be people incapable of seeing an aspect in that way, who had not the capacity to 'see something *as* something': to see the figure as a hexagon or as a cube, say. He emphasizes that, in some cases, being able to see a geometrical drawing (triangle) now like *this*, now like *that*, has for its *substratum the mastery of a technique*:

> In the triangle I can see now *this* as apex, *that* as base – now *this* as apex, *that* as base. – Clearly the words 'Now I am seeing *this* as the apex' cannot so far mean anything to a learner who has only just met the concepts of apex, base, and so on. – But I do not mean this as an empirical proposition.
> 'Now he's seeing it like *this*', 'now like *that*' would only be said of someone *capable* of making certain applications of the figure quite freely.
> The substratum of this experience is the mastery of a technique.[9]

He could only see one aspect and now another if there is mastery of a technique. This capacity depends on a certain training. In many cases it depends on something learned. How you see a figure in descriptive geometry will be different from one who knows nothing about geometry. It is not a question of what the drawing suggests to him, but of how he sees it. Compare an archeologist coming across broken pottery with someone to whom it means nothing.

> Ought he to be able to see the schematic cube as a cube? – It would not follow from that that he could not recognize it as a representation (a working drawing for instance) of a cube. But for him it would not jump from one aspect to the other. – Question: Ought he to be able to *take* it as a cube in certain circumstances, as we do? – If not, this could not very well be called a sort of blindness.
> The 'aspect-blind' will have an altogether different relationship to pictures from ours.
> (Anomalies of *this* kind are easy for us to imagine.)
> Aspect-blindness will be *akin* to the lack of a 'musical ear'.[10]

In this way Wittgenstein is bringing out that 'empirical proposition' is not sharply defined. And similarly for 'describing'. He is discussing, e.g., seeing what is drawn here, and copying what you see with pencil and paper; seeing a similarity between what is drawn here and what is drawn there; seeing this now one way (concave), now in another way (convex), etc. We should speak of *seeing*, in each case, not of *interpreting* what we see.

In some cases, as we have seen, the mastery of a technique is the logical condition of seeing. We can see the triangle as standing up, as having fallen over, or as hanging. 'Seeing as' is not interpreting what you see – but that's how I see it.

> A triangle can really be *standing up* in one picture, be hanging in another, and can in a third be something that has fallen over ... Could I say what a picture must be like to produce this effect? No. There are, for example, styles of painting which do not convey anything to me in this immediate way, but do to other people. *I think custom and upbringing have a hand in this.*[11]

Wittgenstein asks: 'What does anyone tell me by saying "Now I see it as ..."? What consequences has this information? What can I do with it?'[12] Wittgenstein does meet this question with what he goes on to say. But obviously such utterances, and the responses that may be made to them, are different from the 'reporting what he sees' by someone in a look-out or someone at a microscope. It is not that language-game.

If you were asked what you'd learned or come to see in the custom and upbringing Wittgenstein refers to, would you include seeing it under certain aspects? No! It is more like the remark in *On Certainty* that if a child is told someone climbed a mountain some time ago, you aren't taught that the mountain exists. You swallow that down with what you do learn.

Wittgenstein gives many examples of 'seeing as', but there are differences between them. The duck-rabbit – seeing it one way or the other depends on one's experience in *other* contexts, whereas seeing a white cross on a black background or vice versa does not depend on previous experience of that sort at all. These differences are important. Sometimes aspect-blindness depends on the mastery of a technique, but sometimes it doesn't. Suppose you found a people for whom seeing the white or black cross in those circumstances did not occur. We might compare them with the colour-blind, but can we speak of people as aspect-blind? There may be no physiological defect. (There is a physical theory to explain colour-blindness.)

Wittgenstein is interested in how seeing one aspect and now another bears on understanding words. 'Seeing' and 'thinking' as concepts run into one another often in bewildering ways. Seeing is just as puzzling as thinking. It is not a simple matter. You may be struck by an expression on a man's face. 'Is being struck looking plus thinking? No. Many of our concepts *cross* here.'[13]

What happens, in these different contexts, to the analogy between 'aspect-blindness' and colour-blindness? There are ways of establishing colour-blindness, since for the most part people agree entirely when they speak of the colours things have. *'This characterizes the concept of colour statements'* – and otherwise 'saying what colour it has', 'being able to tell what colour it has', would not mean what we understand by these expressions now. But *'There is in general no such agreement over the question whether an expression of feeling is genuine or not'*. We might say: the question does not get its sense from any such general agreement. It is not the agreement among people which *gives sense to asking* whether the expression of feeling is genuine or sham.

> There is such a thing as colour-blindness and there are ways of establishing it. There is in general complete agreement in the judgements of colours made by those who have been diagnosed normal. This characterizes the concept of a judgement of colour.
>
> There is in general no such agreement over the question whether an expression of feeling is genuine or not.[14]
>
> 'The genuineness of an expression cannot be proved; one has to feel it.' – Very well, – but what does one go on to do with this recognition of genuineness? If someone says 'Voilà ce que peut dire un coeur vraiment épris'[15] – and if he also brings someone else to the same mind, – what are the further consequences? Or are there none, and does the game *end* with one person's relishing what another does not?[16]

Was he genuine? We may disagree. 'I am sure: *sure*, that he is not pretending; but some third is not. Can I always convince him? And if not, is there some mistake in his reasoning or observations?'[17] If two physicians disagree over a diagnosis, one *must* be wrong. But in disagreement over the expression of feeling: 'He isn't pretending' – 'Eyewash', there is no question of proof. 'It is certainly possible to be convinced by evidence that someone is in such-and-such a state of mind, that, for instance, he is not pretending. But "evidence" here includes "imponderable" evidence.'[18] Such evidence would include tone of expression, facial expressions, etc. This would enter into one's determination of whether he is charming or not. Wittgenstein refers to this as knowledge of human beings, knowledge of people.

Is there such a thing as 'expert judgement' about the genuineness of expressions of feeling? – Even here, there are those whose judgement is 'better' and those whose judgement is 'worse'.

Correcter prognoses will generally issue from the judgements of those with better knowledge of mankind.

Can one learn this knowledge? Yes; some can. Not, however, by taking a course in it, but through '*experience*'. – Can someone else be a man's teacher in this? Certainly. From time to time he gives him the right *tip*. – This is what 'learning' and 'teaching' are like here. – What one acquires here is not a technique; one learns correct judgements. There are also rules, but they do not form a system, and only experienced people can apply them right. Unlike calculating-rules.[19]

(I should have thought – if the teacher is someone from whom one learns here – then it is less from *tips* that I'd learn than by noticing the judgements which the teacher himself makes. I'd have guessed that this is what *OC:* 139 says about examples, and the way in which examples supplement rules: 'Not only rules, but also examples are needed for establishing a practice. Our rules leave loop-holes open, and the practice has to speak for itself.' – But I do not deny that tips may help, may open one's eyes. But then the teacher is rare. And most tips mislead more than they help.)[20]

This is connected with what Wittgenstein calls the game of guessing people's thoughts. Suppose I said that he had guessed my thoughts correctly. This is not like checking quotations against what is written on a certain page:

> I write down a sentence which the other person cannot see. He has to guess the words or their sense. – Yet another: I am putting a jig-saw puzzle together; the other person cannot see me but from time to time guesses my thoughts and utters them. He says, for instance, 'Now where is this bit?' – '*Now* I know how it fits!' – 'I have no idea what goes in here.' – 'The sky is always the hardest part' and so on – but *I* need not be talking to myself either out loud or silently at the time.[21]

But now: 'Let us assume there was a man who always guessed right what I was saying to myself in my thoughts. (It does not matter how he manages it.) But what is the criterion for his guessing *right*?'[22] The criterion is the truthfulness of the person being referred to, not the description of a process.

A dreamer may write down an account of his dream. The first account is more important than a secondary elaboration. But why is the first-person account more accurate? How do you know this? There is no criterion of truth apart from truthfulness. He may be spinning a yarn, but this has nothing to do with correspondence to the dream. Rather, it raises the issue of how we judge people's motives. Suppose we say: only he knows what his motives really are; he alone knows his motives.

We ought to be struck by the language-game in which I tell you my motives. What am I telling you? Aldous Huxley tried to describe the experiences he had after taking mescaline. He talks about looking at certain objects and seeing certain features, or he describes images he had. There one can talk of what is going on in one's mind, but when I tell you what my motives are, it is nothing like that. Telling someone what one's motives are is not like telling the doctor where the pains are. You are not relating experiences.

If I tell you the state of my bank account you can go and check. But in telling you my motives, the *telling* is different: 'I wanted to embarrass him.' This may play an important part in discussion and investigation. I can ask whether the lay-out of a house *corresponds to reality*. Does an account of motives *correspond to reality*? 'Correspond to reality' doesn't mean the same. 'Ask not: "What goes on in us when we are certain that ... ?" – but: How is "the certainty that this is the case" manifested in human action?'[23]

Of course one's judgements in these contexts will have consequences, but these cannot be formulated in a general way.

> There are certainly *consequences*, but of a diffuse kind. Experience, that is varied observation, can inform us of them, and they too are incapable of general formulation; only in scattered cases can one arrive at a correct and fruitful judgement, establish a fruitful connexion. And the most general remarks yield at best what looks like the fragments of a system.[24]

You don't go by any general rule here. If you say that knowledge of men is empirical that is pedantic. What you do not have is anything like knowledge from the experimental sciences. Elsewhere Wittgenstein says that what is ragged must be left ragged.

It is pseudo-science and dogmatism to think that these judgements can be made into something like knowledge from experimental science. Anyone who has a nose for genuineness of feelings would not play around with tests such as personality tests. Generalizations cannot be introduced, but that is not a defect. The defect is trying to assimilate it to a way of investigating or judging which it isn't. 'What is most difficult here is to put this indefiniteness, correctly and unfalsified, into words.'[25]

Suppose you thought this imponderable evidence is unsatisfactory. Suppose you *explain* why. The trouble is that this makes it look as if the alternative made sense.

Seeing the colour 'red'; seeing a white cross on a black background or vice versa; the duck-rabbit; seeing *this* as the apex of the triangle and *that* as the base and vice versa; seeing the schematic cube as a cube; seeing the triangle as standing, hanging or having fallen over; seeing the likeness between two faces; seeing the genuineness in a facial expression; – suppose someone asks: Why is there this variety of language games? Why not explain this variety? – That means nothing at all. Explanation always gets its sense from a particular context. We concentrate on description and do not go in for explanation. As Wittgenstein says: 'We find certain things about seeing puzzling, because we do not find the whole business of seeing puzzling enough.[26] But the role of description in philosophy which Wittgenstein has in mind is very different, as we have seen, from description of a motor accident. It is showing the role concepts play in our language-games. In *On Certainty* Wittgenstein says:

> You must bear in mind that the language-game is so to say something unpredictable. I mean: it is not based on grounds. It is not reasonable (or unreasonable).
> It is there – like our life. (*OC:* 559)

5

THOUGHT AND LANGUAGE

In the previous section we referred to the fact that in Part Two of the *Investigations* Wittgenstein asks: What makes my image of him an image of *him*? 'The mental image is pretty vague. In so far as it is a physical image it could apply to many, but, no, it is an image of *him*. In one place he says that this sums up the problem of the representational character of language' (see p. 18). The section then related this issue to the discussion of seeing different aspects. Later in the section, we discussed the example of a man who always guessed right what I was saying to myself in my thoughts, and asked what is the criterion here for his guessing right. We said: 'The criterion is the truthfulness of the person referred to, not the description of a process' (see pp. 24–5). We then went on to a discussion of this criterion and its grammatical differences from others.

But these passages raise questions about the relation of thought and language which need to be discussed in their own right. These questions involve the assumption that language is the outward attempt to express something which is a hidden process, and logically prior to it, namely, mental processes which have to do with images and thoughts whose intelligibility does not depend on language. This issue is present in *On Certainty*. Its last remark reads:

> I cannot seriously suppose that I am at this moment dreaming. Someone who, dreaming, says 'I am dreaming', even if he speaks audibly in doing so, is no more right than if he said in his dream 'it is raining', while it was in fact raining. Even if his dream were actually connected with the noise of rain. (*OC*: 676)

This clearly raises the question of the relation of thought to language, but this is a question which emerges from the end of Part One of the *Investigations* which one can characterize, though this is true of the rest of the book too, as the intention to discuss the relation of language to reality, and the relation of thought to reality.

In discussing the relation of thought to reality Wittgenstein meant generally to include conceptions such as 'seeing', 'hearing', 'pain', 'temperature', but also 'expecting', 'intending', 'hoping'. He says that those are very different concepts from 'thinking':

> A proposition, and hence in another sense a thought, can be the 'expression' of belief, hope, expectation, etc. But believing is not thinking. (A grammatical remark.) The concepts of believing, expecting, hoping are less distantly related to one another than they are to the concept of thinking.[1]

You might use 'thinking' very generally, but here Wittgenstein is making distinctions which are more specific. In the last paragraph of Part One of the *Investigations* he again makes the distinction between 'meaning' and 'thinking':

> 'When I teach someone the formation of the series ... I surely mean him to write ... at the hundredth place.' – Quite right; you mean it. And evidently without necessarily even thinking of it. This shows you how different the grammar of the verb 'to mean' is from that of 'to think'. And nothing is more wrong-headed than calling meaning a mental activity! Unless, that is, one is setting out to produce confusion. (It would also be possible to speak of an activity of butter when it rises in price, and if no problems are produced by this it is harmless.)[2]

At first it may be hard to see the connection between the remarks just quoted and the following comments on psychology:

> Misleading parallel: psychology treats of processes in the psychical sphere, as does physics in the physical.
> Seeing, hearing, thinking, feeling, willing, are not the subject of psychology *in the same sense* as that in which the movements of bodies, the phenomena of electricity, etc., are the subject of physics. You can see this from the fact that the physicist sees, hears, thinks about, and informs us of these phenomena, and the psychologist observes the *external reactions* (the behaviour) of the subject.[3]

Many people get excited about the term 'behaviourism', but any psychologist studying 'seeing', e.g. colour-blindness, does so by asking the person to identify patterns. He has to go by the person's expressions. If he's concerned with feeling, e.g. depression (not in a physiological sense), he has to study what the people they study do and say, and what they don't do and don't say. The behaviour is not a 'symptom'. The cardiac specialist observes symptoms – he says there is degeneration in cardiac tissue. If the patient dies, a post-mortem may confirm his hypothesis. So the conclusion and the evidence can be observed independently. But that isn't the case with melancholy and depression. It is not a relation of a symptom to what it is a symptom of, but, rather, an internal relation. 'Anger', 'fear', however, are not the names of bodily movements. Wittgenstein's point is that these terms do not stand for objects which the psychologist studies, in the way in which particles or electronic charge stand for something the physicist studies. Wittgenstein is concerned with a conceptual study and this is the point of the last entry in *Investigations* I: 693. Compare Part Two xiv:

> The confusion and barrenness of psychology is not to be explained by calling it a 'young science'; its state is not comparable with that of physics, for instance, in its beginnings ... For in psychology there are experimental methods and *conceptual confusions* ...
>
> The existence of the experimental method makes us think we have the means of solving problems which trouble us; though problem and method pass one another by.

These points are important for the big issues he wants to discuss. For some people it seems natural to discuss the relation of language to reality, or the relation of the language of physical objects to the objects it talks about, in terms of some sort of physical or causal conception. For example, Russell in 'The Limits of Empiricism' is interested in what it means to say that the word 'cat' expresses the object 'cat'. Russell says it is a causal relation. It sounds plausible. Cf. Locke on words. Words are physical sounds or marks. The syntax of verbal expressions is to be described in terms of the relation between physical marks, and even the mechanism between them. What makes it possible for the physical mechanism of language to represent objects?

> One would like to speak of the function of a word in *this* sentence. As if the sentence were a mechanism in which the word had a particular function. But what does this function consist in? How does it come to light? For there isn't anything hidden – don't we see the whole sentence? The function must come out in operating with the word. (Meaning body.)[4]

29

Compare:

> In the use of words one might distinguish 'surface grammar' from 'depth grammar'. What immediately impresses itself upon us about the use of a word is the way it is used in the construction of the sentence, the part of its use – one might say – that can be taken in by the ear. – And now compare the depth grammar, say of the word 'to mean', with what its surface grammar would lead us to suspect. No wonder we find it difficult to know our way about.[5]

We may be tempted to say that, if someone says, 'I hope he'll come', we can only react in this way if the words are given life by the feeling of hope in the person who utters them.

But does the feeling *give the word its meaning*? What does give meaning to the sentences we use? He wants to combat the temptation to seek some sort of source of meaning for words like 'hope'. Get meaning from the feeling with which it is said. But is hope a feeling? If hoping is feeling tired or feeling happy (more complicated) or feeling afraid, these may be certain feelings characteristic of hope, but they do not cover the meaning.

In *Investigations* Part Two: i, he asks whether an animal can hope. You might say, 'It's because he can't talk', but that is rather queer. What he says here is that only those who have mastered a language can hope.

Suppose I say, 'I hope my friend will come the day after tomorrow', but make arrangements to go to Paris on the same day, you would think I was lying.

'We say a dog is afraid his master will beat him; but not, he is afraid his master will beat him tomorrow. Why not?'[6] The reference is to fear. In conversation with me Wittgenstein said: 'That dog intends to bite me if gnashing, etc. But what if someone points to the dog and says, "He intends to bite me tomorrow".'

If I say my neighbour intends to go to London tomorrow, you can ask, 'What makes you think so?', and I can give various answers. All these reasons – diary cancellations, etc. – would be part of a complicated mode of life. So it doesn't take you far to speak of hope as a feeling. 'It won't do to speak of it without feeling' – all right – but can't describe it without reference to hope. Whatever feelings come in are bound up with modes of a complicated form of life in which he does make arrangements for the day after tomorrow.

There are other objections to saying that it is the feeling that gives hope its meaning. What about the negative form, 'I've given up all hope'? It has meaning, but I have no feeling now. So where does it get its meaning from? Consider the following:

But when one says 'I *hope* he'll come' – doesn't the feeling give the word 'hope' its meaning? (And what about the sentence 'I do *not* hope for his coming any longer'?) The feeling does perhaps give the word 'hope' its special ring; that is, it is expressed in that ring. – If the feeling gives the word its meaning, then here 'meaning' means *point*. But why is the feeling the point?

Is hope a feeling? (Characteristic marks.)[7]

Compare

When longing makes me cry 'Oh, if only he would come!' the feeling gives me the words 'meaning'. But does it give the individual words their meanings?

But here one could also say that the feeling gave the words *truth*. And from this you can see how the concepts merge here.[8]

Wittgenstein also speaks of the language-game in which hope has a meaning. If one says it gets its meaning *from the role it plays*, one is tempted to say that it can only play this role because it has meaning. But it is misleading to separate the meaning from what receives it here. It looks like an explanation otherwise, and philosophy should be description.

It is also misleading to say that the expression of hope gets its meaning from the game it enters. It is not as if it gets its meaning *from* the game, since it wouldn't be the game it is without it. It is an internal not an external relation. It has its meaning in the game, and we couldn't understand its meaning outside that game.

Suppose we asked someone 'In what sense are these words a description of what you are seeing?' – and he answers: 'I *mean* this by these words.' (Say he was looking at a landscape.) Why is this answer 'I *mean* this ...' no answer at all?

How does one use words to *mean* what one sees before one?

Suppose I said 'a b c d' and meant: the weather is fine. For as I uttered these signs I had the experience normally had only by someone who had year-in-year-out used 'a' in the sense of 'the', 'b' in the sense of 'weather', and so on. Does 'a b c d' now mean: the weather is fine?

What is supposed to be the criterion for my having had *that* experience?[9]

What does 'discovering that an expression doesn't make sense' mean? – and what does it mean to say: 'If I mean something by it, surely it must make sense'? – If I mean something by it? – If I mean *what* by it?! – One wants to say: a significant sentence is one which one can not merely say, but also think.[10]

Wittgenstein comes back to the question asked in *Investigations* I: 509 in I: 540:

'Isn't it very odd that I should be unable – even *without* the institution of language and all its surroundings – to think that it will soon stop raining?' – Do you want to say that it is queer that you should be unable to say these words and *mean* them without those surroundings?

Suppose someone were to point at the sky and come out with a number of unintelligible words. When we ask him what he means he explains that the words mean 'Thank heaven, it'll soon stop raining'. He even explains to us the meaning of the individual words. – I will suppose him suddenly to come to himself and say that the sentence was completely senseless, but that when he spoke it had seemed to him like a sentence in a language he knew. (Positively like a familiar quotation.) – What am I to say now? Didn't he understand the sentence as he was saying it? Wasn't the whole meaning there in the sentence?

Can I think it will soon stop raining without a language? Couldn't I just think it? Couldn't the experience I had while uttering 'a b c d' give them meaning? Now look back at *Investigations* I: 511 which refers to Wittgenstein's discussions with Ramsey. They had discussions about infinity and set theory. If Wittgenstein said 'Such-and-such is meaningless', Ramsey would reply, 'No, I'm sure I mean something by it'. That gets us nowhere. Meaning is not an activity by which the words we use are *given sense.*

In this connection Wittgenstein raises the issue of silent speech:

Silent 'internal' speech is not a half-hidden phenomenon which is as it were seen through a veil. It is not hidden *at all*, but the concept may easily confuse us, for it runs over a long stretch cheek by jowl with the concept of an 'outward' process, and yet does not coincide with it.[11]

Seeing where 'silent speech' does and does not coincide with saying something out loud is typical of what Wittgenstein means by conceptual analysis. If you say in the course of a discussion, 'A minute ago I told you ...' you could challenge it and other people or a tape-recorder could show you are wrong. But compare: 'When you said that, I was saying to myself ...' – is it simply that this is inaccessible? We can put it like that, but the trouble is with the 'simply'. You aren't referring to something that happened in your mind, or remembering going over the words. Or even if you are, it is not essential to the meaning, since you are not telling me the same sort of thing as when you say, 'A few minutes ago in discussion ...'. You are not reporting or revealing an event when you say, 'I was just saying to myself ...'. This is important, since it belongs to a large family of cases where you make an assertion without referring to anything that corresponds to it, certainly not as a description.

> That what someone else says to himself is hidden from me is part of the *concept* 'saying inwardly'. Only 'hidden' is the wrong word here; for if it is hidden from me, it ought to be apparent to him, *he* would have to *know* it. But he does not 'know' it only, the doubt which exists for me does not exist for him.[12]

In 'saying to myself' you have a genuine language, and therefore the relation of language to reality. But it is not at all like the relation of the word 'flower' to the flower-bed. You have to consider contexts in which people do say 'I was saying to myself ...' and also the criteria by which you'd judge whether people are being truthful.

At this point we'd return to Wittgenstein's discussion of the game of guessing people's thoughts, and the criterion of truthfulness discussed in the previous section (see p. 24–5). This is not like checking quotations against what is written on a certain page.

6

PICTURING REALITY

In sections 4 and 5 we mentioned Wittgenstein's concern with the representational character of language. This is simply another way of expressing what, at the beginning of section 2, we called Wittgenstein's earliest and last concern, namely, what does it mean to say something? We also said, at that point, that 'For Wittgenstein, the earliest asking of this question took the form: What is a proposition?' (see p. 6).

In the *Tractatus* Wittgenstein thought that the big question of the relation of language to reality could be put, conveniently, by reference to the pictorial character of language. From his early work with Russell he wanted to reject the relation between words and things in terms of causal effect and association. But if you don't want to say, as Locke and Russell did, that words call up associations, nevertheless, you still want to say that the description somehow fits what it describes. What is this 'fitting'?

Wittgenstein sometimes asked: how can you know what has happened from what he has told you, since all he has given you is words, for example, in describing landscapes, streets, etc.? You may say that there is an analogy between description and a painting or drawing. We may say that a painting has some resemblance to what it represents. (That isn't obvious since what is meant by 'resemblance' here isn't obvious. A photograph resembles a man, but doesn't a dog resemble him more? You can put the photograph in your pocket.)

In connection with this Wittgenstein spoke of the pictorial character of propositions and of the 'pre-established harmony' of language. Many people speak of a correspondence between language and thought. In the *Tractatus* Wittgenstein spoke of an internal relation between words and things. When Wittgenstein started philosophy again after a gap of eight years after the *Tractatus* he emphasized verification – 'The meaning of a sentence is its method of verification', but threw away this ladder when it was taken up by the Positivists and turned into a rigid thesis. What impressed Wittgenstein was that the verifying, the finding out, took time. This is connected with his later view – 'Don't look for the meaning, look for its use'. Meaning is only found in a word's function or its role in the language-game.

At first sight, the view of propositions as pictures seems crude: propositions picture reality or the facts. Indeed, it is crude in certain ways. The use of 'picture' can become so flexible that it loses its point. On the other hand, in section 4 we saw how Wittgenstein emphasizes the variety involved in what 'picturing reality comes to', or in what is meant by 'the facts'.

What is important to recognize, however, is that Wittgenstein continued to take seriously the analogy between propositions and pictures in his later work, although there are important developments in his use of it. If one emphasizes that meaning is to be found in a word's function or role in a language-game, this seemed to suggest to some people that the proposition didn't have any meaning in itself; that its meaning appears in the use of it. This would appear, in some respects, far from the idea of the proposition as picturing. The emphasis on the function and role of propositions in various language-games is emphasized in Part One of the *Investigations*, and the parallels between Part One and the early parts of Part Two are obvious. But there are important differences between this aspect of propositions and those discussed, as we have seen, later in Part Two.[1] It is those differences which are the concern of this section. They have to do with the way in which words and expressions may have their whole meaning taken up in themselves. This is not a denial of, but a corrective to, the other discussion of propositions.

Words and sentences have their meaning in a language-game, and yet in some cases we want to say that the meaning is in the sentence. The game wouldn't be what it is without the sentence. If you think of examples like chess, we can change the pieces. As long as we adjust the rules this is all right. But try this for poetry or drama. This is connected with understanding pictures. In the early analogy between propositions and pictures in the *Tractatus*, he meant something like geometrical projection. But here he is interested in something else – in how pictures say something. He says in the *Brown Book* that a pattern in a flower-bed says something.

The distinctions which are of concern to Wittgenstein when he discusses 'seeing something as something', and 'the dawning of an aspect' in *Investigations* II: xi, are already raised in discussions in Part One. There he discusses the difference between 'The picture shows the crowning of Napoleon' and 'This picture shows two men sitting on a bench'. In the first picture what it says lies outside itself. He distinguishes between a portrait where what is said is outside it, and Cezanne's *Card Players* where you don't say that – the picture says itself. You might say, 'I don't understand the picture' at first sight, but then gradually come to distinguish between different forms and see their relation to one another. At first it may seem like a jumble of marks.

Wittgenstein makes the essential distinction as follows:

> If we compare a proposition to a picture, we must think whether we are comparing it to a portrait (a historical representation) or to a genre-picture. And both comparisons have point.
>
> When I look at a genre-picture, it 'tells' me something, even though I don't believe (imagine) for a moment that the people I see in it really exist, or that there have really been people in that situation. But suppose I ask: '*What* does it tell me, then?'[2]
>
> I should like to say 'What the picture tells me is itself'. That is, its telling me something consists in its own structure, in *its* own lines and colours. (What would it mean to say 'What this musical theme tells me is itself'?)[3]

Understanding a theme in music is difficult (unless one is dealing with something like the 1812 Overture). One can speak here of 'understanding' or 'not understanding'. One can also say, 'I understand now, but I didn't before'.

> Understanding a sentence is much more akin to understanding a theme in music than one may think. What I mean is that understanding a sentence lies nearer than one thinks to what is ordinarily called understanding a musical theme. Why is just *this* the pattern of variation in loudness and tempo? One would like to say 'Because I know what it's all about'. But what is it all about? I should not be able to say. In order to 'explain' I could only compare it with something else which has the same rhythm (I mean the same pattern). (One says, 'Don't you see, this is as if a conclusion were being drawn' or 'This is as it were a parenthesis', etc. How does one justify such comparisons? – There are very different kinds of justification here.)[4]

You couldn't *say* what it means, but one could bring out comparisons. But although you speak of understanding music, you don't use it as you use a sentence, although there are sentences which have a meaning in themselves, and where one cannot substitute one for another (see Part Two: xi).

We can see why Wittgenstein says, 'Aspect-blindness will be *akin* to lack of a "musical ear"'.[5] What would you miss if you didn't experience the meaning of a word?

'When I read a poem or narrative with feeling, surely something goes on in me which does not go on when I merely skim the lines for information.' – What processes am I alluding to? – The sentences have a different *ring*. I pay careful attention to my intonation. Sometimes a word has the wrong intonation, I emphasize it too much or too little. I notice this and shew it in my face. I might later talk about my reading in detail, for example about the mistakes in my tone of voice. Sometimes a picture, as it were an illustration, comes to me. And this seems to help me to read with the correct expression. And I could mention a good deal more of the same kind. – I can also give a word a tone of voice which brings out the meaning of the rest, almost as if this word were a picture of the whole thing. (And this may, of course, depend on sentence-formation.)

When I pronounce this word while reading with expression it is completely filled with its meaning. – 'How can this be, if meaning is the use of the word?' Well, what I said was intended figuratively. Not that I chose the figure: it forced itself on me. – But the figurative employment of the word can't get into conflict with the original one.[6]

This is a corrective to the *Tractatus* view that a name only has a meaning in the context of a proposition. The word itself seems to be the portrait of its meaning: 'I feel as if the name "Schubert" fitted Schubert's works and Schubert's face'.[7]

In *Investigations* II: xi (p. 218) Wittgenstein speaks of 'The familiar face of a word', not 'physiognomy of a word' as in G. E. M. Anscombe's translation. The image of 'faces' goes through the discussions again and again. He uses it in his discussions of mathematics and logical proof. But he uses the image especially in connection with words.

Wittgenstein is saying something extremely important when he says:

Don't take it as a matter of course, but as a remarkable fact, that pictures and fictitious narratives give us pleasure, occupy our minds.[8]

But there might be people to whom all this is alien; they wouldn't have an attachment to words. How are these feelings shown among us? Answer: by the way we choose our words and value them.

How do I find the right word? How do I choose among words? Without doubt it is sometimes as if I were comparing them by fine differences of smell: *That* is too … , *that* is too … , – *this* is the right one. – But I do not always have to make judgements, give explanations; often I might only say: 'It simply isn't right yet'. I am dissatisfied, I go on looking. At last a word comes: '*That's* it!' *Sometimes* I can say why. This is simply what searching, this is what finding, is like here.[9]

You can't teach this in the way you can teach someone correct grammar. How can I choose my words? Sometimes I can say why it's the right word, but not always. That is what searching and finding are like here. The point is closely connected with remarks made by Wittgenstein in his *Lectures and Conversations on Aesthetics, Psychology and Religious Belief*:

The word we ought to talk about is 'appreciation'. What does appreciation consist in?

If a man goes through an endless number of patterns in a tailor's [and] says: 'No. This is slightly too dark. This is slightly too loud', etc., he is what we call an appreciater of material. That he is an appreciater is not shown by the interjections he uses, selects, etc. Similarly in music: 'Does this harmonize? No. The bass is not quite loud enough. Here I just want something different … ' This is what we call an appreciation.

It is not only difficult to describe what appreciation consists in, but impossible. To describe what it consists in we would have to describe the whole environment.[10]

Why are these issues important for *On Certainty*? It would seem, at first glance, that the relevance is marginal, since the empirical propositions which concern him in the later work would seem to be on the other side of the divide from those propositions which 'say themselves'. This is true, but the point of contact is in the philosophical significance of the appeal to a 'background' in each case. This notion of an 'environment' or a 'background' plays an important part in *On Certainty*:

The propositions, however, which Moore retails as examples of such known truths are indeed interesting. Not because anyone knows their truth, or believes he knows them, but because they all have a *similar* role in the system of our empirical judgements. (*OC:* 137)

We don't, for example, arrive at any of them as a result of investigation.

There are, e.g., historical investigations and investigations into the shape and also the age of the Earth, but not into whether the Earth has existed during the last hundred years. Of course many of us have information about this period from our parents and grandparents; but mayn't they be wrong? – 'Nonsense!' one will say. 'How should all these people be wrong?' – But is that an argument? Is it not simply the rejection of an idea? And perhaps the determination of a concept? For if I speak of a possible mistake here, this changes the role of 'mistake' and 'truth' in our lives. (*OC:* 138)

We have backgrounds of different kinds here. A whole culture is a background against which the value judgements associated with aesthetics could be what they are. It enables us to understand the people and find our feet with them. The other enables us to understand what is being said when people talk about physical objects and physical events. 'Understanding people' and saying 'That's what life is really like' go together. You can't have one without the other.

Understanding a language is not a matter of having a vocabulary, say eight hundred words, syntax, etc. He does not fail to understand the people because their thoughts are hidden, but because he cannot find his feet with them. You might even pass an examination in the language. The lack is not the absence of a common vocabulary. Think again of the notion of a word having a familiar face.

> We also say of some people that they are transparent to us. It is, however, important as regards this observation that one human being can be a complete enigma to another. We learn this when we come into a strange country with entirely strange traditions; and, what is more, even given a mastery of the country's language. We do not *understand* the people. (And not because of not knowing what they are saying to themselves.) We cannot find our feet with them …
>
> If a lion could talk, we could not understand him.[11]

7

WHAT MAKES LANGUAGE LANGUAGE?

The distinctions made in the last section between different senses in which
propositions picture reality are connected with another major theme in
Wittgenstein's work, namely, that it is idle and foolish to ask for a justification of the use of language, thinking or speaking. In particular circumstances we can give answers to questions like 'Why is he speaking?' but if
you make it general to a type or set of types of human activity we don't
know what would be meant by an explanation here. Wittgenstein says that
if we try to explain the way we speak or the explanations we are prone to
accept, the explanation comes to an end very soon and then you say: 'This
language-game has not been predicted – it is simply there as our life is
there'. There is no theory of language. The ways in which we speak are not
hypotheses. Why do we speak as we do? Why do we live as we do? Why is
human life the sort of thing it is? There is not much that can be said in
answer to these questions.

Sometimes, the attempt to answer such questions is bound up with confusion about the sense in which the language in question pictures reality.
Wittgenstein gives a sustained discussion of such confusion in his 'Remarks
on Frazer's *Golden Bough*'. He disparages the attempt to give an explanation of the rituals Frazer is recounting. His primary criticism is that Frazer
is inclined to view these practices as some sort of attempt to introduce a
scientific account or guidance into their lives. Frazer represents these views
as *mistakes*. Was Augustine mistaken when he calls on God on every page
of his *Confessions*, or is a Buddhist monk mistaken? None of them can be
called mistakes because they are not theories. Religious responses aren't
theories. People speak, they draw pictures, sing songs, dance, and they also

perform rituals. One of the things Wittgenstein does in these notes on Frazer is show that you can get much further in understanding the rituals Frazer reports by recognizing them as forms of language, than by thinking of these practices as poor would-be substitutes for science.

'And magic always rests on the idea of symbolism and of language.'[1] This may seem like a tenuous hobby-horse if you do not understand what precedes it. Wittgenstein says: 'Frazer's account of the magical and religious notions of men is unsatisfactory: it makes these notions appear as *mistakes*.'[2] In most cases you wouldn't call these practices theories or mistaken any more than you'd call a dance a mistake. Consider Frazer's comments on the King of the Forest at Nemi. The people thought he had to be put to death when young, otherwise his soul would not retain its freshness. This sounds like a ground and its consequent, whereas all we can say is that they have this practice and this belief – they are found together, that's all. Trouble comes if you say that one is the explanation of the other:

> When he explains to us, for example, that the king must be killed in his prime because, according to the notions of the savages, his soul would not be kept fresh otherwise, we can only say: where that practice and these views go together, the practice does not spring from the view, but both of them are there.[3]

i disagree

The idea doesn't arise from the practice or vice versa. They are both possessed by these people – it is natural to think of them together like that. If you ask: Why this ritual? Why should the priest devote his whole life to this role knowing he is to be sacrificed? Or: What are they trying to achieve by it? Why should they be striving to achieve anything? Various things happen round about or in the lives of these people in primitive societies, which impress them, and are very different from urban or industrial societies. Death is one of them. If you ask: Why should it? – that's your privilege. It may not impress us – Dr Bernhard will see to it. But it *did* impress them.

> That a man's shadow, which looks like a man, or that his mirror image, or that rain, thunderstorms, the phases of the moon, the change of seasons, the likeness and differences of animals to one another and to human beings, the phenomena of death, of birth and of sexual life, in short everything a man perceives year in, year out around him, connected together in any variety of ways – that all this should play a part in his thinking (his philosophy) and his practices, is obvious, or in other words that is what we really know and find interesting.[4]

41

The search for explanations is misplaced. We need only order the facts Frazer presents, without adding anything to them to find that the satisfaction one was searching for in explanations is already there: 'Compared with the impression that what is described here makes on us, the explanation is too uncertain'.[5] Wittgenstein said to Drury that the language Frazer uses isn't the one he would use in describing an imperfect scientific experiment. But if you ask why it took place, the answer is: because it is terrible. You can only describe and say: that's what human life is like.

> I think one reason why the attempt to find an explanation is wrong is that we have only to put together in the right way what we *know*, without adding anything, and the satisfaction we are trying to get from the explanation comes of itself.
>
> And here the explanation is not what satisfies us anyway. When Frazer begins by telling the story of the King of the Wood at Nemi, he does this in a tone which shows that something strange and terrible is happening here. And that is the answer to the question 'why is this happening?' Because it is terrible. In other words, what strikes us in this course of events as terrible, impressive, horrible, tragic, &, anything but trivial and insignificant, *that* is what gave birth to them.
>
> We can only *describe* and say, human life is like that.[6]

We began this section by referring to Wittgenstein's view that it is idle and foolish to ask for a justification for the use of language. Explanations come to an end pretty soon and then you say, 'This language-game has not been predicted – it is simply there as our life is there'. It should not be difficult to see the connection between these remarks and Wittgenstein's discussion of the ritual of the sacrifice of the King of the Wood at Nemi: 'We can only *describe* and say, human life is like that'. It may not be so obvious to see their connection with the very different background Wittgenstein is discussing in *On Certainty* and, in particular, what he wants to say about the peculiar logical role of certain empirical propositions against this background. He is concerned with comparatively restricted empirical judgements. What interests him is 'the fact that about certain empirical propositions no doubt can exist if making judgements is to be possible at all. Or again: I am inclined to believe that not everything that has the form of an empirical proposition *is* one' (*OC*: 308).

As in his discussion of the ritual at Nemi, here, too, Wittgenstein is not offering explanations. He does not suggest for a minute that the propositions he is interested in explain or justify the practice of language or human life.

42

'An empirical proposition can be *tested* (we say). But how? and through what?

What *counts* as its test? – 'But is this an adequate test? And, if so, must it not be recognizable as such in logic?' – As if giving grounds did not come to an end sometimes. But the end is not an ungrounded proposition: it is an ungrounded way of acting. (*OC:* 110)

Wittgenstein said that compared with the impression the slaying of the priest–king at Nemi makes on us, the explanation is too uncertain. The explanation is speculative and doesn't provide satisfaction. Again, there are parallels with *On Certainty*: if I give people reasons for saying that I have two hands they would be less certain than what they are asked to support. In *both* cases, what Wittgenstein asks us to do is to order the material properly.

8

THE LOGICAL AND THE EMPIRICAL

What is new in these remarks in *On Certainty* is the discussion of the 'peculiar logical role of certain empirical propositions' in our speech and language. In 1944 he talked with me for several weeks about the relations of grammatical propositions and empirical propositions.[1] He was working with the idea that the division between them was not a sharp one, and that his own earlier suggestions about this had been wrong or misleading. (This was before Quine had published anything on these lines.) One time, when there was a pause in the discussion, and we were talking in a desultory way, he said he felt it necessary from time to time to go back and criticize and even change his earlier view on various points – 'otherwise I would dry up'.

The discussion of the distinction between grammatical and empirical propositions, as we have seen, had started in earlier lectures and writings, but not taken as thoroughly as they are in *On Certainty*. He asks: 'Is it that rule and empirical proposition merge into one another?' (*OC:* 309). And: 'But wouldn't one have to say then that there is no sharp boundary between propositions of logic and empirical propositions? The lack of sharpness *is* that of the boundary between *rule* and empirical proposition' (*OC:* 319).

Someone might say that the peculiar role of those propositions which interest him here must mean that they are empirical propositions. Wittgenstein would answer that they *can* be used as empirical propositions normally are, as we see when we imagine circumstances in which you might

From Rhees's notes dated 3 March 1970.

say such a thing (assert one of them) to convey information. But the propositions in *On Certainty* generally have this other role he is interested in.

When he says, for instance, that 'a whole body of such propositions' determine the form of our language-game, or of the game in which we make empirical judgements – he does not say much about 'the form of the language-game' except what relates to empirical judgements: basing judgements on observation and experiments; drawing conclusions from experiments in the way that is familiar as 'induction'. He is interested in 'the certainty of the language-game' with empirical judgements, in the possibility of being able to *continue* 'the game of making judgements' (which would include raising doubts, asking questions, testing, etc.).

As we have seen elsewhere, and especially in *Philosophical Investigations* II: xi, Wittgenstein brings out in various ways that 'empirical proposition' itself is not sharply defined. That is why I said that if the section had a title it might have been 'Seeing and Thinking'. He showed, too, that 'describing' is not sharply defined. Let us remind ourselves of some of the distinctions he makes to show their relevance or connection with his later discussions in *On Certainty*.

We have seen how Wittgenstein brought out the difference between seeing what is drawn and copying it with pencil and paper, and seeing a similarity between what is drawn here and what is drawn there. He called the latter 'seeing an aspect'. He also emphasized how one might see something now one way (concave), now in another way (convex). He wanted to insist that we should speak of *seeing* in each case, not of *interpreting* what we see.

This 'seeing a figure or a sign or an object in a certain aspect', or 'noting an aspect I'd never noticed before' – is important for Wittgenstein's discussion of *generality*. (I may look at the plant you show me, and again I may look at it as an *example* of a plant.) These issues are also important for his discussion of 'mathematical problems' and 'mathematical proof'.

As we have seen, Wittgenstein also discussed 'aspect-blindness', and asked whether there might be people who had not the capacity to 'see something *as* something'. This capacity amounts to different things in different contexts. In geometry, to see a figure as a hexagon or a cube, or to see a triangle in different ways, depends on the mastery of a technique. Again, seeing the similarity between two faces, something another may not see, is different from a straightforward reporting of what one sees as a look-out. In other cases, the mastery of a technique is not involved. As we saw, Wittgenstein gave as examples the ways in which we value certain modes of expression, where things couldn't be put in another way, where 'the expression is completely filled with its meaning'. 'How do I find the right word?' Compare: 'The right word for the colour of the sky' with 'The right word for the hen now crossing the road'. In the latter case I cannot be guided just by the rules of a teacher.

We saw in the *Investigations* how Wittgenstein discusses the differences between 'colour-blindness' and 'aspect-blindness'. There are ways of establishing colour-blindness, since for the most part people agree entirely when they speak of the colours things have. There is no comparable agreement, however, on whether an expression of feeling is genuine or not. This is connected not simply with 'knowing what he is showing', but also with what is meant by 'knowledge of human beings'.

For all these reasons I want to return to the importance of the following remark:

> The familiar face [*not* physiognomy as translated] of a word, the feeling that it has taken up its meaning into itself, that it is an actual likeness of its meaning – there could be human beings to whom all this was alien. (They would not have an attachment to their words.) – And how are these feelings manifested among us? – By the way we choose and value words.[2]

Can we imagine a whole society, a people, in whose use of language there was never anything we'd call 'trying to find the right word'? (This is allied to Wittgenstein's question whether there could be a people who spoke a language although all of them were 'aspect-blind' or 'meaning-blind': they never heard or saw single words in one meaning rather than another. 'For we want to ask "What would you be missing if you did not *experience* the meaning of a word?"'[3]

Our first answer might be, that their speech and language would be in some strange way mechanical ... Like people understanding one another in Esperanto.

This would not be the case with the people in the strange land, where we did not understand the *people*, and could not find our feet with them. What we are trying to imagine here, what is lacking, is in some way more fundamental. And if (*per impossibile*) *all* the people in a country *were* in the same position *vis-à-vis* one another, as we are now *vis-à-vis* the people of a strange country as a whole – but still assuming that they had all 'mastered the same language' – ... (You can see why I said *per impossibile*.) Try taking that passage 'The familiar face of a word ... etc.' and substituting 'person' (or 'people') for 'word'.

'These people would lack ...' But in fact this lack is supplied by what *On*

Certainty calls 'practice' ('and the practice has to speak for itself' (*OC:* 139)) or 'acting'. Compare: 'As if giving grounds did not come to an end sometime. But the end is not an ungrounded presupposition: it is an ungrounded way of acting' (*OC:* 110).

'A way of acting.' 'A practice.' Compare: 'the way we choose and value words'. These expressions do not coincide. The divergences between, on the one hand, the empirical judgements Wittgenstein discusses in *On Certainty* and the practice which holds them fast, and, on the other hand, the way we choose and value words, is probably much wider than anything they have in common. Nevertheless, sometimes boundaries are hard to draw. What we call 'value judgement' seems often to be hardly distinguishable from action. (A man may show what he thinks of a particular painting, by going often to the gallery to look at it; perhaps, by always being alone when he does look at it; by refusing to have a copy of it on the wall of his own room; by looking at other pictures from time to time, and then coming back to this one ... etc., etc. So also, a man may show his devotion to his friend, or may show his admiration for someone who is not his friend, through various things he does. Etc.)

Nevertheless, the differences are important. One may appreciate how people deal practically with things and yet find oneself saying, 'I cannot find my feet with these people'. Suppose someone suggested: 'If I could learn how choosing and valuing other men goes in their lives – learn this, in the sense of being able to respond and show it when I was among them – I'd have begun to understand them. (The "valuing" would include dislike or rejection as well as attachment.)'

When Wittgenstein speaks of 'practice' in *OC:* 139 and 140, it is the practice of making empirical judgements. Here, too, the practice has to speak for itself. This is something that has to be learned, but we do not learn it 'by learning rules: we are taught judgements and their connection with other judgements' (*OC:* 140). Now, despite the differences we have noted, compare this with what the *Investigations* says about learning a knowledge of human beings: some people can learn this, but not 'by taking a course in it, but through "*experience*" ... What one acquires is not a technique; one learns correct judgements' (RR: 'to judge correctly').

Choosing and valuing words and people would include dislike or rejection as well as attachment. Similarly, the certainty of the very different language-game, the possibility of being able to continue the game of making empirical judgements, would include raising doubts, asking questions, testing, rejecting, as well as accepting.

9

ON CERTAINTY: A WORK IN LOGIC

Wittgenstein often speaks of 'logic' in *On Certainty*, and of 'a logical question', 'a logical insight', and so on. He would have said that the whole set of remarks (the whole book) is a discussion of logic.

He does not think of logic as a formal system of principles – like *Principia Mathematica*, for example. If we say that the book is a logical investigation – this means that it is a discussion of what logic is, or what logical principles are. But this does not mean: he is looking for a method by which logical principles may be constructed or derived; or that he wants to give 'a mechanical method' for deciding whether a given formula is a logical principle or not.

On the other hand, the discussion of what logic is goes all the way back to the *Tractatus* where he had said something like: 'Our business is not the construction of formal systems, but rather: what it is that makes any such construction possible'. Compare: 'We now have to answer *a priori* the question about all the possible forms of elementary propositions.'[1] But in *On Certainty* he says something very different: 'If you demand a rule from which it follows that there can't have been a miscalculation here, the answer is that we did not learn this through a rule, but by learning to calculate' (*OC:* 44). And then: 'What sort of proposition is: "What could a mistake here be like!"? It would have to be a logical proposition. *But it is a logic that is not used, because what it tells us is not taught by means of propositions. – It is a logical proposition; for it does describe the conceptual (linguistic) situation.*' (*OC:* 51). (My italics.)

From Rhees's notes dated 3 March 1970.

Wittgenstein asks: 'Am I not getting closer and closer to saying that in the end logic cannot be described? You must look at the practice of language, then you will see it' (*OC*: 501). This takes us back to the opening discussion of section 2. He is not saying that there is nothing logical to be seen, but it will not be a description of a set of logical principles. It will be seen in 'describing a language-game', in 'describing what belongs to a language-game'. As we saw towards the end of the discussion in section 2, it is not always easy to be clear about this, but the idea is fundamental. The word 'describe', as we noted, can mislead some: 'If the propositions of logic describe the ways in which people speak with one another, then they are just empirical propositions. Sociology maybe.' But even 'describing a game', describing chess or describing football, is not the description of a particular match or contest.

But Wittgenstein is describing what belongs to a language-game. For example, speculations about the existence of a planet, and trying to establish the existence of my own hands, are importantly different. He wants to show that, for the most part, doubt is ruled out in the latter case, and that this is not a matter of degree in relation to speculations about the planet. 'For it is not true that a mistake merely gets more and more improbable as we pass from the planet to my own hand. No: at some point it has ceased to be conceivable' (*OC*: 54). Again: 'Or are we to say that *certainty* is merely a constructed point to which some things approximate more, some less closely? No. Doubt gradually loses its sense. *This language-game just is like that. And everything descriptive of a language-game is part of logic.*' (Last two sentences, my italics).

These are logical propositions, but not formal principles, and they tell us (describe for us) what the conceptual situation is like. Here is an example of describing what *belongs* to a language-game: 'If I believe that I am sitting in my room when I am not, then I shall not be said to have *made a mistake*. But what is the essential difference between this case and a mistake?' (*OC*: 195). It is the difference between what belongs to a language-game and what does not. A mistake *does* not belong to that language-game.

But, then, Wittgenstein asks: 'But when is something objectively certain? When a mistake is not possible. But what kind of possibility is that? Mustn't mistake be *logically* excluded?' (*OC*: 194). Wittgenstein's way of responding is to say that 'mistake' is not a move in the game at all. He says (or suggests) that 'it is logically ruled out'. But if he had put this by saying that 'it is a logical impossibility' it would have been confusing because of the associations the phrase 'logical impossibility' has. It would change his emphasis from noting what *is* and *is not* said, to talk of what *can* and *cannot* be said – the hardness of the logical 'must'.

For these reasons, when he says of Moore's truisms and propositions: 'What I hold fast to is not *one* proposition but a nest of propositions' (*OC*: 225), he does not speak of them as a nest of logical propositions, though they 'determine the form of the language-game', or 'describe the language-game'. One of these reasons is expressed as follows:

> 'We could doubt every single one of these facts, but we could not doubt them *all*.'
> Wouldn't it be more correct to say: 'we do not doubt them *all*'.
> Our not doubting them all is simply our manner of judging, and therefore of acting. (*OC*: 232)

When faced with a choice between 'but we cannot' and 'but we do not', he prefers the latter because 'could' and 'could not' would not have a clear meaning here; they seem to presuppose some kind of system.

Compare his responses to the question he poses as follows: 'I know that it never happened, for if it had happened I could not possibly have forgotten it' (*OC*: 224). The question is then whether this is a *logical* 'could not'. Wittgenstein responds:

> What I hold fast to is not *one* proposition but a nest of propositions. (*OC*: 225)
> Can I give the supposition that I have ever been on the moon any serious consideration at all? (*OC*: 226)
> Is *that* something that one can forget?! (*OC*: 227)
> In such circumstances people do not say 'Perhaps we've all forgotten', and the like, but rather they assume that ... (*OC*: 228)
> Our talk gets its sense from the rest of the proceedings. (*OC*: 229)

We might compare: 'If you spoke of something as "logically established" or "logically certain" – it would mean nothing then to speak of the *principles* of logic as logically certain.'

Wittgenstein is also showing what belongs to the language-game when he says '"There are physical objects" is nonsense. Is it supposed to be an empirical proposition?' (*OC*: 35). He then provides the clarification we need:

> 'A is a physical object' is a piece of instruction which we give only to some-one who doesn't yet understand either what 'A' means or what 'physical

object' means. Thus it is instruction about the use of words, and 'physical object' is a logical concept. (Like colour, quantity ...) ['the formal concepts' in the *Tractatus* and also later – RR.] *And that is why no such proposition as 'There are physical objects' can be formulated.* (*OC:* 36) (My italics.)

Compare with this *OC:* 352 and 353. The first reminds us of Moore's wanting to say 'I know that that's a tree'. But suppose the person said he wanted to make a logical observation. Wittgenstein replies:

> If a forester goes into a wood with his men and says '*This* tree has got to be cut down, and *this* one and *this* one' – what if he then observes 'I *know* that that's a tree'? – But might not *I* say of the forester 'He *knows* that that's a tree – he doesn't examine it, or order his men to examine it'? (*OC:* 353)

'I know that that's a tree' would not be a logical remark, but 'He knows that that's a tree' might be. In this example, it would be 'describing the language-game'. – And so would 'Trees are physical objects'.

Part II
DISCUSSIONS OF *ON CERTAINTY*

10

Two Conversations with Wittgenstein on Moore

I

I am sitting with a philosopher in the garden; he says again and again 'I know that that's a tree', pointing to a tree that is near us. Someone else arrives and observes this, and I tell him: 'This fellow isn't insane. We are only doing philosophy.' (*OC: 467*)

'I know that that's a tree' is something a philosopher might say to demonstrate to himself or to someone else that he *knows* something that is not a mathematical or a logical truth. Similarly, someone who was entertaining the idea that he was no use any more might keep repeating to himself 'I can still do this and this and this'. If such thoughts often possessed him one would not be surprised if he, apparently out of all context, spoke such a sentence out loud. (But here I have already sketched a background, a surrounding, for this remark, that is to say given it a context.) But if someone, in quite heterogeneous circumstances, called out with the most convincing mimicry: 'Down with him!', one might say of these words (and their tone) that they were a pattern that does indeed have familiar applications, but that in this case it was not even clear what *language* the man in question was speaking. I might make with my hand the movement I should make if I were holding a hand-saw and sawing through a plank; but would one have any right to call this movement *sawing*, out of all context? – (It might be something quite different!) (*OC: 350*)

Rhees wrote these notes on 13 April 1951 and 14 August 1950 from memory of conversations with Wittgenstein. He does not indicate here when the conversations took place, but judging from remarks Rhees makes elsewhere, they probably occurred before 1946. References to *On Certainty* were added later. (Ed.)

Moore has every right to say he knows there's a tree there in front of him. Naturally he may be wrong. (For it is *not* the same as with the utterance 'I believe there is a tree there'.) But whether he is right or wrong in this case is of no philosophical importance. If Moore is attacking those who say that one cannot really know such a thing, he can't do it by assuring them that *he* knows this and that. For one need not believe him. If his opponents had asserted that one could not *believe* this and that, then he could have replied, '*I* believe it' (*OC:* 520)

So when Moore sat in front of a tree and said 'I know that that's a tree', he was simply stating the truth about his state at the time. (*OC:* 532)

Moore used to sit in his garden and say to Malcolm, 'I know that this is a tree'. There is something queer in making a statement of this kind in those circumstances. It is a perfectly good English sentence. And you can think of a great many contexts in which there would be nothing queer about asserting it. If a blind man were to ask, 'Do you really think that this is a tree here?', you might answer, 'I don't think, I know that this is a tree'. Or the question might be asked whether it were really a tree or a stage prop (of which there were several about), and you might say in a particular case, 'I know that this is a tree'. Or the question might be asked in the fog; and so on. In such contexts the statement is perfectly natural and intelligible. But also in such contexts it ceases to have the slightest interest for philosophy:

> But now it is also correct to use 'I know' in the contexts which Moore mentioned, at least *in particular circumstances*. (Indeed, I do not know what 'I know that I am a human being' means. But even that might be given a sense.)
>
> For each one of these sentences I can imagine circumstances that turn it into a move in one of our language-games, and by that it loses everything that is philosophically astonishing. (*OC:* 622)

Moore is protesting against the view that I can know only such propositions as the propositions of mathematics or 'I know I see red now'; he is insisting that I know other things of quite a different kind, e.g., I know that this is a tree.

There is a confusion if you treat knowing as a state of mind – a confusion in grammar. And perhaps to assert 'I know that this is a tree' in such a context shows such a confusion. You can give examples of states of mind: e.g. feeling sad; but also, perhaps, believing, feeling doubtful and feeling certain or sure. If you say, 'I believe that this is a tree', then if you don't believe it you are lying. But you might have said, for example, 'I know that he was in his room at the time'; and if in fact he was not there then you did *not* know that he was – and yet you need not have been lying when you said you did know it. The difference between 'knowing' and 'believing' is not like the difference between 'believing' and 'being sure or certain'; or between 'being doubtful' and 'being certain'.

So we might say that for anyone to *say* 'I know that ...' is irrelevant. Because this does not show whether in fact you do know it or not. And in a law court, for instance, the court would want to know only what you saw and what happened. Whether you know it or not does not depend on anything that goes on in your mind. It depends on considerations that would be relevant for anyone else. And these are what are important – not anything that is subjective.

Whether you know it does not depend in any way on your conviction or your being sure.

But this does not get to what is important about Moore's saying, 'I know that is a tree'.

There are certain experiential propositions such that the opposite is never considered; where anything like doubt or any alternative is simply ruled out. And without this there could not be language-games at all.

> When Moore says he *knows* such and such, he is really enumerating a lot of empirical propositions which we affirm without special testing; propositions, that is, which have a peculiar logical role in the system of our empirical propositions. (*OC:* 136)
>
> Even if the most trustworthy of men assures me that he *knows* things are thus and so, this by itself cannot satisfy me that he does know. Only that he believes he knows. That is why Moore's assurance that he knows ... does not interest us. The propositions, however, which Moore retails as examples of such known truths are indeed interesting. Not because anyone knows their truth, or believes he knows them, but because they all have a *similar* role in the system of our empirical judgements. (*OC:* 137)
>
> I should like to say: Moore does not *know* what he asserts he knows, but it stands fast for him, as also for me; regarding it as absolutely solid is part of our *method* of doubt and enquiry. (*OC:* 151)

You might ask, 'Why should one confine oneself to "I know that this is a tree"? Why should one not say also "I know that my name is Rhees", or "I know that these are words in the English language"; perhaps "I know that this is a sound", and so on?'

You cannot be doubtful – because it makes no sense to 'be doubtful' –

: are some things which you do not doubt. You can imagine
imes in which at every stage, when one speaks or makes a ges-
e something like a shrug and say 'Perhaps he means so and so',
y he means so and so'. But this is possible only by reference to
rison with situations in which he *does* mean so and so and in
which there is no question of 'perhaps'. If this were not so, you could not
even say 'perhaps' here.

I might make gestures, pointing at this and then pointing at the stairs,
and you might think 'Apparently he wants me to take this down to Mrs
Bevan'. And you might do that, and see whether your conjecture was con-
firmed. You might observe people carrying on in this way, and a man might
be punished when what he did was not the right thing to do, and so on.
But you could understand it that way – you would be observing a game
that's all – and it would make sense to speak of what is done as 'punishing',
only by reference to cases in which it is *not* all conjecture.

There can be no game which is only played once; or which is not played,
so to speak, in a context.

This does not mean that there is any specific class of 'things which cannot be doubted'. In fact that is just the point.

You don't doubt that is a gesture. You don't doubt that he is saying
something.

I don't doubt that 'tin' is a word. Not because I have convinced myself
of this, but because the question just never arises. Or if it does – and in
particular cases it may – this is possible only because there are other things
which you do not doubt.

The same goes for 'That is a chair' or 'That is a tree'. Only, these are
generally not the cases in which you would *say* 'There is no doubt about it'
or 'There is no doubt that that is a chair'. Because you say this in cases in
which there *might* be doubt – when you are talking again within a context,
or by reference to other cases about which the question does not arise.

(Might it not seem queer to speak of the sorts of things in question here
as experiential *propositions* – just for this reason? You might almost say that
so long as they are the sorts of things that are not doubted, they are the
sorts of things that are not spoken about.)

II

Moore's propositions in 'The Defence of Common Sense' – 'The Earth
has existed for a great many years' or 'for many years before I was born'. 'I

have a body.' Etc.

Moore says these are things which he *knows*, or which he is *certain* of. True and false. Where there are reasons.

Compare the idea of a general law of inductive inference, or a general law by which inductive inferences are governed. (Have we any reason to think there *is* any such general law?)

If you say 'I know the Earth has existed for many years – for the past 100 years', we might ask how you know this. And similarly if you said 'I know I have a body'. (Actually you would not say 'I know' in such connections, and if I asked, 'Did you come by bus or by train?', you would not say 'I know I came by train', either. But rather simply: 'I came by train'. I do not have any *reason* for saying, 'I came by train'.) Notice that you can always ask, 'How do you know this?'; with 'believe' it is different.

If we consider evidence – what evidence would show that the Earth has existed for the past 100 years? Then the evidence which would show that it has existed for a million years would not show it. The fossils and other geological evidence would not show that the Earth has existed for the past 100 years. It is queer, also, to think of someone's denying it – or of showing that the Earth has *not* existed for the past 100 years. Have we any idea of what that would be?

> There are, e.g., historical investigations and investigations into the shape and also the age of the Earth, but not into whether the Earth has existed during the last hundred years. Of course many of us have information about this period from our parents and grandparents; but mayn't they be wrong? – 'Nonsense!' one will say. 'How should all these people be wrong?' – But is that an argument? Is it not simply the rejection of an idea? And perhaps the determination of a concept? For if I speak of a possible mistake here, this changes the role of 'mistake' and 'truth' in our lives. (*OC:* 138)
>
> It would strike me as ridiculous to want to doubt the existence of Napoleon; but if someone doubted the existence of the Earth 150 years ago, perhaps I should be more willing to listen, for now he is doubting our whole system of evidence. It does not strike me as if this system were more certain than a certainty within it. (*OC:* 185)

If you asked a physiologist how he knows I have a brain, he might refer to specimens he has dissected. But to ask, 'How do you know that what is found there has any bearing in my case?' – would hardly mean much. In any case he would hardly say 'I know that what I have found in examined specimens is true of all human beings'. It is not something which he would be said to *know*. You may say he is *certain*. But the point for him would be

59

that it is 'obvious'. He goes on like that. He has no reason for doing so. This is the procedure be follows – without any reason. And so it is often and constantly.

'How do you know that I have a brain?': this is the same sort as 'How do you know the Earth has existed for 100 years?' (Not a *hypothesis*, certainly.) You may connect it with a feeling of *certainty*, and this feeling may be the same as if you had reasons for it. But you have no reasons for it. We might say it is connected with all sorts of other things we do and believe (although there are not reasons for it).

You would not ask 'Is it true?' or 'Is it false?' Any more than you would ask what shows it to be true, or what shows it to be false. That is why it is somewhat ambiguous to say it is something of which I am certain – especially if you add that it is something I know.

11

PREFACE TO *ON CERTAINTY*

Moore wanted to protest against the philosophical view which says: one can only really *know* mathematical propositions and impressions of one's own sensations and feelings. He wanted to say that he also has knowledge of things in his immediate surroundings – of this tree, for instance – as well as of facts such as, for example, that the Earth has existed since long before his birth.

Wittgenstein comments that even in the case of those propositions which Moore asserts it is incorrect to begin with 'I know ...'. If I am sitting near a tree in my garden, it doesn't occur to me to *doubt* that it is a tree. But just because of this it doesn't occur to me to say to someone that I 'know' it. So Wittgenstein found it remarkable that Moore says it – that he puts forward just those propositions as ones which he 'knows with certainty': so that under *such* circumstances – sitting in front of the tree on a bright day – he repeats that he *knows* it. – Moore probably meant, among other things,

From a preface Rhees wrote for the German edition of *On Certainty* published by Suhrkamp Verlag. Sometime in 1969, Siegfried Unseld, the head of the publishing house, had asked Rhees whether he thought a German edition of *Über Gewißheit* was a good idea. He responded favourably. Unseld also asked him to write a short preface, but Rhees urged his fellow literary executors to write it. In the event, Rhees wrote the preface himself. On 10 May 1970, in a letter to G. E. M. Anscombe, Rhees says that galley proofs of Wittgenstein's work have arrived. They did not include proofs of his preface, but he says that they may come later. For some reason this preface was not published. The German edition includes the preface written by G. E. M. Anscombe and G. H. von Wright for the Blackwell bilingual edition of *On Certainty*. I am grateful to Timothy Tessin for translating the preface and to Mario von der Ruhr who assisted him.

that here all doubt is ruled out: that 'I *assume* that that is a tree', and the like, were senseless. But there is more to it than this; and the very unnatural way of speaking emphasized this for Wittgenstein.

Wittgenstein writes at *OC:* 136, 137:

> When Moore says he *knows* such and such, he is really doing nothing more than listing empirical propositions which we accept without any further investigation; propositions, that is, *which play a peculiar logical role in the system of our empirical propositions.*[1]
>
> Even if the most trustworthy of men assures me that he *knows* things are so and so, this by itself cannot convince me that he knows it. Only that he believes he knows it. That is why Moore's assurance that he knows ... cannot interest us. But the propositions which Moore gives as examples of such known truths are interesting nonetheless. Not because anyone knows, or believes he knows, their truth, but because they all play a *similar* role in the system of our empirical judgements.

We are familiar with certain empirical propositions whose contrary (or negation) never comes into consideration; those for whom any doubt, any question 'is it true or false?', is ruled out. And were this not so, there would be no language-game and no speaking. The propositions which Moore lists, along with many others, are of just this sort. Wittgenstein mentions, for example, 'I know that my name is L. W.' (which sounds queer); that I have lived in this house for months; that I was never in China; that I had parents; that I have a brain; that my body has never vanished and after a period of time reappeared; but also: that I am now writing in English words; that 'head' is a word; that this man is now speaking; that that hand movement is a gesture – and many others.

These have the form of empirical propositions, but as a rule are not used as empirical propositions. No one explicitly taught me that what they say is the case; I have not satisfied myself of their correctness. I do not normally utter and think them in the form in which I just wrote them. I accept them in so far as I act.

> The child doesn't learn that there are books, that there are armchairs, etc., etc., rather, he learns to fetch books, sit in armchairs, etc. (*OC:* 476)

Together these propositions (ways of acting, facts) constitute a system or a whole. We read in *OC:* 143, 144:

62

... [The child] doesn't *learn* that that mountain has existed for a long time; that is, the question whether it is so doesn't even arise. It swallows this conclusion, so to speak, together with *what* it learns.

The child learns to believe a lot of things. That is, it learns, for example, to act on these beliefs. Little by little it constructs a system out of his beliefs, some of which stand unshakeably fast within the system, some are more or less movable. What stands fast does not do so because it is intrinsically obvious or convincing; rather, it is held fast by what lies around it.

We might even say: were there no such empirical propositions which never came into doubt, then there could be no language-game. For example: if we doubt, or make an assumption, then we do this with reference to something which we accept *without* doubt. If I doubt whether something which, in the fog, I take to be a tree really is a tree, there are other perceptions which I don't doubt but which lead me to doubt. We could imagine language-games in which whenever someone speaks or gestures, the other just shrugs his shoulders and says, 'Perhaps he thinks so and so', or 'He probably thinks such and such'. But it would be possible to react in this way only by comparison with other cases in which the other *does* think such and such and 'perhaps' is completely out of the question. Otherwise he could not say 'perhaps' in this case.

Or compare *OC:* 491, 492:

Do I know, or do I only believe, that my name is L. W.?' ...

'Do I know, or do I only believe ...?' could also be expressed like this: What if it *seemed* to turn out that what until now I have taken to be immune from doubt was a false assumption? Would I react as I do when a belief has been proved false? Or *would the grounds of my judgement seem to have disappeared? ...* [2]

Would I simply say 'I should never have thought it!' – or would I (have to) refuse to revise my judgement, because such a 'revision' would amount to the annihilation of all yardsticks?

He speaks, often strikingly, of the 'grounds of our language-game', the 'foundation', the 'background against which all distinctions between true and false are made'. Yet he doesn't want to say that such a system of propositions could justify or *explain* the form of our speaking and investigating. It is not an hypothesis. Thus he writes, *OC:* 167:

... Think of chemical investigations. Lavoisier carries out experiments with substances in his laboratory and concludes that this and that happens when he burns them. He doesn't say that something different might happen at another time. He has got hold of a definite world-picture: not one that he invented, of course; rather, he learned it as a child. *I say world-picture, and not hypothesis, because it is the foundation of his research which he takes for granted and as such is also unarticulated.*[3]

Here the word 'world-picture' is important. But it is clear that Wittgenstein does not present a world-picture in these remarks (still less so that he gives voice to 'his own' world-picture). As he uses the word, there would be no sense in asking whether one world-picture is preferable to another. – He also says nothing about 'the world'; about the form of the world, the structure of the world, etc.

In the Lavoisier example, the concern is with the way in which he carries out and draws inferences from the experiments. 'He doesn't say that something different might happen at another time.' Something we take for granted; and that means: the world-picture that Lavoisier learned as a child shows up in our thinking as well. – Or think of the sentence 'Every man has a brain', and suppose I asked a physiologist how he knows this. He might point to specimens he had dissected. To go on to ask *how* he knows that what he found in these cases shows anything about mine would be empty and senseless. For him it *is* so. This is the way he acts, the way he carries out his research; and above all: that is what he calls an *answer* to such a question. And so do we, of course. To ask, 'Is that a reason to believe that one finds the same thing in other human bodies?' seems silly to us because it is a model of what in such cases we would call 'a good reason'. That just is the way we think.

But if what we call a 'reason' or 'correct inference' belongs to our world-picture, to speak of a foundation or justification of the world-picture itself is to say nothing.

There have been philosophers who taught (if I am not mistaken) that philosophy's task is to decide (find out?) which world-picture is the *right* one. Apparently the word 'world-picture' would be used differently than in Wittgenstein's remarks.

He says here, for example, that a society's prevailing world-picture can change. History provides us with enough examples of this. – In *OC*: 94, 96 he writes:

But I don't have my world-picture because I have satisfied myself that it is correct; nor because I am convinced that it is correct. Rather, it is the inherited background against which I distinguish between true and false ...

We might imagine that some propositions with the form of empirical propositions had solidified and functioned as a conduit for the empirical proposi-

64

tions which had not solidified, but remained fluid; and that this relationship changed over time, so that fluid propositions solidified and the solid ones became fluid.

There is no yardstick here whereby we could distinguish between correct or incorrect *world-pictures.*

He also describes how it would be were two cultures with radically different world-pictures to come into contact. For example, in *OC:* 608, 609, 610:

> Am I wrong to guide my actions by the propositions of physics? Should I say that I lack good grounds for doing so? Isn't this just what we call a 'good ground'?
>
> Suppose we came across some people who didn't regard that as a compelling reason. Now, how are we to imagine this? Instead of the physicist, perhaps they consult an oracle. (And because of this we consider them primitive.) Is it wrong for them to consult an oracle and guide themselves by it? – If we call this 'wrong', aren't we using our language-game to *combat* theirs?
>
> And are we right or wrong to combat it? Of course we will prop up our course of action with all sorts of slogans.

Don't forget that the propositions we are speaking about are empirical propositions. Thus, for example, individual ones can change their role in the language-game – whereby solid propositions become fluid and fluid ones become solid. They don't have the role of logical principles; even if isolated remarks give that impression at first glance. In the example quoted above, Wittgenstein asks whether '*the grounds of my judgement would seem to have disappeared*'. And elsewhere, 'I cannot doubt that without destroying all judgement'. Then *OC:* 572:

> I do seem to know that I cannot be mistaken, for example, about my own name!
>
> That expresses itself in the words: 'If that is wrong, then I'm insane.' Very well, but those are words; but what influence does that have on the application of the language?

Partly in reply, perhaps, he writes in *OC:* 617: 'Certain experiences would put me in a position where I could no longer continue the old language-game. Where I would be torn away from the game's *certainty* ...'

The concept of the language-game's certainty is important (and Wittgenstein himself emphasized the word). As well as: 'I could no longer continue the old language-game.' – 'I couldn't be mistaken about that': this has to be preserved in some form if the language-game is not to become a form of madness. – The expression 'Am I insane?', as Wittgenstein here considers it, is not the same as 'Am I making a mistake?', nor as 'I am confused'. A mistake 'can be incorporated into one's correct knowledge' (*OC*: 74). 'Madness' cannot. I cannot continue the game.

It is not always the same propositions which determine the language-game's certainty. Naturally we could not give a list of sentences and say, '*These* are the foundations without which no language-game would be possible'. We could not *look* for 'the principles of the possibility of language-games (or of the practice of speaking)'. That says nothing. Because of this it is important to recognize that we are concerned here with *empirical propositions*. Not logical principles or 'necessary propositions'. It is not the form itself of propositions which places them beyond doubt for us. It is not for any *reason* that just *these* empirical propositions have this role. (For perhaps they won't always have this role; and in different circumstances they are different propositions.)

We are not saying that there is a certain class of propositions or facts which cannot be doubted. On the contrary.

12

ON CERTAINTY'S MAIN THEME

The main theme of *On Certainty* can be brought out by the way in which Wittgenstein criticizes Moore's propositions.

We can imagine circumstances in which it is perfectly natural to say 'I know it's a tree'. A blind man asks me, hitting the tree with his stick, 'Do you think it's a tree?' I reply: 'I don't think it's a tree, I know it is.' Stage props may have been left around after an open-air performance and I'm told to get a particular one. I reply: 'No, I know it's a tree.' This may be said to convince someone about what one sees in a fog. And so on. These are circumstances in which the expression can be used, but they are of no interest to philosophy.

Moore is not in such circumstances. He is in the garden of the house in which he had lived for many years and says 'I know that's a tree'. What is this in aid of? What is he telling anyone? Moore says what he does because he is perplexed about the use of the word 'know'.

In lectures given in 1938 Wittgenstein said that philosophers want to use the word 'know' in ways entirely different from its use outside philosophy. Why do they do this, since they were supposed to be helping people to understand the word? Wittgenstein says that we use 'know' correctly if we say, 'I know Jones is in his room' – 'How?' – 'I saw him go in a minute ago.' If he was giving evidence in a law court, given that he wasn't blind, drunk or hallucinating, what he said would be taken as correct. But some philosophers say it is incorrect. Why? Because although the man may be speaking conscientiously, it *could* turn out that he is wrong. This is a famil-

From editor's notes on Rhees's seminar, 19 January 1970.

iar state of affairs. We provide for it with the phrase, 'I thought I knew, but I didn't'. You can't say, 'He knew, but he was mistaken'. This feature of our grammar is one of the chief sources of philosophical puzzlement about 'know'. 'I know that there is a rock in that part of the bay.' I may have been justified in saying that, but the rock may have been removed.

The man who said, 'I know Jones is in his room' used 'know' correctly, and we who taught him could not have avoided teaching it in that way. We are correct to teach him 'know' in this way, even though it *could* turn out that he is mistaken.

It is important in many cases to distinguish between knowledge and conjecture. 'Jones is in his room' is not a conjecture. Sometimes people will change what they say if you pull them up: 'Well, I didn't know, but I felt pretty certain'. We shouldn't say we know unless we have examined the matter and said we know as a result. There is blame attached to the use of it when that use turns out to be unjustified.

This is one feature of 'know' which led Moore and others to treat 'I know' as one does 'I believe'. 'I believe it's raining outside.' I may be wrong about *what* I believe, but, unless I'm lying, I *believed* it. 'I know it's raining' – 'It isn't, why did you say you knew?' Moore wanted to consider the two as similar so that, just as it makes no sense to say, 'I didn't believe it', so it would make no sense to say, 'I didn't know'. – If I know, I must know that I know.

If you say this – if you use the expression 'A man really knows that Jones is in his room' in the same way as 'A man really believes that Jones is in his room', two consequences follow: (1) it won't make sense to say that he is mistaken in saying that he knows it; (2) it won't make sense to say that he said he knew it, but it wasn't so. So philosophers have looked for examples of 'know' where it *cannot* be said that it is now so; examples such as 'I know that 2 + 2 = 4' and 'I know this is a red patch'. The contradictory of a proposition in geometry is an absurdity. The psychological experience, 'I am seeing a red patch' could be wrong – someone may not know how to use the word 'red'. But if he does, and has a visual impression of a red patch, then that's that.

Wittgenstein was discussing these questions long before he wrote the remarks in *On Certainty*. They went along with his discussions of the expressions 'mistake' and 'doubt'.

Philosophers who put forward sceptical views usually reveal confusions about 'doubt'. If you are going to talk about doubt, that only makes sense in a certain language-game, system, environment, etc. When philosophers doubt the existence of objects in the physical world, Wittgenstein says that he does not know what 'doubting' is here, let alone grounds for doubt.

Biologists say, 'There have never been any centaurs'. Someone says, 'But I've seen one'. We say, 'You've been taken in'. This is based on our knowledge of other physical objects. 'Are there beings with one eye in their foreheads?' Here, you know the *kind* of thing you are looking for. But: 'Are there any physical objects?' – How would you go about answering this?

Compare the use of 'mistake'. 'I thought that there was a rock' – 'No, you're mistaken.' The mistake can be fitted in to the rest of the beliefs we hold.

'If I open a door in my house, there is a staircase leading to a corridor.' If I open the door and see a beach and the open sea, I wouldn't say, 'I must be mistaken', but 'I must be crazy'. Wittgenstein speaks in more than one place of the difference between being mistaken and being crazy; the difference between a mistake and madness.

Wittgenstein spells out what he finds important in the propositions Moore enumerates in *On Certainty*. 136 and 137:

> When Moore says he *knows* such and such, he is really enumerating a lot of empirical propositions which we affirm without special testing; propositions, that is, which have a peculiar logical role in the system of our empirical propositions.
>
> Even if the most trustworthy of men assures me that he *knows* things are thus and so, this by itself cannot satisfy me that he does know. Only that he believes he knows. That is why Moore's assurance that he knows ... does not interest us. The propositions, however, which Moore retails as examples of such known truths are indeed interesting. Not because anyone knows their truth, or believes he knows them, but because they all have a *similar* role in the system of our empirical judgements.

Should these propositions be called empirical? This is a difficult question. What Wittgenstein is insisting on is that they aren't logical propositions. There are a great many propositions which seem to be empirical, and yet do not play that role at all. If you think of propositions like 'There is a fair amount of oil on Swansea's sands', 'The Mumbles railway runs along the seashore', 'English people are generally complacent', experience might teach you to modify them. Now compare these with 'This is a desk', 'The Earth has existed for many years before I was born'. Wittgenstein extends the list, and it contains a great variety. Although he calls them empirical propositions, he does not call them a *class* of propositions with features in common.

69

If you *did* open the familiar door which leads to a corridor, and see a green field and a river instead, *you wouldn't know what to say.* Wittgenstein's point is that the kinds of propositions Moore is listing play a similar role, namely, that if they are called into question we wouldn't know what to say; we wouldn't be able to carry on language at all.

Wittgenstein gives more examples: 'I have a brain.' What makes one think so? If it turned out that someone else didn't, it would not simply be a mistake. 'Water boils at 100°' or the elementary propositions of chemistry. 'I had parents.' 'My name is Rhees.' – If you told me I was wrong, and I found other people were unanimous in this, I become unstuck, but I'm unstuck in many other ways as well. What measuring rod can I use?

Compare 'This is a piece of wood' or our use of 'red', 'blue', 'square', 'round'. '"Gas" is a word.' '"Wood" is a word.' 'In raising his hand he was making a gesture.' What would it be *like* to doubt these? One never considers doubt in connection with them.

Wittgenstein says that such propositions aren't formulated. 'The Earth has existed before I was born' may never have been taught, but it goes along with a great many things which have been taught. So propositions of this kind underlie the possibility of speaking. *Underlie* – how? *This is the main theme.* He answers this question differently in connection with different examples. He is not treating them as first principles or hypotheses.

Consider 'The Earth has existed for the past one thousand years'. How does he know?

> If Moore says he knows the Earth existed etc., most of us will grant him that it has existed all that time, and also believe him when he says he is convinced of it. But has he also got the right *ground* for his conviction? For if not, then after all he doesn't *know* (Russell).
>
> However, we can ask: May someone have telling grounds for believing that the Earth has only existed for a short time, say since his own birth? – Suppose he had always been told that, – would he have any good reason to doubt it? Men have believed that they could make rain; why should not a king be brought up in the belief that the world began with him? And if Moore and this king were to meet and discuss, could Moore really prove his belief to be the right one? I do not say that Moore could not convert the king to his view, but it would be a conversion of a special kind; the king would be brought to look at the world in a different way.
>
> Remember that one is sometimes convinced of the *correctness* of a view by its *simplicity* or *symmetry*, i.e. these are what induce one to go over to this point of view. One then simply says something like: '*That's* how it must be'. (*OC*: 92 and 93)

Giving reasons belongs to a particular way of life, and so do doubts. Moore couldn't convert the king by talking about geology.

> We don't, for example, arrive at any of them as a result of investigation.
> There are, e.g., historical investigations and investigations into the shape and also the age of the Earth, but not into whether the Earth has existed during the last hundred years. Of course many of us have information about this period from our parents and grandparents; but mayn't they be wrong? – 'Nonsense!' one will say. 'How should all these people be wrong?' – But is that an argument? Is it not simply the rejection of an idea? And perhaps the determination of a concept? For if I speak of a possible mistake here, this changes the role of 'mistake' and 'truth' in our lives. (*OC:* 138)

The evidence that might be taken to show that the Earth existed for a million years, wouldn't show that it has existed for a hundred years:

> 'It is certain that after the battle of Austerlitz Napoleon ... Well, in that case it's surely also certain that the Earth existed then.'
> 'It is certain that we didn't arrive on this planet from another one a hundred years ago.' Well, it's as certain as such things *are*.
> It would strike me as ridiculous to want to doubt the existence of Napoleon; but if someone doubted the existence of the Earth 150 years ago, perhaps I should be more willing to listen, for now he is doubting our whole system of evidence. It does not strike me as if this system were more certain than a certainty within it.
> 'I might suppose that Napoleon never existed and is a fable, but not that the *Earth* did not exist 150 years ago.'
> 'Do you *know* that the Earth existed then?' – 'Of course I know that. I have it from someone who certainly knows all about it.'
> It strikes me as if someone who doubts the existence of the Earth at that time is impugning the nature of all historical evidence. And I cannot say of this latter that it is definitely *correct*. (*OC:* 183–8)

Not that I'm not doubtful, but that I don't know what it would mean to doubt.

'I have a brain.' A physiologist says, 'All human beings have brains'. We press him. He produces a comparatively small number of specimens. (Cf. Harvey and the circulation of the blood.) Wittgenstein's point is that if I were to say to the physiologist, 'You've found brains in the dozen or so you've dissected, but how does it show that I have one?', it would be meaningless. What kind of *showing* am I after? If he'd say

71

anything he would say, 'It's obvious'. He goes on like that without any reason.

This 'going on without any reason' underlies much of life and the language that we use. It is connected with what Wittgenstein says about induction, general laws and with what he says in other contexts: we go on like that without any reason.

13

INDUCTION

I

When people have asked about 'the justification of induction' – this seems to have been like asking: 'Is there any reason to think that because things have gone this way in the past, they will go this way in the future?'

There have always been local choirs in the Welsh villages; therefore there always will be. The soil in this valley has always been fertile, therefore it always will be.

But we criticize assumptions of this sort: we say that they 'ignore factors which they should have taken into account' (i.e. we use induction in our criticism). And it is for *this* reason that we say that 'it happened in the past' is not a good reason for saying *here* (regarding the fertility of the soil) that it will happen in the future. – It happened 'under specific conditions'. And we must know what these were before we are ready to predict one way or another.

We can ask whether this is really a good reason. But then we have some idea of a good reason: we'll be able to recognize that this is a good reason when you've explained it to us – or else we'll see that it's not one. – And to ask whether we are *justified* in being convinced or influenced by what we see as a good reason, would mean nothing.

'Why do you say the stove will stop smoking when the train starts moving?' – 'It always does.' – 'Yes, but *why* does it?' (You could not answer:

From Rhees's notes dated 17 and 18 February 1970.

'Because it always does.') We speak of an investigation into causes. If you answer only that 'it always does', you have not begun to look for a cause.

'Why does it do that?' is like: 'It doesn't just happen – for no reason'; which is like: 'We could imagine something else happening, and *not* this.' We *answer* this question by reference, direct or indirect, to experiments. Experiments which are framed in accordance with a developed technique and accepted theories.

And we do not consider any alternative to this general method. We would not regard consulting a spiritualist medium as an alternative method at all. (We would never say that the methods of experimental science 'are to be preferred' to consulting a medium; still less would we try to show what considerations weighed in favour of experimental methods, etc., etc. – Obviously, this phrase 'considerations which weigh in favour', has its meaning *within* experimental or inductive techniques.)

Consider Wittgenstein's imagined people who have no experimental science; and instead of being guided by the results of science (as we are), they consult oracles and are guided by them. – If I say that our practice is a better one, that this is the right way to proceed, then I am speaking *within* our methods, judging by our criteria: as though those people were really trying to do what we do but they just did not know how to go about it. Whereas in the case imagined we have no reason whatever to think they are trying to do what we do. For this reason, we should not know how to speak of 'better' or 'worse' in connection with their practice.

(*nota bene,* in *OC:* 286, Wittgenstein is not stating his own views. He is expressing *what someone might say.*):

> What we believe depends on what we learn. We all believe that it isn't possible to get to the moon; but there might be people who believe that that is possible and that it sometimes happens. We say: these people do not know a lot that we know. And, let them be never so sure of their belief – they are wrong and we know it.
>
> If we compare our system of knowledge with theirs then theirs is evidently the poorer one by far.

'Do you mean that a people who had no science and no experiments get results just as well by their methods?'

I do not think they would get *these* results as well by other methods. I.e. they would not develop our engineering and our medicine and our industry. They would now know the answers to problems in physics and problems in chemistry and problems in biology by other methods. They would not *have* these problems.

There is a tendency to ask: 'Aren't our methods the best fitted for finding out what there really is; for finding out what the world is like?' Whereas: they are best fitted for finding out what scientists do find out.

II

The queer thing is that even though I find it quite correct for someone to say 'Rubbish!' and so brush aside the attempt to confuse him with doubts at bedrock, – nevertheless, I hold it to be incorrect if he seeks to defend himself (using, e.g., the words 'I know'). (*OC:* 498)

I might also put it like this: the 'law of induction' can no more be *grounded* than certain particular propositions concerning the material of experience. (*OC:* 499)

But it would also strike me as nonsense to say 'I know that the law of induction is true'. (*OC:* 500)

(On the expression 'the law of induction': compare Russell's 'the principle of induction', *The Problems of Philosophy,* pp. 103ff.).

Special confusions have made people 'uncertain of the foundation' in connection with induction (where 'induction' means roughly: framing hypotheses in connection with some scientific problem, performing experiments and drawing conclusions from the experiments). – Peirce formulated the difficulty roughly like this: 'How can we, from knowledge of one fact, pronounce judgement on another fact which was not contained in it?' Here Wittgenstein would say: it would be better to ask 'How *do* we?' Otherwise it is like asking 'How can I walk?'

But suppose the question were, 'How can induction lead us to truth?' Wittgenstein would say: one answer is that it *doesn't* always. You may draw a curve through a series of dots (from experiments already performed), continuing it in the same way, and in fact the next dot may not fall in that curve at all.

But the suggestion that 'you pass on to assertions about facts which seem to have nothing to do with the facts on which you base them' is a blunder, because these are just the circumstances in which you would *not* say they had nothing to do with them.

In terms of Wittgenstein's method of 'supposing a people who did things differently': suppose a traveller from a society which had nothing like our science or experiments. Suppose he found a tribe who drew conclusions from experiments as we do, and acted on them – building bridges, etc. And imagine his asking: 'How can they draw conclusions from experiments in that way, and then go on to get those results?' – He might say it was a very remarkable thing. But would there be sense in his asking how they were *justified* in acting in this way? – Let him say they *aren't* justified. This is what they do, and they get those results.

Wittgenstein's point is: you might be able to answer the question why one method of treating a disease generally leads to cures whereas another method generally does not. But this is a different sort of question from the question why *induction* leads (often) to true results. Could one mention alternatives and ask 'Is it for this reason or for that one?'? (Perhaps this is where some writers bring in probability.)

Suppose someone said, 'It must be because the world is constituted in such a way that inductions (predictions based on experiments, etc.) do turn out right; or: constituted in such a way that experiments increase the probability of hypotheses.' – The question is whether you have said anything more than that inductions do often lead to true results.

Would inductions be possible in a purely chance world? (Cf. C. S. Peirce.) Would induction be possible in a world in which there was no order?

Well, suppose that we could describe a world in which there was no order, or at any rate describe a certain field in which there was no order. Why should we say that inductions could not be made or would have no validity in such a world? How would one find this out? For people might just go on doing what we do.

(With regard to the 'principle of the limitation of independent variety' et al., Wittgenstein would say: such writers seem to be speaking from God's point of view – suggesting that God would see that since there are no uniformities, no amount of investigation *can* make the law probable.)

Consider the case where someone says, 'It is now probable that some forms of cancer are caused by a virus'. 'It is now probable that metal fatigue is a form of ...' (It is important to note that the scientist himself never says this. He describes the experiments he has made; and he may add 'this shows that ...'.) And we may ask whether 'it is now probable' is not redundant.

It will be sensible to say this ('It is now probable that ...') only if we can say what is *not* probable – what the theory in question is opposed to. *And here we take for granted a developed technique.*

Suppose you say that a certain theory is now not probable. Or suppose you want to dispute the claims that have been made for it. You may examine reports of the experiments, and say they do not support the theory: these occurrences could be explained more simply otherwise; this effect was due to something in the apparatus; etc. – Here your criticisms themselves presuppose an accepted technique. You are relying on induction when you say it is '*due to*' something in the apparatus, and so on.

So if anyone were to ask, 'But why does this make it probable that ...', we should wait for him to state his particular objection. And the objection would operate *within* this developed technique of setting up and testing theories.

Contrast this with a situation where some tribe who had never heard of experiments or of putting forward theories to be tested were told what scientists had done. If they were to ask 'But why does that make it probable that ...' – you wouldn't know what to answer, and you wouldn't know what they were asking.

When *we* ask such a question, it is never a question as to why *induction* makes laws probable, because the answer can only be given, and the question is only understood, *in terms of* induction.

If we *defend* a theory we defend it against objections which could only arise themselves within the developed technique of framing and testing theories. And we have no conception of what would make the theory probable to someone who did not follow experimental procedure at all.

14

WITTGENSTEIN'S PROPOSITIONS AND FOUNDATIONS

I

Wittgenstein adds many propositions to Moore's list. There is a great diversity in these propositions. Wittgenstein says:

> The propositions, however, which Moore retails as examples of such known truths are indeed interesting. Not because anyone knows their truth, or believes he knows them, but because they all have a *similar* role in the system of our empirical judgements. (*OC:* 137)

One misunderstanding people make about the propositions which Wittgenstein says cannot be doubted is to try to classify them, or find out what they all have in common. All his examples are dependent on the immunity from doubt of these propositions, and imagining what it means to say that that could be lost. Obviously, they are not propositions or facts that one considers in most of what one says. We do not treat them as postulates or anything of that sort. They aren't even expressed in our thoughts: 'I had parents'; 'The Earth has existed for many years past'. This is why their logical role cannot be brought out except by imagining what would happen if the immunity from doubt were removed.

Section 1 of this chapter is taken in the main from editor's notes on Rhees's seminar, 9 February 1970. Section 2 is taken in the main from Rhees's notes dated 24 February 1970. Section 3 is from editor's notes on Rhees's seminar, 26 January 1970. Section 4 is from a letter to Godfrey Vesey dated 18 July 1973.

What *is* their logical role? There is no single answer. It differs from one proposition to another. It does not amount to saying: 'There is a class of propositions which we can't doubt'. In *OC*: 519 (third paragraph) Wittgenstein warns us against thinking of them as a set of propositions which are the foundation of language:

> But since a language-game is something that consists in the recurrent procedures of the game in time, it seems impossible to say in any *individual* case that such-and-such must be beyond doubt if there is to be a language-game – though it is right enough to say *that as a rule* some empirical judgement or other must be beyond doubt.

Wittgenstein speaks of these propositions as forming a background, or even a foundation, but he is not explaining the fact that there is language at all. He is not advancing complex hypotheses or logical principles on which the meaningfulness of the expressions we use rest.

'The empirical propositions which are the foundation of our language-game.' – These do not *explain* the forms of language game we carry on: the sequences of comments and observations that we regard as sensible, the queries, questions, doubts and investigations that we regard as sensible, what we regard as a strong reason and what a weak reason, etc., etc. At any rate very *many* of them do not, apparently. With 'the law of induction', acting on what I have learned from elementary text-books or encyclopedia articles about physics and chemistry – that water boils at 100 centigrade – or of biology or physiology (that I have a brain – that I have or had two parents, and similarly for all the other people there are) – Wittgenstein speaks somewhat differently. That is, he says that when people speak of having gone to the moon and see no need to answer the questions which we should put, as to how they would overcome the force of gravity of the Earth, how they would live where there is no atmosphere and so on – then 'we should feel ourselves intellectually very distant from someone who said this' (*OC*: 108). Here 'living in a scientific age' does to a considerable extent determine the ways in which we speak and think.

When he speaks of their logically peculiar role of empirical propositions, this is not to be equated with providing a logical foundation for language. Certainly not in the sense in which Russell and Whitehead wanted logical foundations for mathematics.

Wittgenstein says that the ways in which a scientist draws conclusions from experiments forms part of a world-picture, but we can imagine people among whom such recording of the results of experimental science plays no role comparable to that which they play with us. He asks, 'Is it a *mistake* for us to be guided by the results of experiments in physics?' 'Is it a mistake for them to consult oracles?' He wants to bring out the misuse of 'mistake' there.

There's nothing new in the suggestion that people in different historical periods or in different parts of the world *live very differently*. Wittgenstein didn't claim it was new. What *he's* interested in is the use of 'mistake' here, to counter the idea that it would be reasonable to look for a justification of our trust in physics. Compare the attempt of some mathematicians to justify mathematics. There are reasons which tempt one to do that which do not have analogies in physics.

The development of non-Euclidean geometry bothered some mathematicians. Are all geometries equally valid? Is mathematics simply a formal game? In physics, on the other hand, the experiments give you an anchor in reality. The same is true of the application of physics in engineering. Still, it has been suggested that in relying on experiments (induction) you are not justified. The criterion of success in engineering may be a lucky fluke – it doesn't tell us about the nature of reality. Wittgenstein wants to suggest that such justification wouldn't mean anything.

His question here is the same when he asks, 'Am I mistaken in being guided by science?' 'Are they mistaken in consulting an oracle?'

On specific occasions one may ask for justifications. 'Is my patient being honest with me?' Here, it is a mistake to refer to physics. But in relying on physics in engineering we can't ask whether that is a mistake. What would we have in mind? Are we saying that it is not mistaken to follow physics if you don't make mistakes in the physics you're following?

There would be an added absurdity in speaking of 'the logical foundations of science'. We know what the logical foundation is for a specific hypothesis. But a foundation for the way in which you carry out your enquiries – that is queer. The idea that science would be made firm if the foundations could be found.

Hilbert wants to find a certainty for mathematics; a mathematical certainty for mathematics? What would this mean? Reichenbach's attempt to give foundations to science by developing probability calculus.

Consider plotting a graph on the basis of experiments in the way indicated below:

Am I being rash in drawing the curve? If I performed more experiments between the dots the curve might oscillate. So when am I *ever* justified in drawing it? The scientist uses his nose, not logic. We might say, 'If ever you're justified in drawing the curve you're justified now.' But can't we

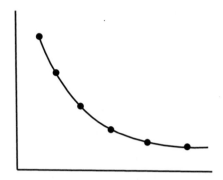

ask: 'Isn't it logically possible to have more experiments and the curve to oscillate?' But *in the circumstances* this may be a pretty meaningless sort of question to ask.

We can't describe this procedure as rash. On the contrary, it is someone who is not a competent scientist who makes rash extrapolations from insufficient evidence. But we know that only because of situations where every competent scientist would say it is not rash to draw the curve.

'Is it rash after a few dissections to conclude that there is a brain in my skull too?' This is *meaningless*. His conclusion from a few specimens *is* a good reason.

The so-called logical foundation would not add anything. *That is how science goes on* – it is natural to them, and to us for that matter. – The certainty with which they go on.

It may be said that we ought to explain the difference between Lavoisier's world-picture which we share, and that of people who consult oracles, so that we can discover why we go about things this way, and why they go about things that way. What would the explanation be? What is sought?

Margaret Mead (it was said) postulated different categories in this connection. People think in different categories and this is *why* they consult oracles. Society is a function of the categories in which people think. That doesn't explain their living in that way at all. Supposing you could say something about the categories in which we think – that wouldn't explain why we think.

This is one of the questions Wittgenstein raises: why do we think? In *Philosophical Investigations* I: 466 Wittgenstein discusses the example of calculating the thickness of a boiler. It might be that fewer boilers have exploded after calculation, than would have exploded had there been no calculation. But, sometimes, boilers explode despite the calculation *and yet* (and this is the point Wittgenstein emphasizes) he would never dream of making a boiler without calculation. He doesn't found his method on the probability of boilers not exploding.

If fire burns your hand, how do you know it will next time? There is no answer, but I'm not putting my hand in again. The action isn't the result of calculation of what is likely or unlikely.

Wittgenstein gives the example of constructing boilers as an example of thinking. It won't do to say that they think in this way because they find it useful. Here an act of thinking is being justified by a further act of thinking. The certainty they show in their actions is not a matter of regarding something as highly probable.

> I am taught that under *such* circumstances *this* happens. It has been discovered by making the experiment a few times. Not that that would prove anything to us, if it weren't that this experience was surrounded by others which combine with it to form a system. Thus, people did not make experiments just about falling bodies but also about air resistance and all sorts of other things.
>
> But in the end I rely on these experiences, or on the reports of them, I feel no scruples about ordering my own activities in accordance with them. – But hasn't this trust also proved itself? So far as I can judge – yes. (*OC:* 603)

Compare *OC:* 600:

> What kind of grounds have I for trusting text-books of experimental physics?
> I have no grounds for not trusting them. And I trust them. I know how such books are produced – or rather, I believe I know. I have some evidence, but it does not go very far and is of a very scattered kind. I have heard, seen and read various things.

Isn't the trust well founded – hasn't it been borne out? Wittgenstein says, 'So far as I can judge – yes'. Wittgenstein's reason for putting it in that way is to show that the certainty he has is *not* of the order – 'So far as I can judge – yes'! The suggestion is meant to serve as an ironic denial of itself.

So my reliance on text-books, etc., is not to be thought as trust on a high probability. This is why Reichenbach's attempt to use the calculus of probability to give a foundation to science is wrong-headed.[1]

Suppose one begins by speaking of different categories (if this were more than empty verbiage) and even if we could say we do speak in categories, this wouldn't explain why we think or why we think in these categories.

Imagine a people who consult oracles. There, examples of thinking would be different; they wouldn't give as a *first* example, calculation etc.

When it is said that the Azande do not think in terms of cause a Westerners do, it might be said that they employ different cate 'employ' is misleading here. In procedures which physicists follo̶v̶. ̶.̶.̶.̶,̶ ̶.̶.̶.̶,̶ use different frames of reference – light-waves or particles. They may switch from one frame of reference to another. This is something they do *within* physics. This can't have any parallel when we talk of our trust in the results of physics, so the use of 'categories' or 'framework' here as an explanation or elucidation doesn't help. A physicist could say, 'I switched to that frame of reference because it was simpler, more convenient, because relations could be made more elegant.' But: 'Why do we rely on science?' No answer.

Why did Spenser write *The Faerie Queene* in the stanzas that he did? Why did Shakespeare choose the sonnet form for his sonnets? Did he *choose* it? Certainly not: 'Shall I write in this way or that?' Why did Rembrandt paint in his style and not in the style of Michelangelo? Why do we think as we do, and why do the Azande think as they do? We can give histories of those societies, but that does not explain it. We aren't claiming that their histories *had* to go that way – they did go that way, that's all.

> You must bear in mind that the language-game is so to say something unpredictable. I mean: it is not based on grounds. It is not reasonable (or unreasonable).
>
> It is there – like our life. (*OC:* 559)

II

There are other empirical propositions of which we have never convinced ourselves and which we keep beyond the reach of any doubt as we act on them. Compared with the influence of science over our thinking, the ways in which these influence the *kind* of discourse that we regard as reasonable is not so plain. And maybe there is little to be said about it. We might have to emphasize that none of them has its 'fixed' position on its own account, but only together with others in a 'nest' of such propositions.

There are cases where we *cease* to ask 'How can we explain this?' or 'What could account for this?' There are cases where 'doubt' and also asking how it could have happened, etc., cease to make sense. One would say something like 'I must be mad'. This is closely parallel to what Wittgenstein says in the following:

This situation is thus not the same for a proposition like 'At this distance from the sun there is a planet' and 'Here is a hand' (namely my own hand). The second can't be called a hypothesis. But there isn't a sharp boundary line between them. (*OC:* 52)

For it is not true that a mistake merely gets more and more improbable as we pass from the planet to my own hand. No: at some point it has ceased to be conceivable.

This is already suggested by the following: if it were not so, it would also be conceivable that we should be wrong in *every* statement about physical objects; that any we ever make are mistaken. (*OC:* 54).

So is the *hypothesis* possible, that all things around us don't exist? Would that not be like the hypothesis of our having miscalculated in all our calculations? (*OC:* 55).

When one says: 'Perhaps this planet doesn't exist and the light-phenomenon arises in some other way', then after all one needs an example of an object which does exist. This doesn't exist, – as *for example* does ...

Or are we to say that *certainty* is merely a constructed point to which some things approximate more, some less closely? No. Doubt gradually loses its sense. This language-game just *is* like that.

And everything descriptive of a language-game is part of logic. (*OC:* 56)

'At this distance from the sun there is a planet' and 'Here is a hand' (namely my own hand) show a different 'conceptual linguistic situation', and that they do *not* differ in degrees of probability or improbability of their contradictories. I can imagine an explanation for the phenomenon which I now take as the appearance of a planet, and say 'Perhaps the light-phenomenon arises in some other way'. But it has no sense to speak of 'explaining', in terms of some other hypothesis, what I am talking about when I say 'Here is a hand' (namely my own hand). It is not that 'hardly anyone *would* doubt such a thing', but that it does not *mean* anything to speak of doubt here. Just as it would not mean anything to *ask* for an explanation if I found green pastures instead of the corridor when I opened the familiar door in my house.

Consider:

But it isn't just that *I* believe in this way that I have two hands, but that every reasonable person does. (*OC:* 252)

And:

Any 'reasonable' person behaves like *this*. (*OC:* 254)

'Reasonable' seems to be connected here with the idea of 'reasonable certainty' and 'reasonable doubt'. But perhaps only superficially, or in a negative way.

Cf. *OC:* 416:

> And here we have an example of this in, say, the proposition that I have been living in this room for weeks past, that my memory does not deceive me in this? – 'certain beyond all reasonable doubt'.
>
> This is connected with 'judging' and 'the game of judging': 'From a child I learnt to judge like this. *This is* judging. (*OC:* 128)
>
> This is how I learned to judge; *this* I got to know as judgement. (*OC:* 129)
>
> But isn't it experience that teaches us to judge like *this*, that is to say, that it is correct to judge like this? But how does experience *teach* us, then? *We* may derive it from experience, but experience does not direct us to derive anything from experience. If it is the *ground* of our judging like this, and not just the cause, still we do not have a ground for seeing this in turn as a ground. (*OC:* 130)
>
> No, experience is not the ground for our game of judging. Nor its out-standing success. (*OC:* 131)

It is also connected with *OC:* 140:

> We do not learn the practice of making empirical judgements by learning rules: we are taught *judgements* and their connection with other *judgements*. A *totality* of *judgements* is made plausible to us.

The use of 'plausible' here is not quite clear to me. But I suppose *rules* would suffice, in many cases, to distinguish a 'meaningful' expression from a meaningless one. We are not simply taught 'how it works'; we are not simply taught grammar: we come to have certain convictions or beliefs.

The rational man would be someone we could understand (with whom we could speak and do business), someone from whom we did not feel ourselves 'intellectually very distant'.

In *OC:* 139 he emphasizes: 'Not only rules, but also examples are needed for establishing a practice. Our rules leave loop-holes open and the practice has to speak for itself.' Apparently 'to establish a practice' and 'to teach *judgements*' come to much the same. And the emphasis is on 'not just *rules*, but examples' – for the reasons that the examples are *applications* of the rules, or are *judgments*.

When the manuscript notebook speaks of 'an agreement in the lives of people' he adds that this is not 'an agreement in opinions' let alone an agreement on opinions about the questions of logic.

III

Take 'The Earth existed six months ago'. It seems silly to say that, but why should that be so? No one doubts it, but it is unclear what that doubt would consist in. Where do you start from? We can raise doubts about life on Mars. We can consider evidence, etc. Doubting or enquiry always takes place in a context, the context of that which one does not doubt. So where the existence of the Earth or of my brain are concerned, where would you begin? Have you any idea what it would be? What is the evidence that I have a brain? The physiologist replies: 'You are a human being, your head is like other heads.' Suppose someone said, 'Is that any good reason why …'? But isn't that *the sort of thing one calls a good reason*? You don't have anything else which one *might call* a good reason. That such investigations have been carried out (and I don't doubt *that*) is part of the context in which we carry out our doubts and conjectures.

Likewise with the existence of the Earth. The evidence that shows that it has existed for the last million years, does not show that it has existed for the last hundred years. But if someone said that the Earth hadn't existed for the last hundred years, we wouldn't know what he was saying.

But it is odd to say we believe it – we don't even formulate it in our thoughts. It is the fixed background of our thoughts.

> I cannot possibly doubt that I was never in the stratosphere. Does that make me know it? Does it make it true? (*OC:* 222)

'The Earth has existed for the last 100 years' doesn't come into the traffic of our thoughts at all.

> Now it gives our way of looking at things, and our researches their form. Perhaps it was once disputed. But perhaps, for unthinkable ages, it has belonged to the *scaffolding* of our thoughts. (Every human being has parents.) (*OC:* 211)

None of these propositions in themselves gives us our way of thinking, but together these things give us a system (not a formal system) – a whole lot of facts which together gives us the way we go about things.

OC: 167 is an important paragraph:

It is clear that our empirical propositions do not all have the same status, since one can lay down such a proposition and turn it from an empirical proposition into a norm of description.

Think of chemical investigations. Lavoisier makes experiments with substances in his laboratory and now he concludes that this and that takes place when there is burning. He does not say that it might happen otherwise another time. He has got hold of a definite world-picture – not of course one that he invented: he learned it as a child. I say world-picture and not hypothesis, because it is the matter-of-course foundation for his research and as such also goes unmentioned.

The second paragraph of 167 is important. Cf. the physiologist making his dissections. He doesn't say, 'It might be different next time'. What is important here is *what goes unmentioned*. All this belongs to what he calls 'world-picture'. He learned it as a child. What does this mean? Not that he had it in a course of instruction.

Consider *OC:* 143–4:

I am told, for example, that someone climbed this mountain many years ago. Do I always enquire into the reliability of the teller of this story, and whether the mountain did exist years ago? A child learns there are reliable and unreliable informants much later than it learns facts which are told it. It doesn't learn *at all* that a mountain has existed for a long time; that is, the question whether it is so doesn't arise at all. It swallows this consequence down, so to speak, together with *what* it learns.

The child learns to believe a host of thing. I.e. it learns to act according to these beliefs. Bit by bit there forms a system of what is believed, and in that system some things stand unshakeably fast and some are more or less liable to shift. What stands fast does so, not because it is intrinsically obvious or convincing; it is rather held fast by what lies around it.

He doesn't even raise the question whether the mountain has existed for a long time – you swallow that with the rest that you drink. You couldn't learn these other things and be in doubt about this – the question just wouldn't arise.

Compare *OC:* 144 with 229: 'Our talk gets its meaning from the rest of our proceedings.'

Compare 476:

Children do not learn that books exist, that armchairs exist, etc., etc. – they learn to fetch books, and sit in armchairs, etc., etc.

Later, questions about the existence of things do of course arise. 'Is there such a thing as a unicorn?' and so on. But such a question is possible only because as a rule no corresponding question presents itself. For how does one know how to set about satisfying oneself of the existence of unicorns? How did one learn the method for determining whether something exists or not?

In this way a system is formed (*OC:* 144). Those empirical propositions underlie, form a background to, the way we speak, the way we think, and what we call 'good reasons'. But they do not do this singly but as a system, a nest of propositions. 'What I hold fast to is not *one* proposition but a nest of propositions' (*OC:* 225).

'I cannot possibly doubt that I was never in the stratosphere. Does that make me know it? Does it make it true?' (*OC:* 222). If you asked me whether I'm sure I wouldn't understand you. Wittgenstein said that he could not doubt whether he had been on the moon. These remarks were written in 1951 when people weren't even thinking about it. That the situation changed does not invalidate what he is saying here.

Certain things need to be emphasized about what he calls 'a nest of propositions'. Although they underlie or form the foundations of doubting and asking questions, such that if, by some way or other, I came to doubt these things, I shouldn't know what to believe – if *that* is doubtful I don't know what is doubtful and what isn't. If I doubted my name, it would be a collapse that would bring down all my measuring-rods with it – despite all this, *it would be an entire mistake to imagine that what Wittgenstein is saying is that these are principles which give language its sense.* Without the fixity of those propositions there could be no distinction between truth and falsity, but this does not mean that you could deduce *what* is true or false from these features. Neither are they hypotheses (see end of *OC:* 167). It is not that he *first* sees the world-picture and then makes experiments. No, the world-picture *is* making experiments in that way. Lavoisier does not invent the picture; it is not personal to him and it is not an hypothesis. The whole use of hypotheses and finding supporting or conflicting evidence is part of what he is calling a world-picture. 'Is it wrong for me to be guided in my actions by the propositions of physics? Am I to say I have no good ground for doing so? Isn't precisely this what we call a "good ground"?' (*OC:* 608).

But, then, see *OC:* 609:

> Supposing we met people who did not regard that as a telling reason. Now, how do we imagine this? Instead of the physicist, they consult an oracle. (And for that we consider them primitive.) Is it wrong for them to consult an oracle and be guided by it? – If we call this 'wrong' aren't we using our language-game as a base from which to *combat* theirs?

Here we have a people who do not regard as good reasons what we regard as good reasons. They consult oracles, not physics. He asks whether we aren't using our world-picture to combat theirs. All you can have is a conflict. You can't convince them by offering reasons; at least, not by the kind of thing called 'reasons' in science (what we call 'reasons' in politics is another matter).

610. And are we right or wrong to combat it? Of course there are all sorts of slogans which will be used to support our proceedings.

611. Where two principles really do meet which cannot be reconciled with one another, then each man declares the other a fool and heretic. (*OC*)

I don't want to say, 'They who follow the oracle are right' any more than I want to say that they are wrong. Compare: is it right for me to be guided by the propositions of physics? The point is: can you raise doubts about it?

Wittgenstein is *not* talking about presuppositions in all our thinking. *NO*. He is talking of something involved *in* our thinking.

No world-picture is *the* right one. What does that mean? Wittgenstein is not presenting a form of relativism: each man has the right to regard his world-picture as *the* right one. That is not Wittgenstein's use of world-picture.

In 'A Defence of Common Sense' Moore wanted to formulate as precisely as possible what propositions can be known to be true. Some philosophers deny their truth. So this was a major philosophical task for Moore. But this is the essential difference between Moore and Wittgenstein. Moore wants to be free from error. One might imagine someone saying that Moore is presenting a picture of the world in so far as it can be known – what can be known about reality. This picture of the world shows how he differs from other philosophers. (Moore doesn't use this expression 'picture of the world'.)

If one says this of Moore, his use of 'know' in connection with these propositions, and his taking the task of philosophy to establish what can be known, could be taken as saying that the task of philosophy is to establish which world-picture is the right one.

Wittgenstein's whole use of 'world-picture' is different from that. Wittgenstein wouldn't say that it is the task of philosophy to *establish* a world-picture, to show that it was the *right* one, or that it could be *known*. He wouldn't call it *the* right one, since it may undergo changes. There are also the differences between peoples. So Wittgenstein wasn't saying anything about *the* structure of the world. Wittgenstein is not meaning by 'world-picture' an environment – an analogy with our physical environment. That is a bad mis-interpretation. Take the example of the child who learns to fetch books and to sit on chairs. Well, aren't books and chairs part of his environment? Yes, but he means a good deal else which is *not* part of the physical environment. For example, reasoning in certain ways – as in the physical sciences. It is so much part of our world-picture that we find it difficult to imagine how it was before this was so. For example, think of scholastic philosophers proving the immortality of the soul by formal reasoning. This seems bizarre to us. A young monk may have become *convinced* about immortality. We know what it is to *believe* in immortality, but to be *convinced* about it? We are so saturated with technology, fiddling with bikes, taps, etc., we can't think in other ways – not that we aren't willing to – we can't. So Wittgenstein is not *speaking of taking a physical environment for granted*.

IV

> Certain facts would put me into a position in which I could not go on with the old language-game any further. In which I was torn away from the *sureness* of the game.
>
> Indeed, doesn't it seem obvious that the possibility of a language-game is conditioned by certain facts? (*OC:* 617)

Wittgenstein says this after imagining that I observe a multitude of facts and events which force me into doubting certain things which in fact I never call into question, any more than I call in question whether I am speaking the language when I ask you something. He gives examples in *OC:* 613 and the last one in the paragraph is the strongest:

> If I now say 'I know that the water in the kettle on the gas-flame will not freeze but boil', I seem to be as justified in this 'I know' as I am in *any*. 'If I know anything I know *this*'. – Or do I know with still *greater* certainty that the person opposite me is my old friend so-and-so? And how does that compare with the proposition that I am seeing with two *eyes* and shall see them if I look in the glass? – I don't know confidently what I am to answer here. – But still there is a difference between the cases. If the water over the gas freezes, of course, I shall be as astonished as can be, but I shall assume some factor I don't know of, and perhaps leave the matter to physicists to judge. But what could make me doubt whether this person here is NN, whom I have known for years? Here a doubt would seem to drag everything with it and plunge it into chaos.

90

If you were talking with some colleague whom you see every day, can you imagine any circumstances which would make you doubt (make you really uncertain, not just make you say 'of course it's logically possible') that this is someone whom you've known for a long time? 'Here a doubt would seem to drag everything with it and plunge it into chaos.'

Or as he puts it in the first part of *OC*: 617: 'I was torn away from the *sureness* of the game'. Here 'the sureness' just means whatever it is that I have when I say something; when I speak. I am speaking the language, I am writing a sentence here, I am saying something. And of course: I am speaking the language that other people speak, the people to whom I am speaking, etc.

If we say the possibility of this is determined by certain facts, Wittgenstein's point is still, I think, that it is determined by our *not calling in question* certain facts. At least this is the point he is emphasizing most of the time here.

'Is conditioned by' or 'depends on certain facts' does also have the sense which is in the immediately following paragraph, *OC*: 618:

> Then can one say that only a certain regularity in occurrences makes induction possible? The 'possible' would of course have to be '*logically possible*'.

This is one of the main themes of *On Certainty*. I am inclined to say it is for Wittgenstein the most important of the whole discussion. In some ways it is *unlike* the examples he gives in *OC*: 613 – e.g. 'I am seeing with two *eyes* and shall see them if I look in the glass'; because 'regularity' seems more general. But in *OC*: 619 he goes on:

> Am I to say: even if an irregularity in natural events did suddenly occur, that wouldn't *have* to throw me out of the saddle. I might make inferences then just as before, but whether one would call that 'induction' is another question.

I am trying to say one thing, and I am being verbose. What makes a language-game possible is not 'certain facts' but *our never calling in question* certain facts.

'Depends on' or 'is determined by' or 'is conditioned by certain facts' – can too easily invite the misunderstanding: 'There are certain facts on which the possibility of language depends' – as though we could then justly ask: 'And which facts are these? What *are* the facts on which the possibility of language depends?'

This is the misunderstanding which is *most commonly* made by people who read *On Certainty*.

Another version of it is: 'When Wittgenstein says that there are certain propositions which have the form of empirical propositions, which are never called in doubt; and that unless this were so we could not speak with one another, we should not have a language – he is saying that there is a specific set of propositions (with the form of empirical propositions) which cannot be doubted.'

Of course he is *not* saying this. He is denying it. This is the chief point of his discussion.

15

LANGUAGE AS EMERGING FROM INSTINCTIVE BEHAVIOUR

I

I have just been reading your paper.[1] Like your other writings, it is so well written that it is as easy to read as it would be to listen while you talked. The only danger in this is that I may think I have understood points when I have missed them.

I wanted to speak to you about the paper somehow. The theme of it interests me immensely. And if I can say anything at all, you may be able to show me where I have gone wrong.

[It is curious that Malcolm does not discuss or emphasize 'that human beings *agree* in their reactions' (which, *nb*, is not a necessary proposition); and that they agree *im Handeln* (in actions) (in einer Handlungsweise, in ihren Handlungen ...) which is often 'ein spontanes *Mitgehen*' (a spontaneous *following*).

The passages in Wittgenstein which come first to my mind were from *Bemerkungen ü.d. Grundlagen der Mathematik*, Teil VI, but there are as many and just as important passages in *Philosophical Investigations* and in *Über Gewißheit* and elsewhere.]

When Wittgenstein says (in the passage which has been pasted into *Zettel* as P541) that trying to tend and ease the painful place in another person's

---

Section 1 of this chapter is from a letter by Rush Rhees to Norman Malcolm dated 19 January 1981. Rhees gave the title to his letter. I have inserted the translations. Section 2 is from a letter to Norman Malcolm dated 7 April 1982, *after* the publication of Malcolm's paper, included in Rhees's paper published in *Philosophical Investigations*.

body is 'ein primitives Verhalten' ('a primitive reaction') and in P541: 'daß sie der Prototyp einer Denkweise ist und nicht das Ergebnis des Denkens' ('That it is the prototype of a way of thinking and not the result of thought') – it has sense to refer to 'ein *Prototyp* einer Denkweise', or to ein Prototyp at all, only when the behaviour is seen already as within – as something akin to a gesture within – a language: as *belonging to* the thinking and speaking with other people.

If we find such behaviour in animals, perhaps in monkeys, this may have striking analogies with that behaviour in human beings which is the 'Prototyp einer Denkweise' (prototype of a way of thinking). But in the animals it *isn't* the prototype of 'a way of thinking', and we should not say 'daß ein Sprachspiel *auf ihr* beruht' ('that a language-game is based *on* it'): you wouldn't know what was meant by that. If you see someone who has been knocked down, and see that his leg is giving him great pain, you may call to him, ask him, and ask other people who come along: discuss what we'd better do, how we can ease it in the meantime; *also*: if you saw that I had seen the man knocked down and that I could see that his leg was hurting him terribly, and that I just shrugged my shoulders and started to walk on, you might say: 'Wait a minute! Can't you see he's hurt? You can't just *leave* him here.' Etc. I might reply, 'I know him. He's shamming, he isn't hurt at all.' Etc., etc. How would *this* behaviour 'emerge' from the instinctive behaviour in an animal?

'I can't help thinking about that man we saw in the street. I wonder if they were able to help him.' We can call this a *Denkweise* (a way of thinking), and also *primitiv*.

You also quote from P545 in *Zettel*: '... – Sicher sein, daß der Andre Schmerzen hat, zweifeln ob er sie hat, u.s.f., sind soviele natürliche instinktive Arten des Verhältnisses zu den andern Menschen ... Unser Sprachspiel ist ein Ausbau des primitiven Benehmens. (Denn unser *Sprachspiel* ist Benehmen.) (Instinkt.)' ('Being sure that someone is in pain, doubting whether he is, and so on, are so many natural, instinctive kinds of behaviour towards other human beings ... Our language-game is an extension of primitive behaviour. (For our *language-game* is behaviour.) (Instinct.)')

You will say that '*Ausbau*' (extension) supports your interpretation. But the remark in parenthesis almost suggests that it is the Ausbau eines *Sprachspiels* (the extension of a language-game). And I think it must mean this.

If the second parenthesis means that the *Sprachspiel* is not, for instance, 'das Ergebnis des Denkens' (the result of reflection), this would be in line with the passage you have quoted more than once in other connections, namely, *On Certainty*, P559:

Du mußt bedenken, daß das Sprachspiel sozusagen etwas Unvorhersehbares ist. Ich meine: Es ist nicht begründet. Nicht vernünftig (oder unvernünftig). Es steht da – wie unser Leben.

(You must bear in mind that the language-game is so to say something unpredictable. I mean: it is not based on grounds. It is not reasonable (or unreasonable).

It is there – like our life.)

In *this* context it would make no sense to ask, 'From what did it *emerge*?' And still less, 'From what did *language – Sprache –* emerge?'

You begin your article with the last sentence of *On Certainty* P475: 'Die Sprache ist nicht aus einem Raisonnement hervorgegangen' ('Language did not emerge from some kind of ratiocination'). This says it wasn't the result or outcome of reasoning. But it does not say that it *was* the outcome of instinct, or 'emerged' from instinct. And I do not think Wittgenstein would have said this. Or not without explaining what it would mean. – (Otherwise it would sound as though he were putting forward a theory in *explanation* of language, instead of describing it.)

I think in that remark – 'I want to regard man here as an animal; as a primitive being to which one grants instinct but not ratiocination. As a creature in a primitive state' (*On Certainty* P475) – he is speaking of *ein primitives Wesen* ... in einem primitiven Zustande (a primitive being ... in a primitive state) – but in a situation in which he is living together with other 'primitive beings': beings which *understand* one another – understand one another's actions and reactions, if you like – in the sense in which *we* understand one another in what we say and do, or the sense in which we understand the language we speak. (If you say: 'Understand the form of life in which we live' this comes to the same thing.) In P475, for me the important sentence is:

Denn welche Logik für ein primitives Verständigungsmittel genügt, deren brauchen wir uns auch nicht zu schämen.

(Any logic good enough for a primitive means of communication needs no apology from us.)

May I repeat

welche Logik für ein primitives Verständigungsmittel genügt
(logic good enough for a primitive means of communication)

We may speak of many of the reactions of animals as instinctive. If my dog burns his foot or his nose on a hot brick, he will draw away quickly, perhaps yell, and avoid that brick at least for a little while. If he is in a field with other dogs and two dogs start fighting, he may start barking and yelling and daring to join in. But in these reactions we do not find *ein Verständigungsmittel* (a means of communication) which characterizes (or *is*) the life which dogs lead with one another.

The sentence before that one, in P475: 'Als ein Wesen in einem primitiven Zustande' ('As a primitive creature in a primitive state'). This *Zustand* (state) is, or includes, ein *Sprachspiel* (a language-game). Wittgenstein does not speak of any development from something prior to a Sprachspiel. – The primitive reactions may become important *within* a Sprachspiel, they show in the character of certain moves in the Sprachspiel. Wittgenstein speaks (*Philosophia* p. 392)[2] of 'looking in the direction of the cause' ('looking in the direction the sound came from' as '*eine* Wurzel des Ursache – Wirkung Sprachspiels' (italics Wittgenstein's) ('*one* root of the cause–effect language-game' [p.409]).

In another place (*Philosophia* p. 403) he says that 'die primitive Form des Sprachspiels *ist* eine Reaktion' (my italics) ('the primitive form of the lan-guage-game is a reaction' [p. 420]). Would he have said here as well that this '*Reaktion*' was ein *Verständigungsmittel*? (a means of communication). It may be so among *us*, of course.

He then goes on to give the sentence which many would take to support your case: 'Die Sprache – will ich sagen – ist eine Verfeinerung, "im Anfang war die Tat"' (p. 403). ('Language – I want to say – is a refinement, "im Anfang war die Tat"' ['In the beginning was the deed'] p. 420). I wonder what he would have given as examples of language as a *Verfeinerung* of (refinement of) … (of what?).

In his *Notes for Lectures on 'Private Experience'* he speaks of 'the *natural* expression' of a feeling (say), much as he speaks of 'instinctive reactions' in the passages we have been looking at. And when he speaks of these as 'expressions which can't lie' or '… which don't lie', this is similar to his remark (*Philosophia* p.394): 'Irgendwo müssen wir – ohne zu zweifeln – sagen: *das* geschieht aus *dieser* Ursache' ('At some point we have to say – without doubting: *that* results from *this* cause' [p. 412]).

The child may learn to sham pain, but this comes later. 'The language-games with expressions of feelings (private experiences) are based on games with expressions of which we don't say that they may lie.'[3]

Later: 'Suppose I said: The expressions get their importance from the fact that they are not used coolly but that we can't help using them. This is as though I said: laughter gets its importance only through being a *natural* expression, a natural phenomenon, not an artificial code' (ibid., p. 281). A half page later: 'Why should I say the "expression" derives *its meaning* from the feeling behind it – and not from the circumstances of the lang[uage] game in which it is used? For imagine a person crying out with pain alone in the desert: is he using a language? Should we say that his cry had *meaning?*' (ibid.) (Wittgenstein's italics).

(a) crying out with pain alone in the desert;
(b) crying out with pain when there are people within hearing; or perhaps: when you are being tortured.

Is (b) an example of a Verfeinerung (A refinement)? (assume that the cry is not a sham, in either example).

He said: 'Die Sprache ... ist eine Verfeinerung' (*Philosophia* p. 403) ('Language ... is a refinement' [p. 420]) just after 'die primitive Form des Sprachspiels ist eine Reaktion' (p. 403) ('the primitive form of the language-game is a reaction' [p. 420]).

On the next page, 404: 'Ich will sagen: es ist charakteristisch für unsere Sprache, daß sie auf dem Grund fester Lebensform regelmäßigen Tun's emporwächst.' ('I want to say: it is characteristic of our language that the foundation on which it grows consists in steady ways of living, regular ways of acting' [p. 420]).

Here he says feste *Lebensformen* (steady ways of living) – as though these were what he had meant just now in speaking of *Reaktionen* (reactions). And he brings in *Regelmäßigkeit* (regularity). And what the more refined forms grow out of, are still *Lebensformen* (forms of life).

Wittgenstein uses the phrase 'Verständigung durch die Sprache' (e.g. *Philosophical Investigations* I-242) ('language as a means of communication'). Suppose we said that 'zur Verständigung durch die Sprache gehört ... ('communication through language involves ...') – that people should *agree* in their reactions'. So far, so good. And when Wittgenstein tries to suggest what 'eine *Sprachverwirrung*' ('linguistic confusion') would be like, he sometimes imagines a situation in which no two people would react in the same way to the question whether this is the same colour as that, or whether his whistle went on for a longer or a shorter time than the other man's, whether this man was pronouncing the same sound as the other man, etc., etc. 'We couldn't talk to one another.'

But if we say, 'In general they agree in their reactions' – then we are not speaking of the agreement there is between many reactions of the animals of a given species – say, dogs, or cats – or between animals of many different species: lying down when tired, becoming restless when long without food, starting in fright at a sudden loud noise, fixing attention on a moving light in the dark, etc. But if most dogs (or – to eliminate the human influence – most foxes) 'agree' in the ways they react in such circumstances, this agreement does not belong to an understanding or a language between them.

It may not interest my dog, whether my neighbour's dog does or does not react in the same way, e.g. whether he sneezes when exposed to a strong whiff of exhaust fumes or not. But if my 'instinctive reaction to something as the cause' is eine Wurzel des Ursache – Wirkung Sprachspiels (one root of the cause and effect language-game), then it *is* important that I and other people agree in einer Lebensform (a form of life) – that the reaction was an action, eine Handlung in einer Lebensform (within a form of life), – that people who are with me may notice and ask questions and perhaps take steps to do something about it.

If it is eine Wurzel des Ursache – Wirkung Sprachspiels (the root of the cause and effect language-game) – then it is *understood* (recognized, treated, reacted to ...) in the Ursache -Wirkung Sprachspiel (the cause and effect language-game). I learn, or have learned, to use a certain expression for it – 'cause' or some other. – This does not mean that the reaction itself – turning and pointing at *that* as the cause – is the outcome of reasoning and investigation.

And it does not mean that I must have had some 'innate language' before I could learn to speak, or that I must have had some innate awareness of essential grammatical structure, enabling me to distinguish ... etc. There is no suggestion of anything innate or *a priori*.

In a conversation once, Wittgenstein imagined, as so many have, a human being who, before he had learned to speak, was abandoned on an island where there were no other human beings. If we landed there, what communication could we have with this human being? (Wittgenstein spent only a few minutes on it.) There are questions which come into Wittgenstein's writings in 1929/30 such as the distinction between *'primären Zeichen'* ('primary signs'), such as gestures, which do not have to be taught, and *'sekundären Zeichen'* ('secondary signs') which are taught or explained by reference to the *'primären'*. He became distrustful of this distinction, partly because it seemed to assume that the 'primären Zeichen' could not be *mis*understood – that they were 'unmißverstehbar' ('incapable of being misunderstood'); but more especially because the whole way of speaking was too nearly modelled on physics, on speaking of 'elementary particles' in terms of which we may hope to *explain* physical phenomena: 'daß sie eine Erklärung der wirklich bestehenden Sprache erwartet, statt der bloßen Beschreibung' ('that it expects an explanation of the actually existing language, rather than a mere description'). (For my nose, the same might be said of certain treatments of 'instinctive reactions' as *fundamental'*.) – There is no reason to think that there are any gestures which *must* (logically?) be understood by anyone who sees them. And there is no reason to think that any gestures would serve as a starting ground for teaching the island man to speak and understand some part of the language we speak. Suppose I went through the motions of putting food in my mouth and chewing it: perhaps the island man would bring me food (perhaps he would run away, perhaps he would attack me ...). If he did, he might not do so a second time.

Wittgenstein said in this connection: 'Unless someone understands the meaning of *"and so on"* (or of some equivalent expression or gesture), it will be impossible to *teach* him the meaning of *"and so on"*.'

At an elementary stage, how do you teach someone what things are called? How do you explain the meanings of 'blue' and 'orange' and 'round'? Or when a child picks up the meanings by watching and hearing people, when do you say he knows the meaning of the colour word? Roughly, when he does 'go on in the same way', when he, on his own, uses the words for the right things as they come along. He understands 'and so on', in the same sense Wittgenstein was speaking of this. We may have to correct the learner sometimes, but after a few times he is all right. In other words, he understands 'and so on' in the same way as you do. This is what is important. He *might* have called something else 'going on *so*'. Übereinstimmung (Agreement).

('"Übereinstimmung" ('agreement') and "Regelmäßigkeit" ('regularity') are cousins.') BGM, VI, ⊦45.

In Wittgenstein's use 'Übereinstimmung' covers a considerable family. One of the most important uses comes when he speaks of Übereinstimmung im Handeln (agreement in actions) or of Übereinstimmung in einer Lebensform (agreement in a form of life).

II

In 'Language as Emerging from Instinctive Behaviour' you quote passages such as *OC:* 204 where Wittgenstein says:

> Giving grounds, however, justifying the evidence, comes to an end; – but the end is not certain propositions' striking us immediately as true, i.e. it is not a kind of *seeing* on our part; it is our *acting*, which lies at the bottom of the language-game.

And there are others like this.

You are saying that certain instinctive reactions are at the foundation of our language. You mention what Wittgenstein often says in asking how it is possible to teach someone (a child) the meanings of colour words, for instance, or the names of elementary shapes. In giving ostensive definitions, and varying them – giving or pointing to various objects which are red and to shades of red – we always depend on 'and so on', or something equivalent in a gesture. He may misunderstand at first, but soon he will go on to call things 'red' which *we* call red. Say to him 'Bring me something of the *same* colour as this', and he will do so. It is conceivable that he should *not* do so, but this practically never happens. All of us who have been taught, find it natural to call *this* the same colour as we called red before. So we recognize this as the correct use; we speak of what the word means; and we know that anyone who knows the word understands it so. If it were not that practically everyone reacts in the same way to 'Would you call this the same colour?' there would not be our concept of colour ... our colour concepts.

But this account is schematic like a diagram. It does not describe ways in which those words come into what people tell one another, in their discussions, reports, etc. I could identify this or that colour, use the right word, and yet be uncertain of the occasions on which it would have sense to do so. To describe the part they play in our life is to describe a 'practice'.

In *OC:* 139 and 140:

> Not only rules, but also examples are needed for establishing a practice. Our rules leave loop-holes open, and the practice has to speak for itself.
> We do not learn the practice of making empirical *judgements* by learning rules: we are taught *judgements* and their connection with other *judgements*. A *totality* of *judgements* is made plausible to us.

Compare also:

> I am not more certain of the meaning of my words than I am of certain *judgements*. Can I doubt that this colour is called 'blue'?
> (My) doubts form a system. (*OC:* 126)
> No, experience is not the ground of our game of judging. Nor is its outstanding success. (*OC:* 131)

Sometimes what he says of *judging* is closely related to what he says of our *world-picture*. See especially *OC:* 167 where he speaks of Lavoisier making experiments with substances in his laboratory, and then concludes that in combustion this and that happens. This is an *Urteil*: 'He has got hold of a definite world-picture – not of course one that he invented: he learned it as a child. I say world-picture and not hypothesis, because it is the matter-of-course foundation for his research and as such goes unmentioned.'

'The matter-of-course foundation for his research' – which Wittgenstein will not call an *hypothesis* because it is *'matter of course'* and because it *'goes unmentioned'*.

Wittgenstein also speaks of 'the foundation of all judging' (*OC:* 614) and 'the ground on which I stand in making any *judgements*' (*OC:* 492). (I quote both of these paras here below.) He also says that the 'foundation of all judging' lies in the fact that certain propositions which have the form of empirical propositions are withdrawn from doubt, are 'beyond the reach of doubt'. This does not mean that we are absolutely convinced of the truth of these propositions; or: absolutely convinced of these facts. On the contrary.

Many of his examples of these propositions are found in Moore's list of truisms at the start of 'A Defence of Common Sense', especially 'The Earth had existed for many years before I was born', 'My body was born at a certain time in the past and has existed continuously ever since'; but prominent also, 'My name is L. W.'. And I needn't remind you that Wittgenstein supplies even more examples of his own.

> I have a telephone conversation with New York. My friend tells me that his young trees have buds of such and such a kind. I am now convinced that his tree is ... Am I also convinced that the Earth exists? (*OC:* 208)
> Does my telephone call to New York strengthen my conviction that the Earth exists?
> Much seems to be fixed, and it is removed from the traffic. It is so to speak shunted onto an unused siding. (*OC:* 210)

On the other hand, if something which I can't imagine did make me doubt the Earth's existence I should not know how to make sense of anything.

> ... we are interested in the fact that about certain empirical propositions no doubt can exist if making *judgements* is to be possible at all. (*OC:* 308)

See also *OC:* 613:

> If I now say 'I know that the water in the kettle on the gas-flame will not

freeze but boil', I seem to be justified in this 'I know' as I am in *any*. 'If I know anything I know *this*. – Or do I know with still *greater* certainty that the person opposite me is my old friend so-and-so? And how does that compare with the proposition that I am seeing with two *eyes* and shall see them if I look in the glass? – I don't know confidently what I am to answer here – But still there is a difference between the cases. If the water over the gas freezes, of course I shall be as astonished as can be, but I shall assume some factor I don't know of, and perhaps leave the matter to physicists to judge. But what could make me doubt whether this person here is NN, whom I have known for years? Here a doubt *would seem to drag everything with it* and plunge it into chaos. (Last italics mine.)

OC: 614:

> That is to say: If I were contradicted on all sides and told that this person's name was not what I had always known it was (and I use 'know' here intentionally), then in that case *the foundation of all judging would be taken away from me*. (My italics.)

See also especially the third remark after this – *OC:* 617:

> Certain events would put me into a position in which I could not go on with the old language-game any further. In which I was torn away from the *sureness* of the game.
>
> Indeed, doesn't it seem obvious that the possibility of a language-game is conditioned by certain facts.

Similarly in *OC:* 490:

> When I ask 'Do I know or do I only believe that I am called …?' it is no use to look within myself.
>
> But I could say: not only do I never have the slightest doubt that I am called that, but there is no *judgement* I could be certain of if I started doubting about that.

And then *nota bene OC:* 492:

> 'Do I know or do I only believe …?' might also be expressed like this: What if it *seemed* to turn out that what until now has seemed immune to doubt was a false assumption? Would I react as I do when a belief has proved to be false? or would it seem to knock from under my feet the ground on which I stand in making any *judgements* at all? – But of course I do not intend this as a

prophecy:

Would I simply say 'I should never have thought it!' or would I (have to) refuse to revise my *judgement – because such a 'revision' would amount to annihilation of all yardsticks?* (Last italics mine.)

And the next remark but one, *OC:* 494.

I cannot doubt this proposition without giving up all *judgement.*

But what sort of proposition is that? ... (namely, the proposition, 'My name is L. W.' (RR)) ... It is certainly no empirical proposition ...

In other passages he seems to say that this, and other propositions which have the same 'logical role', for example, that 'the Earth existed for many years before I was born', have the form of empirical propositions, although he is not satisfied with this; and he never finds a description which gives the 'role' of which he is speaking. See *OC:* 401 – and then the one which follows it:

I want to say: propositions of the form of empirical propositions, and not only propositions of logic, form the foundation of all operating with thoughts (with language). – This observation is not of the form 'I know ...'. 'I know ...' states what *I* know, and that is not of logical interest.

In this remark the expression 'propositions of the form of empirical propositions' is itself thoroughly bad; the statements in question are statements about material objects. And they do not serve as foundations in the same way as hypotheses which, if they turn out to be false, are replaced by others.

(... und schreib getrost
'Im Anfang war die Tat')[4]

Perhaps you will say that this shows that Wittgenstein was speaking of instinctive reactions here. I do not think it does – unless you widen 'instinctive' beyond recognition. And if you suggested that Wittgenstein is holding that Moore's 'truisms' are 'instinctive utterances', this would not refer *at all* to that characteristic of them which does preoccupy Wittgenstein here: to the sense or the way in which they are *'fundamental'.* I think of *OC:* 512:

Isn't the question this: 'What if you had to change your opinion even on

103

these most fundamental things?' And to that the answer seems to be: 'You don't *have* to change it. That is just what their being 'fundamental' is.

'Instinct' does not include that. And neither does 'acting confidently'; which might serve if we *were* acting on some hypothesis. '"Here I have arrived at a foundation of all my beliefs. This position I will *hold*!" But isn't that, precisely, only because I am completely *convinced* of it? – What is "being completely convinced" like?'

Wittgenstein speaks of these propositions as 'not accessible to doubt', 'beyond the reach of doubt' (and other similar phrases). If he called them 'facts which we never doubt', this would suggest that we might have some idea of what it would be to doubt them, even though we regard such doubting as preposterous. It would treat them as though they were pieces in the game. Whereas they are the table on which the game is played.

> Can't an assertoric sentence, which was capable of functioning as an hypothesis, also be used as a foundation for research and action? I.e. can't it simply be isolated from doubt, though not according to any explicit rule? It simply gets assumed as a truism, never called in question, perhaps not even formulated. (*OC:* 87)
>
> It may be for example that *all enquiry on our part* is set to exempt certain propositions from doubt, if they are ever formulated. They lie apart from the route travelled by enquiry. (*OC:* 88).

Wittgenstein speaks of this as 'the peculiar logical role of certain empirical propositions'. And *this* is what chiefly interests him about those propositions of Moore's.

There is the point: (1) it is not that these are facts of which we can see that they cannot be doubted; rather they are '*withdrawn*' from doubt and from assertion; as it were out of range; shifted into an unused siding: And yet: (2) these propositions withdrawn from doubt are '*fundamental*' in the sense that if, through some hardly imaginable situation, I *were* to doubt any of them this would bring an earthquake in the foundations of acting and thinking, destroying all yardsticks.

You speak of Wittgenstein's criticisms of Moore's use of 'know' in 'I know that this is a human hand' and in connection with the propositions at the beginning of 'A Defence of Common Sense'. This is important, but it was not for *these* reasons chiefly that Wittgenstein found Moore's propositions interesting.

See first of all *OC:* 136:

When Moore says he *knows* such and such, he is really enumerating a lot of empirical propositions which we affirm without special testing; propositions, that is, which have a peculiar logical role in the system of our empirical propositions.

Then *OC:* 137:

Even if the most trustworthy of men assures me that he *knows* things are thus and so, this by itself cannot satisfy me that he does know. Only that he believes he knows. That is why Moore's assurance that he knows ... does not interest us. The propositions, however, which Moore retails as examples of such known truths are indeed interesting. Not because anyone knows their truth, or believes he knows them, but because they all have a *similar* role in the system of our empirical *judgements.*

I would add only Wittgenstein's remark when talking to me about this on 13 April 1951 – a fortnight before the last entry in *OC:* 'This does not mean that there is any specific class of "things which cannot be doubted". In fact that is just the point.'

I do not question at all your point that Wittgenstein thought of instinctive reactions as fundamental for language; for the speaking and understanding which is the form of this way of life. By the way, you might have found *Philosophische Grammatik*, p. 109, starting with: 'Wir überlegen uns Handlungen ...' an illustration of certain points.

I have mentioned especially your attention to Wittgenstein's point that people (a) agree in their reactions, and (b) they agree in what they call 'going on in the same way'. – And I go along with everything you say in the first part of your paper (including, incidentally, the polemics with Chomsky and Fodor).

But when Wittgenstein speaks in these passages of propositions which have the form of empirical propositions which belong to the grounds of all 'Operieren mit Gedanken (mit der Sprache)' ('operating with thoughts (with language)'), or when he speaks there (and in other passages I haven't quoted) of 'the foundation of all acting and thinking', of 'the foundation of all judging' – you cannot say that the grounds or the foundation is an instinctive reaction.

When you say: 'Wittgenstein is trying to call attention to something that underlies all language-games' – the 'something' is vague, and I think two different things are confused in it.

16

WORDS AND THINGS

Bertrand Russell seems to think that someone who discusses language as Wittgenstein does has left the relation between words and things out of account.[1] Russell was anxious to keep an almost tangible relation between the use of words on the one hand, and what they are supposed to be talking about on the other hand. He therefore wanted to maintain that there is a causal relation between words and what I am expressing by them. Only by a causal relation can language interact with what it describes.[2]

Earlier Wittgenstein had raised the question: at what point does a sign connect with reality? To pass from a system of signs to reality it seems that reality must be part of your system of signs. Compare sense-data: the primary data from which or in terms of which all language and meaning starts, must be analysed and explained.

The start is in terms of propositions. Russell uses the proposition, 'There is a cat'. The explanation would have to be finally in terms of certain sense impressions. In the analysis of propositions and logically proper names, the demonstratives 'This' and 'That' would play a central part. They do not have an independent meaning. They get their meaning from what they point to, and so sense-data are brought into the analysis.

There are various reasons why Russell says that the analysis must get down to the sense-data. 'I see a yellow surface or patch', 'I hear a squeaky noise', etc. These are statements to which it seems impossible to attach any doubt. 'It may be that there isn't a piece of paper there (Wittgenstein would

From editor's notes on Rhees's seminar, 2 February 1970.

deny this) but there is no doubt about the white patch.' It seems to give an unshakeable foundation for the meanings we're concerned with, and an answer to the question, 'What is expressed?'

What is meant by saying that the word 'cat' expresses what you see? With 'There is a cat', how is the verbal knowledge derived from sensible experience? This indicates the problem he is up against. How is verbal knowledge derived from sense-data (by which philosophers usually mean vision)? How does the vision of a grey patch give verbal knowledge?

'I said there was a cat because I saw a cat.' There seems to be a cause–effect relation involved. But when I say 'I saw a cat' I don't know that a large number of similar words have been followed by similar consequences.

'Virus is the cause of certain kinds of cancer.' This is shown by establishing a regular sequence. But that is *not* what I am asserting. What I assert doesn't go outside what is happening here. Russell says that the causal relations which enter *after* language has been learned are things which can be perceived. So we needn't go outside the happening. This is essential since knowledge is required for the connection of sensible appearances with the verbal assertion of them. If we *don't* admit the causal relation, Russell argues, it seems impossible to explain the connection, or how words express. Otherwise, we can't show that there is a connection between *these* words rather than any others such as 'I had a cup of tea'. Two critical comments can be made:

1   It looks as if the connection between what a person says and what he sees depends on him. But this is queer. The criticism which Wittgenstein brought to bear on this was to ask why Russell wanted to speak of 'cause' here at all. He says only that he perceives the chair; that he is simply aware of it. We can't perceive the causal relation that he perceives. Why did Russell use the term 'cause' here? How did he learn it? Suppose he says that it fits. But that isn't for him to decide. It is public property – it belongs to the meaning the term has in our language.
2   'My words express what I see.' What does this explain? If visual sensations cause me to utter certain words, then I may put you as another psychological subject before the cat, for example, and see what happens. Need it be the same? Why couldn't it be different in many cases? Would we have any grounds for calling one correct and the other incorrect?

Consider other causal relations called associations. An experimenter in a psychological laboratory utters certain words and the subject writes down that with which he associates the word. Different people may have different associations. This is sometimes spoken of as a causal relation. All right, but you can't call it correct or incorrect. You can use a word wrongly or give it the wrong meaning, but what would having the wrong association be? Similarly with Russell: why shouldn't the words cause different things?

Russell might reply, 'But it doesn't work like that – people generally say the same thing'. Perfectly true, but this doesn't need all this causal machinery. All you need to know is that most people would say the same if you asked them what a cat is when they are confronted by one: 'That's a cat.'

This is clear where colour words are concerned. 'What colour is the book?' – 'Red' – 'Correct.' The difference between 'correct' and 'incorrect' depends on the fact that most people who have been taught in that way will say, 'The book is red'. If it weren't so, our language would be very different. Compare *Philosophical Investigations* 242:

> If language is to be a means of communication there must be agreement not only in definitions but also (queer as this may sound) in *judgements*. This seems to abolish logic, but does not do so. – It is one thing to describe methods of measurement, and another to obtain and state results of measurement. But what we call 'measuring' is partly determined by a certain constancy in results of measurement.

Not just definitions, i.e. colour charts, but agreement in *judgments*, i.e. in what they do. The agreement is prior to any distinction between 'correct' and 'incorrect'. That agreement is all that is needed – you don't need the causal connection Russell is talking about.

But Russell would say that we must have 'cause' for without it the word doesn't connect with the thing pointed to. But what *is* the connection here? Do you want the causal connection? The connection is achieved by ostensive definition. This enables me to go on to use it in situations where it would be correct to use it.

Russell wants a foundation beyond doubt – the foundation in the sense-data. *Russell confuses what he rightly feels is the certainty of the language we use and causal necessity which is irrelevant.* Russell is trying to account for the appropriate and inappropriate use of 'There is a cat'.

Suppose someone says 'That is red' and you ask, 'How do you know?' or 'Can you be sure?' – that would be stupid. You are asking for reasons, but what kind of reasons could I give you? I could say, 'Because I know the language', but that isn't the kind of answer you want. 'That's red' in favourable light conditions, etc., is immune to doubt. *That* certainty is essential to the doubt when colours are seen under sodium lights.[3]

In *Philosophical Investigations* I: 498 Wittgenstein has this to say about a causal account of meaning:

> When I say that the orders 'Bring me sugar' and 'Bring me milk' make sense, but not the combination 'Milk me sugar', that does not mean that the utterance of this combination of words has no effect. And if its effect is that the other person stares at me and gapes, I don't on that account call it the order to stare and gape, even if that was precisely the effect that I wanted to produce.

Philosophers speak of 'evidence of the senses'. I may interpret snapshots and postcards, but there is nothing like this in perception. 'All we know is what the senses tell us' – do they tell us anything? Even if they do provide pictures, they do not provide sentences in which the pictures appear. Only *I* say things. If they *did* say anything, we couldn't translate them.

How did people come to speak like this? Wittgenstein considered the case of a conjuring trick. You saw things, but what happened? The film would give you the entire performance. But in the case of seeing a cat there isn't anything to be explained. The only reason why sense-impressions have been introduced is that they want an unshakeable foundation for the way we use words – the sense-impressions are what are unshakeable.

In the *Investigations* Wittgenstein spoke of rules of grammar which we find in the use of various language-games. But in *On Certainty* we have a new development, namely, that in this use *we accept certain facts* as beyond doubt, not simply as true. But in order to recognize what is meant *these facts* must be recognized which are not rules of grammar.

But what is a foundation in one way of living needn't be that in another. 'And one might almost say that these foundation-walls are carried by the whole house' (*OC:* 248). There is no specific class of indubitable propositions, the foundations of all our language. Kant searched for the indubitable, but this is very different from what Wittgenstein was doing.

Wittgenstein's use of 'world-picture' cannot be equated with 'view of the world' (Weltanschauung). 'Humour is a Weltanschauung' – it is a way of looking at things. This is not the kind of thing which would be called a world-picture. Lavoisier, on the contrary, is said to work in a way that *showed* a world-picture – not a personal matter. Other chemists took it as obvious as he did. If you said that humour is a way of viewing the world, that would hold of an individual. Also, in the *Tractatus*, Wittgenstein says that the world of happy people is a different world from the world of the unhappy. So you could have the same world-picture, and yet the worlds of individuals would be different. So we have to contrast a form of life and a view of life. In considering the life of a tribe one might note their hunting, their marriages – all right, they lived like that. A view of life would be different – a pessimistic or optimistic view of life – but sharing the same form of life.

17

NOT WORTH MENTIONING?

Many people might give a rough paraphrase of the queerness or 'absurdity' of statements like Moore's, 'I am standing and not sitting down', 'I am wearing clothes and am not naked', – that such utterances seem absurd only because they are so obvious that there is no need to make them.

But consider *OC:* 552–3:

> Do I know that I am now sitting in a chair? – Don't I know it?! In the present circumstances no one is going to say that I know this; but no more will he say, for example, that I am conscious. Nor will one normally say this of the passers-by in the street.
>
> But now, even if one doesn't say it, does that make it *untrue*??
>
> It is queer: if I say, without any special occasion, 'I know' – for example, 'I know that I am now sitting in a chair', this statement seems to me unjustified and presumptuous. But if I make the same statement where there is some need for it, then, although I am not a jot more certain of its truth, it seems to me to be perfectly justified and everyday.

Without special occasions the statements seem unjustified or presumptuous. We can imagine special circumstances – such as coming out of an anaesthetic. *OC:* 554:

> In its language-game it is not presumptuous. There, it has no higher position than, simply, the human language-game. For there it has its restricted application.

Taken in the main from a letter to Peter Winch, 23 January 1970.

But as soon as I say this sentence outside its context, it appears in a false light. For then it is as if I wanted to insist that there are things that I *know*. God himself can't say anything to me about them.

' … that there are things I *know*' – that, Wittgenstein thought, was Moore's mistake.

If you stand on a lecture platform and say '"I am standing and not sitting down" is obviously true', this would suggest that you could have said '"I am not standing but sitting down" is obviously false' – i.e. that we should have *understood* you if you had said 'I am not standing but sitting down'. Whereas I do not think we should know what the speaker meant at all. Still less, that we could try to show him that he had fallen into a mistake: explain to him where he had gone wrong, perhaps. We should not know what he was doing with these words at all. (If you say 'He was using them to illustrate a philosophical point' – well, all right, but that is irrelevant: it does not help to show what could be meant by calling them obviously true or obviously false.)

Compare:

> The reason why the use of the expression 'true or false' has something misleading about it is that it is like saying 'it tallies with the facts or it doesn't', and the very thing that is in question is what 'tallying' is here. (*OC:* 199)
>
> Really 'The proposition is either true or false' only means that it must be possible to decide for or against it. But this does not say what the ground for such a decision is like. (*OC:* 200)

For one thing, the propositions or utterances in question are not obviously true or obvious at all, in those contexts in which they are philosophically interesting. And in contexts where they are natural and informative, they aren't 'obviously true'.

More important, I think: the idea that 'there is no *need* to assert propositions because everybody knows them; and this is what makes them seem absurd' – this helps to obscure what (in Wittgenstein's view) is interesting about them.

In the first place, there are things which everyone that's listening to you knows – 'You have invited me to speak to you', 'This lecture is scheduled to stop at 11 o'clock – which would not generally have the sort (or sorts) of role which Wittgenstein is considering.

Compare:

'I know that that's a tree.' Why does it strike me as if I did not understand the sentence? though it is after all an extremely simple sentence of the most ordinary kind? It is as if I could not focus my mind on any meaning. Simply because I don't look for the focus where the meaning is. As soon as I think of an everyday use of the sentence instead of a philosophical one, its meaning becomes clear and ordinary. (*OC:* 347)

Just as the words 'I am here' have a meaning only in certain contexts, and not when I say them to someone who is sitting in front of me and sees me clearly, – *and not because they are superfluous,* but because their meaning is not *determined* by the situation, yet stands in need of such determination. (*OC:* 348). (The first italics are mine, the second is in the text.)

If someone said, '... it's just because they are so *obviously* true', I should want to ask 'what makes them so obviously true?'
Compare:

The child learns to believe a host of things. *I.e. it learns to act according to these beliefs.* (I have italicized this because I want to come back to it.) Bit by bit there forms a system of what is believed, and in that system some things stand unshakeably fast and some are more or less liable to shift. What stands fast does so, *not because it is intrinsically obvious or convincing;* it is rather held fast by what lies around it. (*OC:* 144) (My italics)

'What lies around it' he sometimes calls 'a nest of propositions', or, as in the quotation just given, 'a system of beliefs'. But he also connects this, as here, with what he calls 'Action' or 'Practice'.

Our talk gets its meaning from the rest of our proceedings. (*OC:* 229)

Why do I not satisfy myself that I have two feet when I want to get up from the chair? There is no why. I simply don't. That is how I act. (*OC:* 148)

Sure evidence is what we *accept* as sure, it is evidence that we go by in *acting* without any doubt.

What we call 'a mistake' plays quite a special part in our language-games, and so too does what we regard as certain evidence. (*OC:* 196)

Compare:

If I say 'Of course I know that that's a towel' I am making an *utterance.*[1] I have no thought of a verification. For me it is an immediate utterance.

I don't think of past or future. (And of course it's the same for Moore, too.)

It is just like directly taking hold of something, as I take hold of my towel without having doubts. (*OC:* 510)

113

As if giving grounds did not come to an end sometime. But the end is not an ungrounded presupposition: it is an ungrounded way of acting. (*OC:* 110, last two sentences)

Children do not learn that books exist, that armchairs exist, etc., etc. – they learn to fetch books, sit in armchairs, etc., etc.

Later, questions about the existence of things do of course arise. 'Is there such a thing as a unicorn?' and so on. But such a question is possible only because as a rule no corresponding question presents itself. For how does one know how to set about satisfying oneself of the existence of unicorns? How did one learn the method for determining whether something exists or not? (*OC:* 476)

Does a child believe that milk exists? Or does it know that milk exists? Does a cat know that a mouse exists? (*OC:* 478)

And in explanation of 'what lies around it':

A child learns there are reliable and unreliable informants much later than it learns facts which are told it. It doesn't learn *at all* that that mountain has existed for a long time: that is, the question whether it is so doesn't arise at all. It swallows this consequence down, so to speak, together with *what* it learns. (*OC:* 143, from third sentence on)

I do not explicitly learn the propositions that stand fast for me. I can *discover* them subsequently like the axis around which a body rotates. This axis is not fixed in the sense that anything holds it fast, but the movement around it determines its immobility. (*OC:* 152)

If now we look back we can see how little is said and something of what is left out by: 'We are concerned here (in "that's a tree", for instance) with propositions which differ from others only in that they are so obviously true that nobody would have occasion to assert them.' Wittgenstein might add something like: 'as though we could speak of "propositions" without ever considering what we do with them; or whether we do anything with them at all: whether you would want to say that they play any part in our life and language.' – As I have suggested, the part that they do play in our life and language – the difference there would have to be, for instance, if we recognized some way or form of being doubtful about them – this is the chief theme of *On Certainty*.

Wittgenstein is not saying that we have to take 'our environment' for granted; and certainly not that we have to take our *physical* environment for granted. It is not clear what this would mean, in terms of Wittgenstein's discussions, anyway. See, for example, the remarks in *Investigations* II: xii and the following remarks in *Remarks on the Foundations of Mathematics*.

But what things are 'facts'? Do you believe that you can show what fact is meant by, e.g. pointing to it with your finger? Does that of itself clarify the part played by 'establishing' a fact? – Suppose it takes mathematics to define the *character* of what you are calling a 'fact'!

'It is interesting to know *how many* vibrations this note has!' But it took arithmetic to teach you this question. It taught you to see this kind of fact.

Mathematics – I want to say – teaches you, not just the answer to a question, but a whole language-game with questions and answers. (p. 173)

'Calculating, if it is to be practical, must be grounded in empirical facts.' – Why should it not determine what *are* empirical facts? (p. 174)

The point (for Wittgenstein, anyway) about such propositions as 'the Earth has existed for many years before I was born' or 'since it was born my body has been either on the surface of the Earth or not far from the surface of the Earth' – is not that these are propositions one knows about one's environment. When he insists that 'know' and 'doubt' and 'be certain' are always 'used within a context', he does not mean 'within a physical environment'. The 'context' may of course include descriptions (a way of looking at, a way of treating) of this or that in one's physical environment; but generally 'the context' includes 'propositions' of other sorts as well: 'My name is L. W.', '"foot" is a word', etc., etc. – This is why the notion of *Weltbild* (world-picture) is important – or if you like, of *Lebensform* (form of life), which comes to much the same. See, to begin with, the remark about Lavoisier in *OC*: 167: 'He has got hold of a definite world-picture – not of course one that he invented: he learned it as a child. I say world-picture and not hypothesis, because it is the matter-of-course foundation for his research and as such goes unmentioned.' Our world-picture includes, for instance: recognizing this and that as *reasons* for so and so (or: reasons for doing such and such), recognizing that as a ground for doubting, and so on. And this is not description of an environment.

What is important in Moore's remark 'I know that that's a tree' is not that we take for granted the existence (reality) of trees because they are regularly or constantly part of our environment. The point is Moore's 'I *know* that that's a tree'. The way in which doubt, or asking 'How can you be sure?', is ruled out here. And of course, to answer 'Because I see trees here, there and everywhere every day of my life', would just show a misunderstanding of the point. Moore and Wittgenstein both were considering a case in which there *is* no 'because'. It may be that my meeting trees constantly in my environment is to some extent a *causal* explanation of this feature of our grammar – although, I suppose, it need not be.

115

Perhaps Moore's own discussion in the 'Defence of Common Sense' does not make this clear, although I think that what he says suggests it.

The 'Defence of Common Sense' shows a way of doing philosophy, or a conception of philosophical enquiry, which is (in many respects) sharply different from the idea of philosophy which we get in these last remarks of Wittgenstein's. Moore gives lists of propositions which he says he knows with certainty to be true. And he defines his relation to other philosophers by reference to this.

If a philosophical inquiry is trying to determine 'What can be known?' or 'What sorts of things (propositions) do I really know?' – or perhaps without the 'sorts of', just: 'What do I really know?' – there is something about this which reminds me of science. Of course it does not aim at discovering processes or particles that had never been known before. But it does make me think of 'setting forth a picture of the world', or what we know about the world, in a series of carefully formulated statements; and this seems to be the *aim* of the inquiry. – I say 'seems to be', and perhaps I should have said 'may be taken to be'; for I do not know that Moore himself would have said this. But I am not sure. I am thinking of what he said in his 'Reply to my critics' in the Schilp volume, *The Philosophy of G. E. Moore*, where he defended his preoccupation with the logical analysis of propositions on the ground that such analysis 'shows us something about reality'.

Suppose he did speak of 'setting forth a picture of the world, or what we know about the world, in a series of statements'. – If he had, then he would have added (in the mid-1930s at any rate) that philosophy should try to give the *right* picture of the world. In a similar way, he used to say that in philosophy we try to give, not just '*an* analysis', but *the* analysis, or the *right* analysis of the propositions we consider. Although, apparently, he did not think that anyone had ever succeeded in doing so. And his work in philosophy was tentative, uncertain and probing in trying to get clear as to the right method of getting there (i.e. of completing the right analysis).

But I am not sure if Moore ever used the phrase 'picture of the world' in this connection. But I think he might have, and I have introduced it because here it would have to be used so differently then from the way Wittgenstein uses it.

To ask 'Are we right in thinking in terms of the world picture that we do; in representing the world as we do; in speaking as we do; in looking on *this* as speaking or as language (saying something); – would be somewhat analogous to: 'Are we right in calling this red?'; or in closer analogy: 'Are we right in understanding the word "red" as we do?' 'Does this word – "red"

116

– have any connection with what is really there?' Cf. Russell's causal theory, etc., discussed in the previous section.

Our world picture is shown, e.g. in what we take as an *explanation*. I am told: 100 years ago the idea of *progress* was prominent in the thoughts of those who wrote on social policies or on the state of society at the time. This idea is not nearly so influential in the thoughts and writings of social planners, social revolutionaries et al. at the present time. The Government is asked to explain this. The explanation is ... two world wars, congestion, pollution of natural scenes and resources (voice from the rear: and the Government), etc., etc. *This is the sort of thing we regard as an explanation.*

If I say, 'That's not really an explanation of it; what you ought to have mentioned and amplified is ...' – then I am still asking for an explanation of the same general sort of form.

But it would not mean much if someone asked WHY we regard something of this sort as an explanation. Perhaps such an explanation would have meant nothing to members of the University of Paris in the thirteenth century.

Or put it so: you understand *why* we speak in this way, why we regard this as an explanation ... when you yourself are able to speak in this way, to see it as an explanation; (when you are convinced by an explanation of that form, or suggest a better one).

The way to show someone why the calculations in arithmetic have the form that they do ... is to teach him to calculate.

18

CERTAINTY AND MADNESS

I

The notion of 'I must be mad' and of 'being unable to continue the language-game in which I have been speaking and acting'; of being unable to 'go on with the old language-game any further. In which I was torn away from the *sureness* of the game' (*OC:* 617).

Sometimes I have been sure of something for a long time – perhaps that the dome which you can see in this direction from Parliament Hill is St Paul's – and I meet evidence that makes me revise my judgement. (Perhaps someone will convince me that the new buildings make it impossible to see St Paul's from there at all.) But there are other cases in which I would not revise my judgement on *any* evidence; in which I would say 'If this is not true, then I'm crazy'.

Wittgenstein once put it in this way: I might say, 'If you walk through that door you get into the street'. If I went with you to the door and then found not street but green pastures, I'd say 'I must be mad'. In other words: here we should not play the game as we *would* play it in cases which *seem* different only in degree. If I say 'I'm sure there was a tree there, but now I don't see it', I may try to think what the explanation could be; and I may say 'After all, I was mistaken'. If I saw no street, but green pastures,

Section 1 is from Rhees's notes dated 25 February 1970. Section 2 is from editor's notes on Rhees's seminar, 2 February 1970, with a modest amount of editorial insertion in linking certain passages.

when I opened the door, I should *not* say 'After all I was mistaken', and I should not try to think what the explanation could be – *because here I should not know what was MEANT by an explanation.* (Or in other words: I'd no longer know what was meant by 'revising my judgement'.)

We might say: 'There is no move I could make' (I should not ever know what to ask). Which is the sense of: 'I could not continue the language-game'.

Again in other words: it is *not* just a difference of degree. Compare the discussion in *OC:* 52–6 where he contrasts

> 'At this distance from the sun there is a planet' and 'Here is a hand' (namely my own hand). (*OC:* 52)
> For it is not true that a mistake merely gets more and more improbable as we pass from the planet to my own hand. No: at some point it has ceased to be conceivable. (*OC:* 54)

It is not just that hardly anyone *would* doubt such a thing (regarding my own hand), but that it does not *mean* anything to speak of doubting here. Just as it would not mean anything to *ask* for an explanation if I found green pastures instead of the street when I opened the door.

Notice that we are not asking here whether it is a 'meaningful sentence', as though this could be determined by rules of syntax or construction.

This is connected with the use, in this book, of 'rational' and 'reasonable': speaking of 'reasonable doubt' (or: of what is 'beyond all reasonable doubt' (*OC:* 416), or every reasonable man believes (*OC:* 252) saying 'Any "reasonable" person behaves like *this*' (*OC:* 254), acts in *this* way, and so on).

Sometimes 'reasonable' is the better translation of the German 'vernünftig', sometimes 'rational'. Perhaps 'rational' is better in most cases.

Examples are:

> There cannot be any doubt about it for me as a reasonable person. – That's it. (*OC:* 219)
> The reasonable man does *not have* certain doubts. (*OC:* 220)
> But it isn't just that *I* believe in this way that I have two hands, but that every reasonable person does. (*OC:* 252)
> Any 'reasonable' person behaves like this. (*OC:* 254)
> So rational suspicion must have grounds?
> We might also say: 'the reasonable man believes this'. (*OC:* 323)
> Thus we should not call anybody reasonable who believed something in despite of scientific evidence. (*OC:* 324)

119

When we say that we *know* that such and such ..., we mean that any reasonable person in our position would also know it, that it would be a piece of unreason to doubt it. Thus Moore too wants to say not merely that *he* knows it that he etc., etc., but also that anyone endowed with reason in his position would have it just the same. (*OC:* 325)

But who says what it is reasonable to believe in *this* situation? (*OC:* 326)

So it might be said: 'The reasonable man believes: that the Earth has been there since long before his birth, that his life has been spent on the surface of the Earth, or near it, that he has never, for example, been on the moon, that he has a nervous system and various innards like all other people, etc., etc.' (*OC:* 327)

It would not be unreasonable to doubt if that was a tree or only ...

My finding it beyond doubt is not what counts. If a doubt would be unreasonable, that cannot be seen from what *I* hold. There would therefore have to be a rule that declares doubt to be unreasonable here. But there isn't such a rule, either. (*OC:* 452)

I do indeed say: 'Here no reasonable person would doubt.'

– Could we imagine learned judges being asked whether a doubt was reasonable or unreasonable? (*OC:* 453)

There are cases where doubt is unreasonable, but others where it seems logically impossible. And there seems to be no clear boundary between them. (*OC:* 454)

One doesn't say: he is in a position to believe that.

But one does say: 'It is reasonable to assume that in this situation' (or 'to believe that'). (*OC:* 556)

A court martial may well have to decide whether it was reasonable in suchand-such situation to have assumed this or that with confidence (even though wrongly). (*OC:* 557)

This sort of 'rationality' belongs to what makes it possible for us to speak with one another and understand one another. Or rather: we can speak with one another where we can speak of rational talk and action *or* of irrational (unreasonable) talk and action. Contrast the example in *OC:* 108: 'We don't know *how* one gets to the moon, but those who get there know at once that they are there; and even you can't explain everything', and the concluding comment: 'We should feel ourselves intellectually very distant from someone who said this'. We should *not* say that that man's remarks were unreasonable – as though we might suggest how they might be amended to make them rational. We should not make anything of his remarks at all.

This does not mean that his remarks could not be expressed as 'well formed formulae'.

(Wittgenstein sometimes used the expression when talking about the relations of logic and mathematics: '... The point is that if I get contradictory reports, then whether you think me rational or irrational will depend on what I do with these ...' Recognizing the law of contradiction would come to: acting in a certain way which we call 'rational'. *vide* also *Remarks on the Foundations of Mathematics* I: 148–52:

148. Very well: but what if they piled the timber in heaps of arbitrary, varying height and then sold it at a price proportionate to the area covered by the piles?

And what if they even justified this with the words: 'Of course, if you buy more timber, you must pay more'?

149. How could I show them that – as I should say – you don't really buy more wood if you buy a pile covering a bigger area? – I should, for instance, take a pile which was small by their ideas and, by laying the logs around, change it into a 'big' one. This *might* convince them – but perhaps they would say: 'Yes, now it's a *lot* of wood and costs more' – and that would be the end of the matter. – We should presumably say in this case: they simply do not mean the same by 'a lot of wood' and 'a little wood' as we do; and they have a quite different system of payment from us.

150. (A society acting in this way would perhaps remind us of the Wise men of Gotham.)[1]

151. Frege says in the preface to the *Grundgesetze der Arithmetik*: '... here we have a hitherto unknown kind of insanity' – but he never said what this 'insanity' would really be like.

152. What does people's agreement about accepting a structure as a proof consist in? In the fact that they use the words as *language*? As what we call 'language'.

Imagine people who used money in transactions; that is to say coins, looking like our coins, which are made of gold and silver and stamped and are also handed over for goods – but each person gives just what he pleases for the goods, and the merchant does not give the customer more or less according to what he pays. In short, this money, or what looks like money, has among them a quite different role from among us. We should feel much less akin to these people than to people who are not yet acquainted with money at all and practise a primitive kind of barter. – 'But these people's coins will surely also have some purpose!' – Then has everything that one does a purpose? Say religious actions.

It is perfectly possible that we should be inclined to call people who behaved like this insane. And yet we don't call everyone insane who acts similarly within the forms of our culture, who uses words 'without purpose'. (Think of the coronation of a King.)

This is connected also with the way in which he speaks of *judgements* (and not of 'propositions' or 'sentences') in *On Certainty*: 126–31 and *OC:* 139–40.

'Judgements' would be, e.g., expressing beliefs or acting on belief. He speaks in *OC:* 140 of 'A *totality* of judgements', and he might have spoken of 'a whole body of judgements' or 'a system of judgements', as he speaks of 'our game of judging' (*OC:* 131). – And when he speaks in *OC:* 617 of being able – or unable – to 'go on with the old language-game', he might have said 'to continue the game of judging' – *But this would not have been the same as 'being able to continue the calculation' or 'being able to continue the series of calculations'.*

And in *OC:* 139 and 140 he emphasizes that we learn a practice or a way of acting – and in this we learn to make certain judgements – and for this we need not just definitions and rules, but *examples* (in which we can see what the *application* of the rules and definitions is). We are not simply taught grammar. We come to have serious convictions or beliefs.

In an earlier manuscript (probably 1941 or 1942) he speaks of an agreement in judgements (*vide Investigations* I: 242: 'If language is to be a means of communication there must be agreement not only in definitions but also (queer as this may sound) in judgements. This seems to abolish logic, but does not do so.'), but more often of 'an agreement in the lives of people' (in a society speaking the same language). And he speaks of this sometimes as presupposed where there is logic: but this 'is not an agreement in *opinions,* and especially not in opinions on questions of logic'.

And, parallel to what was just said about 'rationality': there would be agreement in the lives of people if I could call someone's action or comment *un*reasonable, no less than if I were to call it reasonable.

II

In *OC:* 167 Wittgenstein speaks of 'world-pictures'. He contrasts people who consult physics with people who consult oracles. He speaks here of *different* world-pictures. With relation to our own he says that we did not acquire it by satisfying ourselves as to its correctness.

The propositions presenting what Moore 'knows' are all of such a kind that it is difficult to imagine *why* anyone should believe the contrary. E.g. the proposition that Moore has spent his whole life in close proximity to the Earth. – Once more I can speak of myself here instead of speaking of Moore. What could induce me to believe the opposite? Either a memory, or having been told. – Everything that I have seen or heard gives me the conviction that no man has been far from the Earth. Nothing in my picture of the world speaks in favour of the opposite.

But I did not get my picture of the world by satisfying myself of its correctness, nor do I have it because I am satisfied of its correctness. No: it is the inherited background against which I distinguish between true and false. (*OC:* 93–4)

Wittgenstein suggested once that a people trying to understand one another, when they don't have a common language, might do so by means of gestures – 'He wants me to take that book and put it on the table'. That is an interpretation of the gesture – an hypothesis. You might put forward other hypotheses to see if this hypothesis was right. You might reward him for taking the book to the right place, and punish him for taking it to the wrong place. But you can only describe it in that way by depending on or appealing to meanings *which are not a matter of conjecture*. Conjectures of this kind presuppose carrying on language which is not conjecture. That is a requisite of carrying on language at all.

This is one of the main features of what Wittgenstein is discussing here and it raises problems.

These problems arise, partly, as we have seen previously, from attempting to treat all Wittgenstein's examples in *On Certainty* in the same way. With respect to the tribe who claim to have been on the moon, Wittgenstein says that he would feel at a great intellectual distance from them. The fact that people have gone to the moon is different from the example of the tribe, but, in any case, does not affect Wittgenstein's point. Empirical changes and discoveries can have occurred which then become part of the scaffolding of our thoughts.

It might be imagined that some propositions, of the form of empirical propositions, were hardened and functioned as channels for such empirical propositions as were not hardened but fluid; and that this relation altered with time, in that fluid propositions hardened, and hard ones became fluid. (*OC:* 96)

Wittgenstein recognizes that, sometimes, there is no sharp boundary between what is fixed and what is fluid:

123

The mythology may change back into a state of flux, the river-bed of thoughts may shift. But I distinguish between the movement of the waters on the river-bed and the shift of the bed itself; though there is not a sharp division of the one from the other. (*OC:* 97)

But this does not mean that everything, from the distance of the planets to looking at my hand, is a matter of degree. Wittgenstein says:

Certain events would put me into a position in which I could not go on with the old language-game any further. In which I was torn away from the *sureness* of the game.
    Indeed, doesn't it seem obvious that the possibility of a language-game is conditioned by certain facts? (*OC:* 617)

As we have seen, again and again, it is the way in which these considerations are developed which constitutes what is new in *On Certainty*.
    When Wittgenstein says, 'Certain facts would put me ...', it is important to recognize that his concern is not with *prophecy*.

'Do I know or do I only believe ...?' might also be expressed like this: What if it *seemed* to turn out that what until now has seemed immune to doubt was a false assumption? Would I react as I do when a belief has proved to be false? or would it seem to knock from under my feet the ground on which I stand in making any judgements at all? – But of course I do not intend this as a *prophecy*.
    Would I simply say 'I should never have thought it!' – or would I (have to) refuse to revise my judgement – because such a 'revision' would amount to annihilation of all yardsticks? (*OC:* 492)

Here, as throughout *On Certainty*, Wittgenstein's concerns are *logical*. He is not concerned with asking, 'What would happen if ...'. In envisaging circumstances in which I'd say 'I must be crazy', his interest is not in these circumstances, but with the *sureness* involved in the various ways in which we *do* judge and act.

124

Appendix 1

COMPARISONS BETWEEN *ON CERTAINTY* AND WITTGENSTEIN'S EARLIER WORK

I

Compare the LPA [*Tractatus*] distinction between *what can be said* and *what cannot be said but only shown* with:

> But I did not get my picture of the world by satisfying myself of its correctness; nor do I have it because I am satisfied of its correctness. No: it is the inherited background against which I distinguish between true and false. (*OC:* 94)
>
> I want to say: it's not that on some points men know the truth with perfect certainty. No: perfect certainty is only a matter of their attitude. (*OC:* 404)
>
> If I say '*we assume* that the Earth has existed for many years past' (or something similar), then of course it sounds strange that we should *assume* such a thing. But in the entire system of our language-games it belongs to the foundations. The assumption, one might say, forms the basis for action, and therefore, naturally, of thought. (*OC:* 411)

In connection with the expression 'background of language' (meaning, thinking) see *OC:* 94. Cf. Plato's notion of 'recollection'.
Philosophical Grammar, p. 82:

> You will say: 'But he certainly can't be wrong when he says that he didn't understand the word'. And that is an observation about the grammar of the

These passages are extracted from scattered notes in German by Rhees in the late 1960s.

statement 'I didn't understand the word'. It is also an observation about grammar when we say, 'Whether he understood, is something he knows which we cannot *know* but only guess'. Moreover the statement 'I didn't understand the word' doesn't describe a state at the time of hearing the word; there are many different ways in which the process characteristic of not understanding may have taken place later.

In *On Certainty* he would not have thought this account of 'he cannot be mistaken' was satisfactory.

Also *Philosophical Grammar*, pp. 85–6

43. Isn't it like this? First of all, people use an explanation, a chart, by looking it up; later they as it were look it up in the head (by calling it before the inner eye, or the like) and finally they work without the chart, as if it had never existed. In this last case they are playing a different game. For it isn't as if the chart is still in the background, to fall back on; it is excluded from our game, and if I 'fall back on it' I am like a blinded man falling back on the sense of touch. An explanation provides a chart and when I no longer use the chart it becomes mere history.

Compare (or *contrast* with *OC*) *Philosophical Grammar*, p.87:

(In our study of symbolism there is no foreground and background; it isn't a matter of a tangible sign with an accompanying intangible power or under-standing.)

Compare *Tractatus* 'what cannot be said, but can only be shown' with *OC:* 51

What sort of proposition is: 'What could a mistake here be like!'? It would have to be a logical proposition. But it is a logic that is not used, because what it tells us is not taught by means of propositions. – It is a logical propo-sition; for it does describe the conceptual (linguistic) situation.

Cf. *Philosophical Grammar*. 'But can't someone say "He is certain that he has toothache"?'

II

Anticipations of these discussions in lectures and discussions in earlier years:
Philosophical Investigations.

242. If language is to be a means of communication there must be agreement not only in definitions but also (queer as this may sound) in judgements. This seems to abolish logic, but does not do so. – It is one thing to describe methods of measurement, and another to obtain and state results of measurement. But what we call 'measuring' is partly determined by a certain constancy in results of measurement.

241. 'So you are saying that human agreement decides what is true and what is false?' – It is what human beings *say* that is true and false; and they agree in the *language* they use. That is not an agreement in opinions but in form of life.

Philosophical Grammar, p. 88:

That one empirical proposition is true and another false is no part of grammar. What belongs to grammar are all the conditions (the method) necessary for comparing the proposition with reality. That is, all the conditions necessary for the understanding (of the sense).

Ibid., p. 154:

What makes us think that a thought, or a proposition we think, contains the reality? It's that we're all ready to pass from it to the reality, and we feel this transition as something already potentially contained in it (when, that is, we reflect on it), because we say 'that word *meant him*'. We feel this transition as something just as legitimate as a permitted move in a game.

Ibid., p. 160:

110. Thinking plus its application proceeds step by step like a calculus. – However many intermediate steps I insert between the thought and its application, each intermediate step always follows the previous one without any intermediate link, and so too the application follows the last intermediate step. It is the same as when we want to insert intermediate links between decision and action. ...

111. It is as a calculus that thinking has an interest for us; not as an activity of the human imagination.

Ibid., pp. 157–8:

(I go to look for the yellow flower. Suppose that while I am looking a picture

127

comes before my mind, – even so, do I need it when I see a yellow flower? If I say: 'as soon as I see a yellow flower, something as it were clicks into place in my memory' – rather like a lever into a cog in the striking mechanism of a clock – can I foresee, or expect, this clicking into place any better than the yellow flower? Even in a particular case it really is true that what I'm expecting isn't what I am looking for, but some other (indirect) criterion, that certainly isn't an explanation of expectation.)

'Belong to a whole culture': Cf. *Lectures on Aesthetics* I-20: 'It is not only difficult to describe what appreciation consists in, but impossible. To describe what it consists in we would have to describe the whole environment.'
Philosophical Grammar, p. 165:

115. So what the picture tells me is itself. Its telling me something will consist in my recognizing in it objects in some sort of characteristic arrangement. (If I say: 'I see a table in this picture' then what I say characterizes the picture – as I said – in a manner which has nothing to do with the existence of a 'real' table. 'The picture shows me a cube' can e.g., mean: It contains the form.

Asked 'Did you recognize your desk when you entered your room this morning?' – I should no doubt say 'Certainly!' and yet it would be misleading to call what took place 'a recognition'. Certainly the desk was not strange to me; I was not surprised to see it, as I should have been if another one had been standing there, or some unfamiliar kind of object.

'Something is familiar if I know what it is.'

'What does it mean: "this object is familiar to me"?' – 'Well, I know that it's a table.' But that can mean any number of things, such as 'I know how it's used', 'I know it looks like a table when it's opened out', 'I know that it's what people call "a table".'

What kind of thing is 'familiarity'? What constitutes a view's being familiar to me? (The question itself is peculiar; it does not sound like a grammatical question.)

I would like to say: 'I see what I see.' And the familiarity can only consist in my being at home in what I see.

Ibid., p. 166

No one will say that every time I enter a room, my long-familiar surroundings, there is enacted a recognition of all that I see and have seen hundreds of times before.

Ibid., pp. 168–9:

119. Familiarity gives confirmation to what we see, but not by comparing it with anything else. It gives it a stamp, as it were.

On the other hand I would like to say: 'what I see here in front of me is not *any old* shape seen in a particular manner: what I see is my shoes, which I know, and not anything else.' But here it is just that two forms of expression fight against each other.

This shape that I see – I want to say – is not simply *a* shape; it is one of the shapes I know; it is a shape marked out in advance. It is one of those shapes of which I already had a pattern in me; and only because it corresponds to such a pattern is it this familiar shape. (I as it were carry a catalogue of such shapes around with me, and the objects portrayed in it *are* the familiar ones.)

But my already carrying the pattern around with me would be only a causal explanation of the present impression. It is like saying: this movement is made as easily as if it had been practised.

And it is not so much as if I were comparing the object with a picture set beside it, but as if the object *coincided* with the picture. So I see only one thing, not two.

Cf. the discussion in *OC:* 512ff. to 570 with *Philosophical Grammar*, p. 127:

If a proposition is conceived as a picture of the state of affairs it describes and a proposition is said to show just how things stand if it's true, and thus to show the possibility of the asserted state of affairs, still the most that the proposition can do is what a painting or a relief does: and so it can at any rate not set forth what is just not the case. So it depends wholly on our grammar what will be called possible and what not, i.e. what the grammar permits. But surely that is arbitrary! Certainly; but the grammatical constructions we call empirical propositions (e.g. ones which describe a visible distinction of objects in a space and could be replaced by a representational drawing) have a particular application, a particular use. And a construction may have a superficial resemblance to such an empirical proposition and play a somewhat similar role in a calculus without having an analogous application; and if it hasn't we won't be inclined to call it a proposition.

Compare *OC:* 558:

We say we know that water boils and does not freeze under such-and-such circumstances. Is it conceivable that we are wrong? Wouldn't a mistake topple all judgement with it? More: what could stand if that were to fall? Might someone discover something that made us say 'It was a mistake'?

Whatever may happen in the future, however water may behave in the future, – we *know* that up to now it has behaved *thus* in innumerable instances. This fact is fused into the foundations of our language-game.

with *Philosophical Grammar*, p. 95:

If the use of the word 'red' depends on the picture that my memory auto-matically reproduces at the sound of the word, then I am as much at mercy of this reproduction as if I had decided to settle the meaning by looking up a chart in such a way that I would surrender unconditionally to whatever I found there.

If the sample I am to work with appears darker than I remember it being yesterday, I need not agree with the memory and in fact I do not always do so. And I might very well speak of a darkening of my memory.

and with *Philosophical Grammar*, p. 96:

If I'm told: 'look for a red flower in this meadow and bring it to me' and then I find one – do I compare it with my memory picture of the colour red? – And must I consult yet another picture to see whether the first is still cor-rect? – I see the colour of the flower and recognize *it*. (It would naturally be conceivable that someone should hallucinate a colour sample and compare it, like a real sample, with the object he was looking for.)

But if I say 'no, this colour isn't the right one, it's brighter than the colour I saw there' that doesn't mean that I see the colour in my mind's eye and go through a process of comparing two simultaneously given shades of colour. Again, it isn't as if when the right colour is found a bell rings somewhere in my mind and I carry round a picture of this ringing, so as to be able to judge when it rings.

Searching with a sample which one places beside objects to test whether the colours match is one game; acting in accordance with the words of a word-language without a sample is another. Think of reading aloud from a written text (or writing to dictation). We might of course imagine a kind of table that might guide us in this, but in fact there isn't one, there's no act of memory, or anything else, which acts as an intermediary between the written sign and the sound.

Wittgenstein said (21 January 1949): 'Scientific questions can interest, but never really grip (intrigue) me. Only conceptual or aesthetic questions do that for me. The solution of scientific questions is a matter of indiffer-ence to me; but not the other, former, questions.'

Appendix 2

SOME PASSAGES RELATING TO DOUBT AND CERTAINTY IN *ON CERTAINTY*

126. I am not more certain of the meaning of my words than I am of certain judgements. Can I doubt that this colour is called 'blue'?

(My) doubts form a system.

524. Is it essential for our language-games ('ordering and obeying' for example) that no doubt appears at certain points, or is it enough if there is the feeling of being sure, admittedly with a slight breath of doubt?

That is, is it enough if I do not, as I do now, call something 'black', 'green', 'red', *straight off*, without any doubt at all interposing itself – but do instead say 'I am sure that that is red', as one may say 'I am sure that he will come today' (in other words with the 'feeling of being sure')?

The accompanying feeling is of course a matter of indifference to us, and equally we have no need to bother about the words 'I am sure that' either. – What is important is whether they go with a difference in the *practice* of the language.

One might ask whether a person who spoke like this would always say 'I am sure' on occasions where (for example) there is sureness in the reports we make (in an experiment, for example, we look through a tube and report the colour we see through it). If he does, our immediate inclination will be to check what he says. But if he proves to be perfectly reliable, one will say that his way of talking is merely a bit perverse, and does not affect the issue. One might for example suppose that he has read sceptical philosophers, become convinced that one can know nothing, and that is why he has adopted this way of speaking. Once we are used to it, it does not infect practice.

Rhees assembled these passages for his own use. I have simply reproduced them as reminders which may be usefully combined with appendix 1.

522. We say: if a child has mastered language – and hence its application – it must know the meaning of words. It must, for example, be able to attach the name of its colour to a white, black, red or blue object without the occurrence of any doubt.

523. And indeed no one misses doubt here; no one is surprised that we do not merely *surmise* the meaning of our words.

526. If someone were to look at an English pillar-box and say 'I am sure that it's red', we should have to suppose that he was colour-blind, or believe he had no mastery of English and knew the correct name for the colour in some other language.
If neither was the case we should not quite understand him.

527. An Englishman who calls this colour 'red' is not 'sure it is called "red" in English'.
A child who has mastered the use of the word is not 'sure that in his language this colour is called …'. Nor can one say of him that when he is learning to speak he learns that the colour is called that in English; nor yet: he *knows* this when he has learnt the use of the word.

528. And in spite of this: if someone asked me what the colour was called in Germany and I tell him, and now he asks me 'are you sure?' – then I shall reply 'I *know* it is; German is my mother tongue.

529. And one child, for example, will say, of another or of himself, that he already knows what such-and-such is called.

530. I may tell someone 'this colour is called "red" in English' (when for example I am teaching him English). In this case I should not say 'I know that this colour …' – I would perhaps say that if I had just now learned it, or by contrast with another colour whose English name I am not acquainted with.

531. But now, isn't it correct to describe my present state as follows: I *know* what this colour is called in English? And if that is correct, why then should I not describe my state with the corresponding words 'I know, etc.'?

532. So when Moore sat in front of a tree and said 'I know that that's a tree', he was simply stating the truth about his state at the time …

Afterword

RHEES ON READING ON CERTAINTY

D. Z. Phillips

I

Organizing the Notes for On Certainty

Wittgenstein worked through what became his *Philosophical Investigations* with Rush Rhees. He discussed some parts of it with him many times. Rhees says that these discussions were indispensable to any understanding he arrived at of Wittgenstein's work. Nevertheless, he goes on to say: 'such understanding of it as I have has come more since his death'.[1] Reading these words was a strange experience for me, since I find myself saying the same of my philosophical relation to Rhees's work.

Rhees taught me at Swansea in my undergraduate years from 1952 to 1956. I was only 17 when I began my studies, and 21 when I graduated – far too young for a proper appreciation of Rhees's teaching. From 1956 to 1960, Rhees supervised my two research theses, although for the latter, which became *The Concept of Prayer*, I was at Oxford. By the time I attended his seminars on *On Certainty* in 1970, I had been a university teacher for nine years, at Queen's College, Dundee and University College, Bangor, returning to Swansea in 1965. I mention my association with Rhees because despite it, 31 years later, I have to say that I understand Rhees's discussions of *On Certainty* in a way that I did not then. This calls for some explanation.

With regard to the notes Rhees circulated in the seminars, the delay or development in my understanding does not surprise me. Like Wittgenstein, Rhees demands more of his readers than they, myself included, are prepared to give. It is not an uncommon experience, therefore, to find, not once, but again and again, new insights in Rhees's texts with which one had assumed complete familiarity. There is an enormous amount of compression in his writing. He is the person who wrote 170 pages as the background for his classic paper, 'Wittgenstein's Builders', which is only 13 pages long![2] I have found more and more as I work on his papers that he is not a philosopher whose work can be summarized in a number of theses, or even emphases. As a teacher, he would never allow us to settle in an all-embracing view of things. He has argued, for example, that anyone writing about suffering, from a religious point of view, will ignore much in human affairs. But he adds, immediately, that this will be true no matter what angle one writes from.[3] So the idea of a 'complete account' of human life seems to be a philosophically suspect phenomenon.

The notes I took in Rhees's seminars call for observations of a different kind. How could they help me to understand Rhees *now*, if I didn't understand them *then*? First, I must not exaggerate. It is not that I had no understanding of what was going on. Nevertheless, the notes do speak to me differently now. This was made possible by the fact that I took notes more or less *verbatim*. Rhees spoke slowly in his lectures, and there were often pauses as he tried to work through things again, as though for the first time. I have no doubt, too, that editing Rhees's work, especially *Wittgenstein and the Possibility of Discourse*, has been the activity through which 31-year-old notes have come alive for me in a new way.

This afterword has four sections. In the fourth, I advance suggestions as to how Rhees develops Wittgenstein's notions of 'form of life' and 'world-picture'. In the third section, I indicate how Rhees's reading of *On Certainty* differs from some other readings of that work. Some of those differences are related to how one perceives the relation of *On Certainty* to Wittgenstein's earlier work. The second section of the afterword is devoted to Rhees's understanding of that relation.

II

Groundlessness and Language-games

Why does Rhees insist that Wittgenstein's interests in *On Certainty* are not new? His insistence is no historical quibble. Rhees would not have expended energy on arguing, for its own sake, whether Wittgenstein's interest in the topics he discusses originated in 1949 when he discussed G. E.

Moore with Norman Malcolm during a visit to America. Neither would Rhees have been interested in determining whether Wittgenstein's aim was to wage a polemic against Moore. Rhees's only interest in showing that the questions raised in *On Certainty* go back as far as 1930, is because this brings out the *kind* of questions they are – that they are questions in logic, not questions in epistemology.

It is no accident that I chose as the motto for Rhees's work a remark from *On Certainty* which captures the continuity between it and Wittgenstein's earlier concerns: 'You must bear in mind that the language-game is so to say something unpredictable. I mean: it is not based on grounds. It is not reasonable (or unreasonable). It is there – like our life' (*OC:* 559). What would it be for our language-games to have grounds? What would the grounds be? But if there are no grounds, aren't the language-games arbitrary? We seem to have nothing but words, when what we need is the sureness of a link, a reliable foundation, between our words and the world. How is that need to be satisfied? Some have thought it necessary to show that the language-games are determined by the structure of the world, and that there is some kind of pre-established harmony between them. But what of that harmony itself? Does it, in turn, need to be grounded in a sure foundation? Some have sought such a foundation in the existence of a God who is no deceiver. Others, while denying that any such prior proof is necessary, arrive at belief in God as an argument to the best explanation of the harmony between our minds and the world. For those who reject any kind of religious foundationalism, the link between our experiences and the world is found in the nature of our constitution as human beings. Some find the direct causal connection they seek between experience and the world in an incorrigible sense experience.

If no such grounds can be found, if we take Wittgenstein at his word when he says that our language-games are unpredictable, does that mean that we do not care whether they are grounded in reality or not? Can we say or do what we like? Surely not. Is not what we say governed by rules, by a logic which determines what can and cannot be said? But, once again, it will be said, we need more than words. So we are led to enquire into the relation not only of logic to language, but of language to reality. These questions become central in philosophy. They are Wittgenstein's concerns from first to last.[4]

Rhees argues that Wittgenstein addresses these issues by asking the following question: what does it mean to say something? That question runs throughout his work. In the *Tractatus*, it is found in his asking: what is a proposition? In his last work, *On Certainty*, he is still discussing certain

135

propositions and what he calls 'the peculiar role' they play in language. Long before that last work, however, Wittgenstein is denying that our language-games have grounds, the very grounds philosophers have thought to be necessary if those language-games are to tell us anything about the world. He tells us that the language-games are unpredictable, neither reasonable nor unreasonable; that they are there like our life. Rhees's work, it might well be said, is concerned with the philosophical significance of that remark.

Searching for Primary Links Between Language and Reality

In the *Tractatus* Wittgenstein searches for the essence of a proposition. If 'saying something' doesn't always mean the same, doesn't that make the whole thing arbitrary? It seems necessary, then, to seek what all propositions have in common; that which makes a proposition a proposition. In his elementary propositions Wittgenstein was looking for something which is simply 'given'; whose meaning cannot be misunderstood. As for the link between the form of language and the structure of the world, that is said to be established by a kind of pre-established harmony said to exist between them.

Rhees tells us that around 1930, Wittgenstein began to feel dissatisfied with the way philosophers talked of logical possibility and logical impossibility, and the implication that logic determines what can and cannot be said. He is still wrestling with that dissatisfaction in *On Certainty*, where he is denying that there is a sharp distinction between logical and empirical propositions, and where he is asking whether logic can be described.

For a short period after the *Tractatus*, however, Wittgenstein entertained a very different conception of logic. He thought that a certain kind of logical analysis could show how language is grounded in the world. The analysis would culminate in immediately experienced sense-data whose sense is simply 'given'. Thus an incorrigible link would have been established between our experience and the world. In his later work, Wittgenstein is bringing out the logical incoherence of a self-referential sign, whether that sign is found in elementary propositions or primary data. He called this a magical view of signs; the view that the meaning of a sign resides in the datum itself, in a mark, sound or image. This is to be contrasted with a logical view of signs; the view that a sign has its sense in the context in which it is used. Wittgenstein, Rhees argues, is not searching for primary 'ultimates', he is not searching for anything like Russell's ultimate furniture of the world, or Quine's ontology.

136

Logical Positivism is seen best as another attempt to ground our experience in the world. That is why the Positivists argued that such a ground is guaranteed in what they claimed to be 'pure observation' or 'pure seeing'. In a somewhat similar way, Moore worried about what it means to say 'That's a tree'. He wanted to know what the 'that' refers to. In the *Investigations* Wittgenstein shows how the dream of 'pure observation' or 'pure seeing', as conceived by the Positivists, is an empty one. He begins by addressing the context where it might be thought that the Positivists' conception has an obvious application, namely, seeing colours.

It might be thought that all we need do is to look at a red patch to know that it is red. Doesn't the colour stand in a one-to-one causal relation to the person who perceives it; a relation which simply 'gives' him or her the perception 'red'? But, as Wittgenstein shows, we do not learn what 'red' is simply by looking at a red patch. The misconception is in thinking that the meaning of 'red' is simply 'given' in a way that cannot be misunderstood. What fixes our concept of colour is the way we react to colours, reactions which show an agreement *in* our judgements. This is not an agreement we made with each other, or arrived at, but one that is shown in the judging itself.

It is tempting to think that were this agreement in our judgements not present, one person might say, 'This flower is red', while another might say of the same flower, 'This flower is blue'. But, as Wittgenstein points out, whatever they are saying, they are not using our notions of 'red' and 'blue'. These concepts are not arrived at by consensus. It is not that every individual saw the flower as *some* colour or other, and then the majority perception prevailed. We have only to ask *what* colour the individual saw. Without the agreement in our judgements, the individual would have no conception of colour. Wittgenstein says: 'There is such a thing as colour-blindness and there are ways of establishing it. There is in general complete agreement in the judgements of colour made by those who have been diagnosed normal. This characterizes the concept of a judgement of colour' (*Investigations* II: xi, p. 227).

The characterization of the concept of colour shows us the place of colours in our world. Rhees says that Wittgenstein would call a remark like 'There can't be a reddish green', 'a concept-forming phrase since it helps to fix our conception of "red" and "green"' (see p. 13). But, now, suppose we ask whether that remark is an empirical or a logical observation, is there a clear answer? Certainly, it is not a logic which determines what we *can* say about colours, since the remark only has force in what we *do* say about colours; that is, in the actual judgements we make. On the other hand, the remark does cast light on the linguistic and conceptual situation. For example, it shows us why it makes no more sense to wait for a reddish-green to turn up, than it would to wait for a round square. Already we are seeing the abandonment of a sharp distinction between the logical and the empirical which is so prominent a feature of *On Certainty*.

What links Wittgenstein's discussion of colours with a major theme in *On Certainty*? Rhees argues that it is an interest in the *sureness* of our language-games. This emphasis on logical or conceptual issues shows that Wittgenstein's primary concern is not epistemological. If his argument is appreciated, we see why it makes no sense to ask whether our colours really are what we take them to be. The request for a further justification is shown to be quite empty. Our colours are there, like our life.

Seeing

Wittgenstein explores the implications of recognizing that there is no primary datum of 'seeing' in Part One of the *Investigations*, but he does so especially in Part Two section xi where he discusses what he calls 'seeing an aspect'. Given the array of examples Wittgenstein provides, it is easy to forget their logical purpose, namely, to show how the Positivists' conception of 'pure seeing' or 'pure observation' cannot be used as the primary link between ourselves and the world. Rhees expresses the logical purpose as follows: 'If the idea of "seeing" is not as unitary or simple as analysis in terms of sense-data suggests – if the concept of seeing itself stands in need of conceptual analysis – it does not have the unquestioned character that seems to qualify it as the basis for all analysis' (p. 8). Behind this is the longer purpose of showing that nothing unitary or simple is going to be the basis of 'what is to be seen' in our world.

By 'seeing an aspect' Wittgenstein means 'seeing something *as* something'. This is important even in connection with colours. For example, it is connected with issues of generality there: the difference between seeing something as the description of a colour, and seeing something as a sample of a colour. But Wittgenstein's discussion of 'seeing an aspect' is meant to show how 'what it is to see something' is a far more heterogeneous notion than a concentration on our agreement in colour-judgements would suggest. Even these judgements are more varied than one might think. We would make little progress in understanding 'what it is to see something', and, therefore, in understanding our world, if we gave no consideration to 'seeing an aspect'.

The examples Wittgenstein discusses are extremely varied, and one cannot say the same about them all. For example, he speaks of how, when we look at a triangle, we might see *this* as the apex, now *that*. Seeing the triangle under different aspects depends on something like the mastery of a technique. It would mean nothing to someone with no knowledge of geometry. But a mere elementary knowledge of the subject might be insufficient to see aspects of more complicated geometrical figures. Notice how many of our concepts cross over here. Compare how an archeologist can see in an earthenware pot what others cannot. Yet, we are still talking of 'what it is to see something'.

In other examples Wittgenstein discusses, no mastery of a technique is involved. This applies to the duck-rabbit phenomenon, and to seeing a white cross on a black background and vice versa. Even here there are differences. The duck-rabbit phenomenon depends on one's acquaintance with ducks and rabbits in other circumstances, whereas seeing the white or the black cross does not.

In further examples the notion of a technique is even less applicable, as the notion of a culture becomes central in understanding 'what it is to see something', although the differences need not be sharp in all cases. For example, although we have noted the general agreement which marks our colour judgements, colour-discernment of a different, but related kind is involved when we consider aesthetic considerations. Wittgenstein asks us to imagine someone choosing a colour from a tailor's book of samples, saying, 'No. This is slightly too dark' or 'No. This is slightly too loud'. Such appreciation, he tells us, has a complex culture as its background. It is against such a background that sense can be made of 'seeing x as the right colour'. Similar considerations apply to seeing something as the right word for what we want to express, or to seeing why a musical theme develops in the way it does.

Finally, Wittgenstein asks us to think of examples which involve a context for which even the word 'culture' may be too restrictive. He has in mind certain features of what might be called 'our lives or living together'. Consider the case of two people who make excellent copies of two faces they are drawing, but where only one of the copiers sees a likeness between the two faces. This marks an important grammatical difference in the grammar of 'object of sight', where one is talking, on the one hand, of the copies, and, on the other hand, of the likeness. This is connected with wider contexts where some people see likeness between things, and others do not. Again, think of differences relating to what it is to see something in a person's face. Is it a genuine expression or not? One person says it is, while another says it is plainly sham. Wittgenstein asks whether we can speak of greater knowledge in such cases. He says that we can, but that we couldn't take a course in it. He calls it a greater knowledge of human beings. Here, it would not be appropriate to speak of mastering a technique. Neither do these judgements exhibit the same agreement as our colour-judgements. Nevertheless, such judgements of human beings are central to anything we'd call acquaintance with the world.

What is the point of parading and analysing these various examples? We miss Wittgenstein's concern with issues of logic, language and reality, if we settle for saying, important though it may be, that he simply wants to rescue us from our craving for generality. Rescuing us from a search for the essence of 'what it is to see something' serves these deeper logical issues. Seeing a colour, seeing something as the apex of a triangle, seeing the duck, the rabbit, the white cross or the black cross, seeing the right colour, seeing the right word, seeing the musical development, seeing a likeness, seeing a facial expression – Wittgenstein insists that these are all cases of 'seeing'. Paying attention to them gets us to see how hopeless it would be to try to capture all this in the Positivists' notion of 'pure observation' or 'pure seeing'. Not that Wittgenstein's examples, of course, are meant as examples of 'impure seeing'. The point of his examples is twofold: first, they are meant to wean us away from a primary seeing which establishes, in itself, an incorrigible contact with the world; second, and equally important, they are meant to stop us from thinking that we ought to get behind them to something more fundamental on which they depend. Once again, Wittgenstein is telling us, with respect to these modes of seeing, that they are there like our life. Our judgements vary, some exhibiting general agreement, others not. But in all cases we are shown the kind of judgements they are, and, at the same time, different aspects of what it is to see something in our world.

Wittgenstein realizes that to those who want single answers to questions such as 'What is "seeing"?', 'What is "thinking"?', 'What is "experience"?', his wide-ranging examples will seem disappointingly indefinite. Rhees points out that what Wittgenstein says of 'seeing' could be said just as easily of 'thinking' and 'experiencing', since it has been shown how many of our concepts cross over in these contexts. If Part Two section xi of the *Investigations* had a title, Rhees says that it could well be 'Seeing and Thinking'. Wittgenstein is well aware, too, that his difficulty will be to convince his readers that in presenting such varied examples he is pursuing, not forsaking, his concern with central issues in logic: how our life with our words is, at the same time, our life in our world.

140

Logic and Practice

Towards the end of his seminars on *On Certainty* Rhees says, 'Suppose someone asks: Why is there this variety of language-games? Why not explain this variety? – That means nothing at all. Explanation gets its sense from a particular context. We concentrate on description and do not go in for explanation' (p. 26). Wittgenstein is arguing that what brings the clarity we need is not explanation, for example, attempts to show that our language-games are determined by something called the structure of the world, or are dependent on something called the nature of the human constitution. What we need is description, by which he means an elucidation of the place a concept occupies in our language-games.

Many have been puzzled by this notion of description, thinking that Wittgenstein has turned away from philosophy in favour of some kind of descriptive sociology. But in showing the roles concepts play in our language-games, Wittgenstein is showing the sureness which belongs to them. One important aspect of this 'sureness', an extremely important one in *On Certainty*, concerns what is *ruled out* in the language-game. What is ruled out is not ruled out by logic, but by the language-game; or, if you like, by the logic of the language-game. One of the central claims of *On Certainty* is that logic cannot be described in abstraction, but is seen if we pay attention to our practices.

The sense in which certain questions are ruled out by a language-game can be illustrated by Wittgenstein's much misunderstood example of moon travel. At the time of these remarks, of course, no one had been on the moon. Wittgenstein said that we would reject any claim to have done so. It flies in the face of too much. How would one overcome the force of gravity? How could one live without an atmosphere? But now that these obstacles have been overcome, some have scoffed at Wittgenstein's example of 'what is ruled out' as a premature dogmatism. This response is based on a misunderstanding. It mislocates what is being ruled out in the example.

It is important to remember that Wittgenstein does not say the same of all the examples he discusses in *On Certainty*. He does not think that they can all be treated in the same way. The moon-travel example is interesting because it illustrates this complexity within its own bounds. If we ask what made Wittgenstein so sure that no one had been on the moon, one might say that that judgement was held fast by the scientific and technological culture which surrounded it. But that culture is one which is characterized by change and development. Wittgenstein never denied this. Indeed, he emphasizes how what does not make sense, at a given time, may shift as the result of scientific or technological advances. The example of moon-travel illustrates the point. It still does not follow that it made sense to claim one had been on the moon at the time Wittgenstein made his remarks. But if we remain with this conclusion, we miss an equally important aspect of Wittgenstein's discussion of the example. We may be led to think that the differences between overcoming technological obstacles, on the one hand, and *other* conceptions of moon-travel he discusses, on the other hand, are simply a matter of degree. This is not so.

I said that the scientific and technological culture which surrounds judgements concerning moon-travel is one which allows for development and change with respect to such judgements. This should not obscure the fact, however, that the considerations by which such development and change are recognized themselves have features which are not questioned. Furthermore, those features rule out certain responses to moon-travel as nonsensical *tout court*, not simply as nonsensical given the present state of scientific knowledge. In concentrating on the fact that human beings reached the moon, discussions of Wittgenstein's example often miss the fact that he goes on to discuss a bizarre response when a claim to have been on the moon is challenged. The person who claims to have been on the moon replies, 'We don't know *how* one gets to the moon, but those who get there know at once that they are there; and even you can't explain everything' (*OC:* 108). The difference between this response and those which emphasize practical obstacles to getting to the moon is not a difference in degree. Wittgenstein's reaction to the response is extremely important, 'We should feel ourselves intellectually very distant from someone who said this' (*OC:* 108). We wouldn't know what to make of him. As Rhees says, 'We want to ask certain questions, and if someone says that they aren't relevant, we find it hard to see what relevance could mean' (p. 13). By contrast, the questions Wittgenstein asked about obstacles to getting to the moon *were* relevant, and recognized as such in the *same* scientific culture in which those obstacles were eventually overcome.

The strange response, on the other hand, is ruled out in the language-game. Shall we say 'logically' ruled out? That conjures up misleading associations; the thought that it has been ruled out by logical principles. What rules it out is a language-game in the context of a scientific world-picture in which standards of relevance play a crucial role. Human beings went to the moon, but we can make nothing of the suggestion that *how* they got there is of no relevance. If someone asked *why* this was relevant we would be nonplussed. We would be bereft of reasons. We would wonder what world that person was living in.

Pictures, Propositions and Reality

In describing the roles concepts play in our language-games, Wittgenstein is endeavouring to give us a clearer understanding of what we mean by 'the world' at the same time. As we have seen already, the descriptions he gives are extremely varied. He shows us differences in our world. I want to pursue this point by following Rhees in showing how, despite Wittgenstein's later criticisms of the so-called picture theory of propositions in the *Tractatus*, he continued to take the analogy between pictures and reality seriously.

In Part One of the *Investigations* (para 522), Wittgenstein makes a distinction between pictures which are historical representations, and what he calls genre pictures. He wants to insist that comparisons with the relation of language to reality have a point with respect to *both* kinds of pictures. In a picture which is a historical representation, such as the crowning of Napoleon, Wittgenstein emphasizes that what the picture says lies outside itself. This is not the case with a genre picture such as Cezanne's *The Card Players*. Wittgenstein wants to relate this distinction to two views of language he finds in the *Investigations*.

When Wittgenstein took up philosophy again eight years after the *Tractatus*, he placed great emphasis on the verification of a proposition. He thought this emphasis became unprofitable once the Positivists had turned it into a rigid thesis. What Wittgenstein found important in the notion is that verification *takes time*. The meaning of a word or a proposition is not given to us all at once. We must look for it in the function they have in the language-game to which they belong. These functions vary. We are confronted by a vast array of them. This emphasis on the function of words and propositions is prominent in Part One of the *Investigations*, and there are clear parallels in Part Two. But in Part Two, Rhees argues, there is also a corrective to this view of language. Moreover, it is a corrective which has to do with Wittgenstein's claim that a genre picture says itself.

It is easy to misunderstand the contrast Wittgenstein is drawing. Wittgenstein is not saying that the meaning of the genre picture is given all at once. His emphasis on verification was meant to combat *that* view. Here, the place occupied by 'function' in that context, is now occupied by 'culture'. One could not appreciate a great painting if that were the only painting one had seen. To see why a painting is a profound treatment of its subject one would have to compare it with other paintings of lesser significance. I do not mean, of course, that the comparison has to be made on the occasion of seeing the great painting, though that might occur. But one brings to one's seeing of a great painting one's acquaintance with other

143

paintings. Similar points could be made with respect to great literature and music, and nothing Wittgenstein says is meant to deny this.

What, then, does Wittgenstein mean when he says that a genre picture says itself? He wants to emphasize that the picture cannot be explained in terms of its function. In many contexts, the functions our words perform could be fulfilled by different words. But this is not true in poetry or drama. Wittgenstein speaks of words whose whole meaning is taken up into themselves. But his point is not confined to literary or artistic contexts. Think of the ways in which people express themselves in their day-to-day conversations with each other – the telling phrases, striking expressions, thoughtful responses, sarcasm and humour – all play such a crucial role. But it is not a role which can be captured in terms of function. It is not as though what is said could be said in another way. Such modes of expression enter into our relationships with each other, and, at times, are constitutive of them. Rhees asks what language would be like if words weren't valued in this way. He thinks it would be something mechanical, like Esperanto. A world with such a language would be very different from ours.

Wittgenstein's distinction between words which perform a function, and words whose whole meaning seems to be taken up in themselves, may seem to create a difficulty. Rhees has been emphasizing that instead of seeking explanations of why our language is what it is, Wittgenstein has been showing, by means of description, the confusions involved in striving for such an explanation. But is Wittgenstein now saying that with respect to certain forms of language, where words are clarified by reference to the function they perform, explanation *is* what we need, but that with respect to those forms of discourse in which we value words, only description is necessary? What has become of the insistence that with respect to *all* our language-games what we need is description, not explanation? This worry is based on a misunderstanding.

Rhees goes some way towards addressing this issue by pointing out that the distinction between words which have a function and words which say themselves, is not a sharp one. There are times when expressions of value judgement are hardly distinguishable from action, as when someone shows his appreciation for a painting by going often to a gallery to see it, by always being alone when he looks at it, by refusing to have a copy of it in his house, and so on. Admiration for a friend may show itself in the various things one does with respect to him. Without denying what Rhees says, it does not get to the heart of the problem, or address it in the fundamental way he does elsewhere in the text, where, despite the sharp distinctions which do exist between the different modes of discourse, he endeavours to

144

show that in *both* contexts, description, and not explanation of our practices is what we need to bring out sureness in our language-games, and, thus, the sureness in our world.

This claim may seem unlikely, since in drawing the contrast we have discussed, Rhees, somewhat unfortunately, calls words and propositions which can be elucidated functionally, 'practice', and calls words and propositions which say themselves, 'the way we choose and value words'. He insists, quite rightly, given these senses, that the expressions 'practice' and 'the way we choose and value words' do not coincide. Rhees goes further: 'The divergencies between, on the one hand, the empirical judgements Wittgenstein discusses in *On Certainty* and the practice which holds them fast, and, on the other hand, the way we choose and value words, is probably much wider than anything they have in common' (p. 000). If the divergencies are so great, why does Rhees spend so much time arguing for connections between them? Why should seeing these connections be important in seeing a relation between *On Certainty* and Wittgenstein's earlier work?

The answer to the apparent difficulty, I believe, is Wittgenstein's insistence that in considering the relation of language to reality, the analogy with pictures has a point, *both* in relation to representational and genre pictures. Rhees says:

> We have backgrounds of different kinds here. A whole culture is a background against which the value judgements with aesthetics would be what they are. It enables us to understand the people and to find our feet with them. The other enables us to understand what is being said when people are talking about physical objects and physical events. 'Understanding people' and saying 'That's what life is really like' go together. You can't have one without the other. (p. 39)

It seems to me, however, that Rhees's last sentence must be applied to *both* backgrounds he discusses. In both he is concerned with what Wittgenstein means by his wider use of 'practice' to mark conceptual differences between forms of discourse.

Discussion of diverse contexts shows Wittgenstein's abiding interest in the issue of our being in the world. He is suggesting that there is an analogy between aesthetics and logic; an analogy which is not discussed often enough. The question 'Why do we paint as we do?' may have more affinity than we think to the question 'Why do we think as we do?' Neither is a matter of choice. We could not adopt a culture at will, or simply choose to paint, let us say, like the Egyptians. In the case of culture, the system of

145

empirical judgements discussed in *On Certainty*, and language generally, we are tempted to get behind what we do to something more fundamental, when what we need is a clarifying description of the place of concepts in our lives. This is one of the major connecting themes between *On Certainty* and Wittgenstein's earlier work.

Forms of Life

Many readers of Wittgenstein may find it hard to see any connection between the concerns in logic I have mentioned, and his 'Remarks on Frazer's *Golden Bough*'. It is easier to settle for saying that his main concern in the latter work is to avoid condescending misunderstandings of ways of living other than our own. He finds such condescension, it may be said, in what Frazer says about the slaying of the priest–king at Nemi. Yet, concerned though he is about such condescension, it is important to see that Wittgenstein is still pursuing issues in logic even here. He is still showing why we should resist the desire to get behind a distinctive form of life, to show whether it has a rational foundation or not. In the case of the slaying of the priest–king, this may come about by subliming functional activities, and treating them as though they were *the* criterion by which all other activities are to be assessed. We cannot get behind distinctive ways of acting. When we think we have, we are often elevating one of them to a spurious space outside the appropriate language-games from which it purports to give us an absolute conception of the world.

Frazer tells us that the king has to be killed in his prime in order to keep his soul fresh. It looks as though we are given an explanation in terms of a ground and its consequent, whereas, Wittgenstein insists, belief and practice go together here. The ritual slaying says itself. The idea does not arise from the practice, nor vice versa.[5] Rhees says:

> If you ask, Why this ritual? Why should the priest devote his whole life to this role knowing he is to be sacrificed? or What are they trying to achieve by this? Why should they be trying to achieve anything? Various things happen round about in the lives of these people in primitive societies, which impress them, and are very different from urban or industrial societies. Death is one of them. If you ask, Why should it? – that's your privilege. It may not impress us ... But it *did* impress them. (p. 41)

That is part of their lives – an expression of them. If *we* are impressed by the ritual, it is that impression, not the explanation that we think we need, that we ought to concentrate on. Rhees tells us: 'Wittgenstein said to Drury that the language Frazer uses isn't the one he would use in describing an imperfect scientific experiment. But if you ask why it took place, the answer is: because it is terrible. You can only describe and say: that's what human life is like' (p. 42).

But suppose we ask: what *is* human life like? Is it not clear that it contains *both* functional practices *and* practices which say themselves? As we have seen, we may confuse them, but they are related in our lives nevertheless. One may misunderstand the character of rain dances in thinking of them as failed scientific experiments to cause rain. The dances occurred when the rains were due. They celebrated their coming. If one asks 'Why waste time doing that instead of getting on with the job?' – that's one's privilege. People sing, dance, celebrate, perform rituals. Here are activities which say themselves. But, clearly, they are related to purposive, functional activities. People are dependent on the rain whose coming is celebrated. The celebration would not mean much otherwise. The dance is related to the lives of people who need rain to live, people who sow, reap and harvest. This interlocking intelligibility of different forms of discourse is one of the major themes of Rhees's *Wittgenstein and the Possibility of Discourse*. The celebratory and functional aspects of our activities are there like our lives. Wittgenstein says that they are simply some of the activities we engage in, some of the language-games we play.

Practices and Parallels

Wittgenstein asks in *On Certainty* (51): 'Am I not getting closer and closer to saying that in the end logic cannot be described? You must look at the practice of language then you will see it.' But what enables us to see it is not the application of principles of logic, but the way in which our practice speaks for itself. This is a point which Wittgenstein makes with respect to practices of very different kinds. As we have seen, with regard to judging the genuineness of human beings, Wittgenstein says that we cannot take a course in it. But in the very different context of the system of empirical judgements he discusses in *On Certainty*, he also says that we do not reach conclusions 'by learning rules: we are taught judgements and their connection with other judgements' (*OC*: 140).

In the case of empirical judgements, it is tempting to fall back on the foundationalist assumption that they must eventually be grounded in propositions that we *know* to be true. Wittgenstein replies:

'An empirical proposition can be tested' (we say). But how? And through what? (*OC:* 109)

   What counts as its test? – 'But is this an adequate test? And, if so, must it not be recognizable as such in logic?' As if giving grounds did not come to an end sometimes. But the end is not an ungrounded proposition: it is an ungrounded way of acting. (*OC:* 110)

Wittgenstein illustrates this with reference to the most famous of Moore's propositions:

It is possible to imagine a case in which I *could* find out that I had two hands. Normally, however, I *cannot* do so. 'But all you need is to hold them up before your eyes!' – If I am *now* in doubt whether I have two hands, I need not believe my eyes either. (I might just as well ask a friend).[6]

Any reason I give, in normal circumstances, in an attempt to show that I have two hands, will be less certain than what it is asked to support. Again, Wittgenstein draws a parallel in very different circumstances: compared with the impression made on us by the slaying of the priest–king at Nemi, any explanation offered is too uncertain.

   Wittgenstein is interested in the kind of sureness involved in our language-games – the sense in which our practices speak for themselves. He does not speak of all his examples in the same way, but central to his logical concerns is the fact that when practice speaks for itself, certain facts and certain procedures go unquestioned. Here is one example:

There are historical investigations and investigations into the shape and also the age of the Earth, but not into whether the Earth has existed during the last hundred years. Of course many of us have information about the period from our parents and godparents, but mayn't they be wrong? – 'Nonsense!' one will say. 'How should all these people be wrong?' – But is that an argument? Is it not simply the rejection of an idea? And perhaps the determination of a concept? For if I speak of a possible mistake here, this changes the role of 'mistake' and 'truth' in our lives. (*OC:* 138)

When practice speaks for itself, the question of whether the Earth has existed for the last hundred years simply does not arise. If someone said that this needs to be investigated, we would not know what to make of him. We would wonder whether he knew his way around the practice. When practice speaks for itself, a person who says that he has been on the moon, but sees no relevance in the question of how he got there, is a complete enigma to us. His rejection of the question's relevance places him outside an inherited tradition in which investigation and standards of relevance play a crucial role. When practice speaks for itself, the question of why death is impressive does not arise.

It is important to note that Wittgenstein is emphasizing what practices *do* say, not what they *must* say. Wittgenstein is not saying that the practices are determined by anything like the structure of the world. If we are inclined to think that a practice gives us an absolute conception of the world, that the world, for example, forces us to have a scientific interest in it, Wittgenstein asks us to imagine a people with no such interest. They have no physics. They consult oracles.

Given the parallels I have noted, what is new in *On Certainty*? Certainly not his renewed attack on foundationalism, though he mentions the term 'foundations' many times. Neither can it be said to be a discussion of Moore's propositions. As we have seen, he discusses the most famous of them in the *Investigations*. But, in relation to those propositions, Wittgenstein explores, with a new thoroughness, his interest in the sureness in our language-games. That interest, as Rhees shows, goes back to 1930. But what Wittgenstein emphasizes now is that that sureness involves certain facts that are not questioned. We are not simply taught the grammar of concepts.

How is our sureness with regard to such facts to be understood? Are they asserted in propositions that we know to be true? If Wittgenstein rejects this use of 'know', does he say that the truth of these propositions is something we believe, assume, presuppose, or take for granted? It is in the way he wrestles with these questions that Rhees's reading of *On Certainty* differs, in important respects, from the readings of other commentators on the work.

III

I am not going to argue for Rhees's reading of *On Certainty*, compared with other readings. That would require a book in itself. Readers may be helped, however, if I simply indicate where some major differences are to be found. I do not claim to be doing justice to the other readings, since I am only highlighting what I take to be differences between them and Rhees. These disagreements do not rule out the possibility of agreement on other points relating to *On Certainty*. I therefore urge readers to read the authors I refer to for themselves. In identifying the disagreements in a sequence of questions, I am, of course, tracing the way I have attempted to find a path through the complexities of *On Certainty*.

Is the Title On Certainty a Happy One?

Rhees says that the title is not altogether a happy one: '"Certainty" is no more prominent a theme than "knowledge", "mistake", or 'what it is to say anything at all"' (p. 3). Jerry Gill, on the other hand, argues that Wittgenstein's central issue is what it means 'to doubt or affirm those "beliefs" which comprise the very framework within which doubting and affirming take place. Or, in other words, what is the nature of the certainty that pervades and undergirds all language, making it possible to doubt or affirm anything at all.'[7] Rhees does say that what interests Wittgenstein is the sureness in our language-games, but is that sureness to be expressed in terms of certainty? Is it a matter of asserting anything? Gill recognizes that these are major issues to be faced. Not that Wittgenstein wants to say that we *know* certain things are certain. His criticisms of Moore are enough to show that. Wittgenstein is not engaged in any attempt to refute scepticism, as Moore is, by responding to the sceptic's 'You do not know' with 'Yes I do know'.

This leads to an important question. It may lead us to think that we need to find an epistemic replacement for 'know'. As Peter Winch says, 'Much of Wittgenstein's discussion seems to take the form of trying to substitute some other word for "know" in these contexts: such as "believe", "assume", "presuppose", "take for granted"'. Rhees agrees with Winch's view of these efforts: 'The outcome of these attempts is that none of these suggestions is satisfactory. But the conclusion is not meant to be that we must look harder till we have found the right word, but that we are looking in the wrong direction altogether.'[8] In comparing Rhees's readings with others, I hope to show the character of that wrong direction.

Is On Certainty a Polemic against Moore?

We cannot appreciate Wittgenstein's concerns in logic if we remain within the parameters of Moore's interests. Wittgenstein's essay, for Rhees, is not a polemic within those parameters. While commentators acknowledge that Wittgenstein's interests go beyond those of Moore, it is suggested frequently that *On Certainty* began through an interest in Moore, an interest created in Wittgenstein's discussions with Malcolm in 1949. Jean-Pierre Leyvraz says, 'In his last years, Wittgenstein fought against the common-sense philosophy of G. E. Moore'.[9] Avrum Stroll suggests that when Wittgenstein began writing *On Certainty* 'his focus was on Moore's work with its propositional emphasis'.[10] Marie McGinn asserts, 'The primary aim of *OC*, ... is to avoid the mistake of "countering the assertion that one cannot know that [that's a tree], by saying 'I do know it'" (*OC:* 521), and to steer a course between the sceptic's doubt and Moore's dogmatism.'[11] Frederick Stoutland claims: 'What inspired Wittgenstein to write on certainty was Moore's "A Defence of Common Sense".'[12]

Rhees says that Wittgenstein 'used to speak of Moore's "Defence of Common Sense" again and again, years before that visit to Malcolm in 1949'. He is not 'questioning the point that his 1949 discussions with Malcolm about Moore's "defence of common sense" interested him, particularly at the period he was writing the notes in *On Certainty*. Rhees's point 'is rather that his 1949 conversations with Malcolm stimulated Wittgenstein to take up thoughts which were not new to him, and to develop them further' (p. 5). With regard to Moore's propositions, Rhees says, 'That aspect of the propositions which so impressed Wittgenstein, Moore did not notice or find very interesting. (Which is not surprising. The seeds bore fruit for Wittgenstein because they fell into the soil of his other thoughts and interests.)' (p. 3). In the second section of this afterword I endeavoured to give some indication of the character of that soil.

Is Wittgenstein's Main Interest in Moore's Propositions the Nature of Nonsense?

If, as Rhees says, Wittgenstein is interested in aspects of Moore's propositions which Moore did not notice, does making those aspects explicit lead simply to the exposure of nonsense? Rhees says, 'We can imagine circumstances in which it is perfectly natural to say "I know it's a tree" ... These are circumstances in which the expression can be used, but they are of no interest to philosophy' (p. 67). But these are not the circumstances in which Moore said, 'I know that's a tree'. He said so sitting in a garden near a tree. Wittgenstein found this proposition both odd and important. But not for the reason suggested by McGinn. She takes Wittgenstein to be saying that while the proposition 'I know that's a tree' makes sense, it is simply inappropriate to assert it in the circumstances depicted. For her, 'the crucial idea, is that there are two distinct notions of meaning – word meaning and speaker's meaning'.[13] As James Conant says, this makes it look 'as if we could know what Moore would be asserting if only he were *per impossibile* able to assert it'.[14] For Conant, Wittgenstein's charge of

'Nonsense!' is directed, not against the sentence, 'but against a failure on the part of the speaker to provide the sentence with something to do on occasion of speaking'.[15] So far, I think Rhees would agree with Conant. The 'failure' Conant refers to would be part of the oddity of Moore's propositions for Wittgenstein and Rhees.

But where do we go from there? Do we end with the recognition that the exposure of the oddity of Moore's response 'I know' to the sceptic's claim, 'You don't know', is simply another instance of success for Wittgenstein's therapeutic techniques? Are we simply prevented from talking nonsense? Rhees would not settle for this. Some of Conant's remarks suggest that we should:

> Wittgenstein's point about Moore and the skeptic is not *pace* McGinn, that it is clear in each case what judgment is in question (concerning which Moore avows and the skeptic disavows knowledge) and that, given the special epistemic status of the judgment in question (its immunity to doubt, its status as a framework proposition, etc.) the 'it' in question is something which can be neither known nor doubted. His point is rather that it is not clear what Moore and the skeptic are doing with their words – i.e., what the context of use is supposed to be – and hence what it is that they are saying. For what your words say depends upon what they are *doing* – how they are at work – in a context of use.[16]

Elizabeth Wolgast has a very different, yet related, argument. She suggests that Wittgenstein gets into trouble with Moore-like propositions in *On Certainty* by forgetting precisely the lesson Conant says Wittgenstein is trying to teach us about Moore and the sceptic. Wittgenstein, she argues, is torn between trying to find a use for the propositions which express our 'comfortable certainties' (as she calls them), while at the same time saying that they have no use. We seem to be so familiar with Moore's propositions. Wolgast argues: 'This sense of familiarity, indeed, seems to account for why the propositions are not used. There is no need to use them; they are secure beyond opportunity for use, just as they are secure against debate.'[17] Wolgast, however, does not allow us an easy acquiescence with these conclusions. She says:

> But wait a minute: How can a proposition be important when it never comes into the working language and is not learned as part of that language. It is precisely its *not* coming into that language as a working proposition that shows its character as fundamental. This is part of the criterion for its being a 'framework proposition'. But this reasoning is circular. Framework proposi-

tions are important partly because they are not used; and they are not used because that is part of their framework role.[18]

Wittgenstein would have avoided this trouble, according to Wolgast, had he remembered the lesson he taught so well in the *Investigations* about the functionality of propositions. If we try to consider propositions in abstraction from their function, we are left with empty words. Wittgenstein is well aware of this wrong turn but, nevertheless, according to Wolgast, falls prey to it in his last work. For her, 'It is ironic that *On Certainty* should be largely devoted to exploring this wrong turn'.[19]

These conclusions would be too negative for Rhees. While recognizing the importance of clarifying conceptual confusions, he always emphasized that, for Wittgenstein, this was in the service of the big questions of philosophy. This is why Rhees disliked Wittgenstein's analogy between philosophy and therapy – he thought it did his work a disservice by obscuring these larger issues. So Rhees would not be content to show, as do Conant and Wolgast, in their different ways, that the sceptic and Moore are talking nonsense, and that the concept of a framework proposition is a pseudo-concept.[20] There is something related to Moore's propositions which Wittgenstein thinks is important for our whole way of thinking about the world. The difficulty is in trying to get clear about what that 'something' is.

Rhees comes back to this question from many different directions, as does Wittgenstein himself. It is not as though Wittgenstein did not come to general conclusions in this context. He said that language is a collection of language-games; that to imagine a language is to imagine a form of life, or a way of living; and that our ways of thinking and acting constitute our world-picture. These issues are as old as Plato. Rhees claims that Wittgenstein was showing the connections between Plato's questions and ours, 'with our understanding and thinking altogether', but says, 'And I would add with our *lives* altogether. Cf.: "to imagine a language is to imagine a form of life" – and, more important, *Investigations* II: xii, p. 230' (p. 9). The latter passage reads:

> If the formation of concepts can be explained by facts of nature, should we not be interested, not in grammar, but rather in that in nature which is the basis of our grammar? – Our interest certainly includes the correspondence between concepts and very general facts of nature. (Such facts as mostly do not strike us because of their generality.) But our interest does not fall back upon these possible causes of the formation of concepts; we are not doing natural science; nor yet natural history – since we can invent fictitious natural history for our purposes.

153

I am not saying: if such-and-such facts of nature were different, people would have different concepts (in the sense of a hypothesis). But: if anyone believes that certain concepts are absolutely the correct ones, and that having different ones would mean not realizing something that we realize – then let him imagine very general facts of nature to be different from what we are used to, and the formation of concepts different from the usual ones will become intelligible to him.

Compare a concept with a style of painting. For is even our style of paint-ing arbitrary? Can we choose one at pleasure? (The Egyptian, for instance.) Is it a mere question of pleasing and ugly?

The point is not to belittle the importance of freeing ourselves from con-ceptual confusion, but to recognize what freedom from confusion brings, namely, according to Rhees, not only a clarity about 'thinking' and 'under-standing', but also a certain kind of clarity about our lives altogether. It was such connections, Rhees argues, that Wittgenstein saw in the oddity of Moore's propositions.

Does Wittgenstein Say that the Propositions he is Interested in Form a Class, and Does he Say the Same of all of Them?

Before answering this question, it is worth reminding ourselves of the propo-sitions which are discussed in *On Certainty*. McGinn provides a useful list:

'My name is L. W.', 'The world existed for a long time before my birth', 'Everyone has parents', 'Everyone has a brain inside his skull', 'I have two hands', 'That's a tree', 'I am in England', 'I have never been on the moon', 'I have never been to China', 'Water boils at 100ºC', 'I know that the water in the kettle on the gas-flame will not freeze but boil', 'I am a human being', 'I flew from America to England a few days ago', 'I am sitting writing at the table'.[21]

McGinn comments: 'the class is very much a motley' and that, as a result, 'the best we can do is offer a very rough characterization of what would constitute the class of Moore-type propositions at a given time and in a scientific context'.[22] But what if the propositions do not constitute a class and that providing any general characterization will lead only to the citing of obvious counter-examples? That is certainly Rhees's view. If he is right, and Wittgenstein is not aiming for a consistent account of all the proposi-tions he discusses, it will be no criticism to say, as John Churchill does, that

'He offers no consistent account whether propositions in that "peculiar logical role" are genuinely empirical propositions or not'.[23] If one thinks that Wittgenstein is, or should be, offering an all-embracing account of the propositions he discusses, it is little wonder that he appears as he does to John Cook, as someone 'constantly changing direction, like a man lost in a maze'.[24]

I shall simply offer a few examples of the trouble which ensues if one attempts a general characterization of the propositions Wittgenstein discusses. Ilham Dilman says of them: 'We do not arrive at them as the result of an investigation; we are taught to believe them.'[25] But, in some cases, what is now accepted without question was arrived at as the result of an investigation, for example, that every skull contains a brain. What is true is that once discovered, it becomes part of what Wittgenstein calls the scaffolding of our thought, such that no one would doubt that every skull contains a brain. As to the general claim that we were taught to believe the propositions Wittgenstein discusses, Lance Ashdown asks, 'in which class or by which adult were we taught the proposition, "The Earth is very old"?'[26] If we were taught some of them, they wouldn't have 'the peculiar role' Wittgenstein is interested in. On the other hand, we are taught that water boils at 100°C.

McGinn, Stoutland and Stroll suggest that in relation to Moore-type propositions, if we are wrong, this is not a matter of being *mistaken*.[27] To be mistaken is to have a false belief, one that can be fitted in to what we already know. If we are wrong about Moore-like propositions, the suggestion is that all one's yardsticks are broken up, and one is dragged into chaos. It is a state akin to a mental disturbance. To all of which Rhees says: it depends.

If someone said that water will freeze, rather than heat, when placed over a fire, we should regard him as being in need of elementary instruction. To doubt that the water would heat would not be to doubt a single proposition. One would be doubting much else besides. But what if the water *did* freeze? No doubt we would be astonished. But an explanation would be sought. In any event, we would go on. It would not overthrow our whole way of thinking. More radically, imagine different plants growing from the same seeds. If over a long period of time, despite the most diligent research, no difference is detected in the seeds, A seeds would become known as the seeds which lead to A plants, and B seeds would become known as the seeds which lead to B plants. One could imagine interest shifting, gradually, from the seeds to the plants. Of course, this would revolutionize botany, but, again, a science of some kind would go on.

On the basis of examples such as these, however, we must not think the differences between them and others Rhees discusses are simply a matter of degree. We do not know what it would be to doubt that the Earth has existed for many years. Further, if I were separated from the sureness that a door in my house leads to a familiar corridor, that this is where I lived, that these were my friends, and so on, I'd think I was going crazy.

Sometimes, Stroll entertains certain criteria for what he regards as foundational propositions. In every case, however, the price of doing so is to ignore some of the propositions Wittgenstein discusses.[28] First, it may be said that the propositions must be characterized by a certain vagueness, and be unspecific. Thus, on this view, though the Earth is said to exist many years before my birth, no specific number of years is mentioned. But this criterion clearly excludes propositions such as 'Here is a hand', or 'That's a tree', which are quite specific and not vague at all. Second, it may be said that foundational propositions are those which most human beings know to be true. Thus, 'There are human beings' would be such a proposition, but not 'I am a human being'. But apart from excluding the latter proposition, this criterion also excludes propositions such as 'There exists a living human body which is my body', and 'I was born'. Third, it may be said that these propositions cannot be negated without absurdity, but we have already discussed counter-instances to that claim. Fourth, it may be said that foundational propositions are not empirical discoveries, but we have also seen that this need not be the case. Fifth, it may be said that foundational propositions are not subject to change. Wittgenstein, on the other hand, discusses changes in the riverbed of our thoughts, some of a more radical nature than others.

In contrast to such attempts at finding criteria for the propositions Wittgenstein discusses, Rhees writes: 'One misunderstanding people make about the propositions Wittgenstein says cannot be doubted is to try to classify them, or find out what they all have in common ... What *is* their logical role? There is no single answer. Wittgenstein says they have "a *similar* role in the system of our empirical judgements" (*OC:* 137)' (pp. 78–9). He does not say that they have the *same* role. For example, he does not treat all specific facts in the same way. Compare what he says about water freezing when heated, with what he says about being deprived of the sense of one's familiar surroundings. Again, the treatment of inductive procedures, or the picture of the Earth as a floating ball is different, as is what Wittgenstein says of the wider contexts of 'form of life' and 'world-picture'.

From this point on it should be borne in mind that my own choice of examples is selective. They are chosen to illustrate specific philosophical issues, but ones, I believe, which are central to Wittgenstein's concerns.

Are Wittgenstein's Propositions Context-free?

In the light of our discussion of the previous question, it is surprising to find Cook claiming that Wittgenstein's thesis in *On Certainty* is that the propositions he discusses are such that 'we must be able to recognize hinge propositions without considering circumstances at all. We must be able to recognize a hinge proposition by considering merely what the proposition says. Indeed, this is what is *meant* by saying that it is a *proposition* that is "exempt from doubt". This is essential to Wittgenstein's conception of hinge propositions.'[29] In chapter 3 Rhees says that Wittgenstein told him once, in a conversation, that the propositions he was interested in, not simply propositions in geometry, but also propositions such as 'There can't be a reddish-green', he held to be self-evident. But Rhees says that Wittgenstein soon retracted this view (see p. 13).

It will be noted that Cook calls Wittgenstein's propositions *hinge* propositions. This is one of the many analogies Wittgenstein employs in discussing them. He also refers to them as the axis (*OC*: 152), riverbed (*OC*: 97) and scaffolding (*OC*: 211) of our thoughts. But, as Winch points out, some analogies are better than others. That of a hinge has certain disadvantages, the very disadvantages that Cook seizes on in attributing a theory of hinge propositions to Wittgenstein. Wittgenstein says, 'the *questions* that we raise and our *doubts* depend on the fact that some propositions are exempt from doubt, are as it were like hinges on which those turn' (*OC*: 341). But, as Winch points out:

> A hinge exists in a fixed position independently and in a sense prior to the motion of the door which hangs on it; the hinge is a causal condition of the door's movement. And though the 'hinge theorists' have by and large, I think, wanted to see this as an example of Wittgenstein's anti-foundationalism, it seems to me a bad example for the purpose and obscures the radical nature of Wittgenstein's position. It suggests that Wittgenstein had not *abandoned* the search for a 'foundation', but is simply pointing to a foundation of a kind different from the usual. For a hinge *is* a kind of foundation.[30]

Earlier, in *On Certainty*, Wittgenstein says, 'I do not explicitly learn the propositions that stand fast for me. I can *discover* them subsequently like

157

the axis around which a body rotates. This axis is not fixed in the sense that anything holds it fast, but the movement around it determines its immobility' (*OC:* 152). Winch thinks, and Rhees would agree, that this analogy is far better suited to express what Wittgenstein wants to say:

> Hinges after all *are* held fast by something besides the movement around them. 'Axis' on the other hand is a purely geometrical concept; not merely the 'immobility' of an axis is 'determined by the movement around it'; *it itself* is so determined. It is a reference point for description of the movement. It has no existence or meaning apart from the movement. We can of course make a mark to indicate where the axis is located. But the mark is not itself the axis.[31]

My point is that Cook's thesis may be aided by his choice of an analogy which serves Wittgenstein's purposes least. But once we note its disadvantages, we can appreciate the difference between Wittgenstein's remarks and the theory Cook finds in them. Cook admits that Wittgenstein, despite his many examples, seldom says, 'This proposition is one of those that are exempt from doubt',[32] but attributes this to Wittgenstein's difficulty in finding a criterion for hinge propositions; propositions recognizable as such independent of circumstances. Considering example after example, Cook has no difficulty in imagining circumstances in which the propositions can be doubted and concluding, triumphantly, that they do not qualify as hinge propositions after all. But as we noted in answering the third question, the circumstances Cook keeps invoking are of no interest to Wittgenstein. They are irrelevant for the issues he is discussing. From an exegetical point of view, it is not encouraging to hear Cook outline his own approach: 'I must begin by giving some account of the theory that has been attributed to Wittgenstein. In order to do this, I will go through Wittgenstein's notes and select passages that seem to belong to the theory. When I come upon passages that seem to undermine the theory, I will simply ignore them.'[33]

Cook claims to reveal a well-kept secret about Wittgenstein that is supposed to account for his having a theory of hinge propositions: 'Wittgenstein, if I may let the cat out of the bag, was a phenomenalist, and his principal concern in *On Certainty* was to figure out how, if at all, a phenomenalist can avoid being a skeptic, can avoid the conclusion that anything we say about a physical object might be disconfirmed by our future experience'.[34]

Many other commentators have found Cook's claims to be bizarre. Rhees certainly did when Cook presented them in seminars at Swansea before their publication. Rhees told us in chapter 2 that for a short period after the

Tractatus Wittgenstein toyed with the idea that a certain kind of logical analysis could show how language is grounded in the world. The analysis would culminate in immediately experienced sense-data said to be an incorrigible link between our experience and the world. It is an elementary fact of Wittgensteinian scholarship that, in his later work, Wittgenstein mounts a massive attack on this assumption, so I will not labour the point here. Readers can consult papers by Norman Malcolm, Deborah Jane Orr and Jon Dorbolo for references to Wittgenstein's philosophical development in this respect.[35] Orr expresses a concern with Cook's exegesis with reference to his claim 'that hinge propositions, although they are propositions about physical objects have the same "logical status" as propositions about "sense-data".'[36] But when we turn to the passage to which Cook refers us, we find Wittgenstein saying, 'So one might grant that Moore was right, if he is interpreted like this: a proposition saying that here is a physical object may have the same logical status as one saying that here is a red patch' (*OC:* 53). The reference is to a 'red patch', not to a sense-datum, and to the possibility of its being used as a sample or a grammatical remark, as well as being used as a description. In either event, as we saw in chapter 2, we do not learn what 'red' means by experiencing a sense-datum.

We saw, *contra* Cook, that 'This is red', so far from having a meaning independent of any circumstances, is dependent on our agreement in colour-judgements for its meaning.

What is the Connection between Wittgenstein's Propositions and Logic?

It is to Cook's credit that he recognizes that the issues Wittgenstein is dealing with are issues in logic. He sees, rightly, that when Wittgenstein says that the propositions he is interested in are exempt from doubt, 'Wittgenstein does not mean that we are incapable of doubting them, as a man might be incapable of doubting his son's innocence ... It is not a matter of psychology that concerns us here but a matter of logic.'[37] But how is this to be understood?

At the end of chapter 2 of Part One, Rhees writes:

> Moore enumerates a number of propositions which he says that he knows, with certainty, to be true. Wittgenstein gives no such list of things that can be known. What interests him is the peculiar role these propositions play. He is investigating what we do with these propositions. The investigation

becomes a concern of logic in asking these questions; in asking what the possibility of going on speaking depends on. (p. 10)

That 'dependence' involves ruling out the possibility of a mistake. Wittgenstein writes: 'What sort of proposition is: "What could a mistake here be like!"? It would have to be a logical proposition. But it is a logic that is not used, because what it tells you is not learned through propositions. – It is a logical proposition; for it does describe the conceptual (linguistic) situation' (*OC:* 51). We may well feel that this leaves things in a rather murky state, and that further elucidation is needed.

We are told that we have an investigation which concerns logic into a form of dependence which is said not to be a logical dependence. When the possibility of a mistake is ruled by our ways of thinking and acting, that seems to be a matter of logic, but of a logic, we are told, which is not used. Whatever we learn, in this respect, it is not through propositions. On the other hand, we are told that a logical proposition is involved, since we are informed of the conceptual situation, and anything that does that is said to deserve the name of logic.

Rhees grapples with these issues, and the way he does so marks further differences between his and other readings of *On Certainty*.

Is Wittgenstein Appealing to Primitive, Pre-linguistic Reactions as the Basis of our Language-games?

In *On Certainty* the propositions Wittgenstein discusses are referred to in a number of ways. They are often said to be the grounds or foundations of our language-games. The problem is in seeing what saying this amounts to. Rhees says that one of the commonest misunderstandings of *On Certainty* is to think that Wittgenstein is looking for a set of basic facts on which language depends. Wittgenstein never says that 'what is beyond the possibility of a mistake' determines the form our language takes. What *is* Wittgenstein saying, then, on this issue?

Despite the criticisms made of him, Cook bequeaths a serious question which goes unanswered by the alternatives proposed by others. For example, John Levett, despite criticizing Cook, still thinks that Wittgenstein is committed, inadvertently, to regarding the propositions he discusses as belonging to an ontology of abstract entities which exist 'independently from any sentential expression they might receive in a language-game.'[38] Levett is influenced by the arguments of Wolgast we have already considered. Like Wolgast, he finds the character of Wittgenstein's propositions extremely elusive: 'Their standing fast in certain contexts is essential to the possibility of discourse. And they can only stand fast when they are not asserted in a language-game. But this requires that such propositions have a meaning – a semantic role – which is not dependent on context or circumstances, something which is not bound up with use in a language-game.'[39] Yet this very requirement, as Levett sees as well as Wolgast, goes against the emphasis on propositions and their use argued so forcibly in the *Investigations*.

Wolgast, however, goes beyond her conclusion that Wittgenstein's propositional view of 'comfortable certainties' is confused. She has an alternative to offer. Certainty, she claims, though it is shown in behaviour, is not a matter of asserting propositions at all. Wittgenstein, she suggests, regards this certainty as akin 'to a natural feeling, something animal and not something reasoned … it can apply to animals and does not require any use of language'.[40]

Similarly, in criticizing Cook, Orr argues that when Wittgenstein uses 'belief' in connection with the propositions he discusses, he is employing 'a very common sense of the verb "believe" by which we say that pre-linguistic children and even animals believe things without attributing a grasp of, or the use of, propositions to them. For instance, we say that a dog is barking because it believes its master has arrived.'[41] Orr argues that 'Cook himself is so deeply committed to a rationalist approach to epistemology that he totally ignores the multitude of references by Wittgenstein to the role of human pre-linguistic and non-linguistic behaviour throughout *On Certainty*'.[42]

Rhees would be sympathetic to much of what Wolgast and Orr say about the difficulty of treating the sureness in our language-games which Wittgenstein is interested in as a matter of asserting certain propositions which express our 'comfortable certainties'. On the other hand, he is strongly opposed to the alternative they offer. For him, the appeal to pre-linguistic, instinctive behaviour as the foundation of language, or as that from which language emerges, is thoroughly confused and takes us away from anything Wittgenstein was emphasizing. Rhees's reasons for this opposition were shown in chapter 15 in his criticisms of Malcolm.[43] I cannot repeat his arguments in detail here, with the textual analyses used to support it, but his main emphases bear repeating, not only because they are extremely important in themselves, but also because they are connected with the developments in Rhees's thought which I discuss later in this afterword.

161

Malcolm, like many others, in the discussion of these matters, is impressed by Wittgenstein's remark in *OC:* 475: 'Language did not emerge from some kind of ratiocination'. Rhees's response is extremely important: 'This says it wasn't the result or the outcome of reasoning. But it does not say that it *was* the outcome of instinct, or "emerged" from instinct' (p. 95). Rhees wants to insist that when something is characterized as primitive or instinctive behaviour, this is always from an already existing language-game. He finds it odd that Malcolm does not emphasize that human beings *agree* in their reactions. That agreement does not indicate a *necessary* proposition. It is an agreement which is to be seen in the language-game. For example, we tend to a painful place in another person's body. In *Zettel:* 541, Wittgenstein says 'That it is the prototype of a way of thinking and not the result of thought'. Rhees's point is that it could not be seen as such a prototype unless the gesture were seen already as a gesture within language, as part of our thinking and speaking with other people. That speaking might involve asking the injured person where it hurts, remonstrating with someone who is indifferent, and so on. How could all that be said to emerge from instinctive behaviour in an animal? The point is that in the latter context the behaviour is *not* the prototype for a way of thinking. It is not taken up in a form of life in which, for example, there is discussion of whether a person's concern with the injury of another is genuine or not.

There may be striking similarities between animal and human behaviour. Both may react strongly to fumes, but the excited barking of a dog is not taken up in a form of life as is a human reaction to a cause, where taking appropriate action, tracing a cause, rectifying the cause, and so on, are an essential part of what we mean by 'reacting to a cause'. But none of this would mean that the reaction itself, pointing at *that* as the cause, is the outcome of reasoning or investigation.

Malcolm emphasizes the importance of instinctive reactions in connection with teaching a language, for example, colour words. His point, Rhees says, is to draw our attention to the following: 'If it were not that practically everyone reacts in the same way to "Would you call this the same colour?" there would not be our concept of colour ... our colour concepts'. Rhees responds:

> But this account is schematic like a diagram. It does not describe ways in which those words come into what people tell one another, in their discussions, reports, etc. I could identify this or that colour, use the right word, and yet be uncertain of the occasions on which it would have sense to do so. To describe the part they play in our life is to describe a 'practice'. (p. 100)

Rhees does not avoid commenting on the two passages to which people are most likely to appeal in support of a position like Malcolm's. One is where Wittgenstein says, 'I want to regard man here as an animal; as a primitive being to which one grants instinct but not ratiocination. As a creature in a primitive state' (*OC:* 475). Rhees argues that the creature in a primitive state envisaged, here, is one

> in which he is living together with other 'primitive beings': beings which *understand* one another – understand one another's actions and reactions, if you like – in the sense in which *we* understand one another in what we say and do, or the sense in which we understand the language we speak. (If you say: 'Understand the form of life in which we live' this comes to the same thing). In P475, for me the important sentence is ... 'Any logic good enough for a primitive means of communication needs no apology from us.') (p. 95)

The second passage Rhees comments on is from *Zettel*: 545, where Wittgenstein says 'Our language-game is an extension of primitive behaviour. (For our *language-game* is behaviour.) (Instinct).' Rhees says that the word 'extension' may seem to support Malcolm's argument, but suggests that the remark in parenthesis indicates that Wittgenstein means 'extension of a language-game'. The language-game which is our behaviour is unpredictable. It is there, like our life. Rhees concludes: 'In *this* context it would make no sense to ask, "From what did it *emerge?*" And still less, "From what did *language – Sprache –* emerge?"' (p. 95).

In a conversation with Rhees, Wittgenstein imagines a human being abandoned on an island before he could learn to speak. He asks us how we, if we landed on the island, could communicate with him. There is no reason to think that any gestures would stand as the ground for teaching the man the language we speak. Rhees says, 'Suppose I went through the motion of putting food in my mouth and chewing it: perhaps the island man would bring me food; (perhaps he would run away, perhaps he would attack me ...). If he did, he might not do so a second time' (pp. 98–9). Wittgenstein said in this context: 'Unless someone understands the meaning of *"and so on"* (or of some equivalent expression or gesture), it will be impossible to *teach* him the meaning of *"and so on".*' A child picks up the meaning of colour words, 'when he does "go on in the same way", when he, on his own, uses the words for things as they come along' (p. 99).

In 1929–30, Rhees says, Wittgenstein entertained a distinction between 'primary signs', such as gestures, which do not have to be taught, and secondary signs which are taught or explained by reference to the primary

163

ones. He became distrustful of this distinction, Rhees tells us, not only because it involved a view of primary signs or gestures as something whose meaning couldn't be misunderstood, but also because the whole view is modelled on something like elementary particles in physics, by means of which one hopes to *explain* physical phenomena.

What is the relevance of all this for Wittgenstein's treatment of Moore's truisms? Simply that we would be committing the same mistakes if we regarded them either as 'instinctive utterances', or as pre-linguistic reactions. Rhees says, 'this would not refer *at all* to that characteristic of them which does preoccupy Wittgenstein' (p. 103).

Wittgenstein speaks of the propositions he discusses as 'beyond the reach of doubt', and of their peculiar role. Rhees says that 'If he called them "facts which we never doubt", this would suggest that we might have some idea of what it would be to doubt them, even though we regard such doubting as preposterous. It would treat them as though they were pieces in the game. Whereas they are the table on which the game is played' (p. 104). It is not that we see that certain facts cannot be doubted, but, rather, that these issues simply do not arise. Yet this is fundamental in that, if, 'through some imaginable situation, I *were* to doubt any of them this would bring an earthquake in the foundations of acting and thinking, destroying all yardsticks' (p. 104).

Talking to Rhees on these matters a fortnight before the last entry in *On Certainty*, Wittgenstein said, 'This does not mean that there is any specific class of "things which cannot be doubted". In fact that is just the point' (p. 105).

What is Meant by the Sureness in Our Language-games?

The discussion of the previous question may help us in answering the present one, and also help us in the issues we left unresolved in our discussion of the connection between Wittgenstein's propositions and logic.

If we think of the sureness in our language-games as constituting propositions we assert, they seem to become matters of knowledge, belief, truth and falsity, and yet that is clearly not the way in which Wittgenstein thinks of this sureness. For this reason, Stroll, like Wolgast, Orr and Levett, finds it difficult to say that Wittgenstein's propositions have any place in our language-games. Stroll argues that when, through the analogies of hinges, axis and scaffolding, Wittgenstein refers to what stands fast for us, he is referring to 'something that is not part of the language-game and therefore is not susceptible to certain sorts of ascriptions: such as being true or false, known or not known, justifiable, revisable, and so forth'.[44] Stroll's reaction to the view that what stands fast for us cannot be part of the language-game, is to say that it must be something outside it. This may make one wonder where that 'outside' is, although, as I shall show later, Stroll's suggestion may lead us to appreciate what Wittgenstein has in mind.

Stroll's own answer is to offer the community, or the background we inherit, as the substratum of our language-games. He says, 'Whether this account actually captures Wittgenstein's thoughts is surely open to discussion, but given the inconclusive nature of the textual evidence it is the best we can do.'[45] Stroll believes his account explains the shift of emphasis from propositions to practices in *On Certainty*. For him, the relation between practices and the community is presuppositional: 'the community makes that set of practices possible. If it didn't exist they wouldn't either.' But no sooner is this said than he continues: 'On the other hand, there is an important logical relationship in the opposite direction. These practices are essential to the existence of the community: we can think of them as necessary conditions.'[46] It is unclear what is presupposed by what. In any case, Wittgenstein is not talking about what is *presupposed* by our ways of thinking and acting, but about what is involved *in* our ways of thinking and acting.

Stroll's reference to 'community' seems to take us away from the particularities of Wittgenstein's examples, various detailed examples, of what stands fast for us. It is odd to say that these particularities are outside our language-games, since, after all, they are held fast by them. This is what Churchill means when he says that Wittgenstein inverts architectural foundationalism. Stroll discovers, in *On Certainty*, 'more than sixty places in which Wittgenstein uses explicitly foundational language'.[47] But, as Churchill points out:

Although Wittgenstein repeatedly uses the term 'foundation', he explicitly disavows the notion that knowledge begins with a basic 'given' ... Wittgenstein writes that the central certainties of a system may be discoverable only after the fact, like the axis around which the body rotates (152). He inverts the foundationalist image of the structure of knowledge: 'I have arrived at the rock-bottom of my convictions. And one might almost say that these foundation-walls are carried by the whole house' (248).[48]

While Rhees would welcome Churchill's comments on Wittgenstein's inverting architectural foundationalism, he would be wary of his talk of 'discovering certainties'. It gives the impression of a prior ignorance concerning them. The point, as Wittgenstein says, is: 'This doubt isn't one of the doubts in our game' (*OC:* 317). Rhees says that what makes a language-game a language-game is not certain facts which are basic to it, but the matters which simply do not arise. That is his emphasis in chapter 14, and in chapter 12, where he is discussing *On Certainty*'s main theme. Rhees says that 'what does not arise', 'what stands fast', is not something we are taught, explicitly, but something which is swallowed down with what we are taught.

If I am driving with you in your car and tell someone about it later, do I include the existence of the car in my account? Did I presuppose the existence of the car, and did I presuppose your existence as I talked to you? These are not propositions I do not doubt, but issues *which do not arise.*[49] That is why the issue of their truth or falsity does not arise. For this reason, it is misleading to speak, as Gill does, of 'tacit' or 'implicit' knowledge in this context, since this encourages the conception of the propositions as the 'shadowy presences' which Wolgast rightly criticizes. This issue also marks a disagreement between Winch and Stoutland, the latter insisting that a minimal conception of truth is still involved: 'In accepting a proposition as true, we are committed to its agreeing with reality only in the truistic sense that a proposition is true (or false) depending on the way the world is'.[50] Winch's argument is that once we raise issues of truth and falsity, question of *how* truth and falsity are established must arise. If I say that while talking to you face to face, your existence must tally with the facts, the difficulty is to say what 'tallying with the facts' could mean.

In this matter Rhees agrees with Winch. He asks us to imagine a person standing on a platform and saying, 'I am standing and not sitting down'. This suggests, Rhees argues, that the person could have said, '"I am not standing, but sitting down" is obviously false'. That suggests, in turn, that had the person said, 'I am sitting down, not standing', we would, at least, have understood what is being said. 'Whereas', Rhees says, 'I do not think we should know what the speaker meant at all. Still less, that we should try to show him that he had fallen into a mistake, explain to him where he had gone wrong, perhaps. We should not know what he is doing with these words at all' (p. 112).

Wittgenstein writes, 'The reason why the use of the expression "true or false" has something misleading about it is that it is like saying "it tallies with the facts or it doesn't", and the very thing that is in question is what "tallying" is here' (*OC:* 199). It is not that 'tallying with the facts' in the examples we have considered is too obvious to mention, but that this notion has no application in the circumstances envisaged. Wittgenstein writes:

'Why do I not satisfy myself that I have two feet when I want to get up from the chair? There is no why. I simply don't. That is how I act' (*OC:* 148).

Winch says that 'to speak of what "stands fast" for me in the language of propositions, *Sätze*, is to obscure the fact – if that is not even too weak a phrase – that it is no part of our practice at this point to *assert* anything'.[51] But if what stands fast for us is not formulated in terms of propositions, is it not odd that we go on to say what these propositions are? But *who* says what they are? Philosophers such as Moore. Wittgenstein was right to find such propositions odd. As we have seen, Winch, Stroll, Wolgast, Orr, Levett and Conant, in their different ways, argue that the philosophers fail to provide an occasion for the use of such propositions. Nevertheless, by re-flecting on these propositions, we can be led to the important conclusion that not all the agreements which show themselves in our ways of acting and thinking are agreements about the truth or falsity of propositions.

Rhees's emphases should help us with the questions we left unanswered in our discussion of the connection between Wittgenstein's propositions and logic. What rules out the possibility of mistake is not a set of logical propositions. *That* logic is unused. Our ways of acting and judging are what rule certain things out of consideration. This is not something we learn by means of propositions. Wittgenstein writes:

'We could doubt every single one of these facts, but we could not doubt them all.'
Wouldn't it be more correct to say: 'we do not doubt them all'?
Our not doubting them all is simply our manner of judging and therefore, of acting. (*OC:* 232)

Winch finds the 'and' intrusive in the last line of the quotation, which he says is rendered better as: 'the ways we judge, that is act'. Rhees empha-sizes that faced with a choice between 'could not doubt' and 'do not doubt', Wittgenstein chooses the latter. If we opt for 'could not' that invites the question: what stops us? Winch replies:

But it isn't that anything stops us: rather that whatever anyone did, we *would not* call it 'doubting all these facts'. Behaviour, however superficially similar to behaviour that expresses doubt, counts as expressive of doubt only in the right circumstances. In particular, we look for contrasts: certain things are doubted against the background of our *not* doubting certain other things. And these contrasts are not haphazard.[52]

167

Wittgenstein asks, 'Can I doubt at *will?*' (*OC:* 221).

What stands fast or is ruled out for us, are not determined by rules of logic, but by practice. We are not merely taught grammar, but judgements. Wittgenstein writes: 'Not only rules, but also examples are needed for establishing a practice. Our rules leave loop-holes open, and the practice has to speak for itself' (*OC:* 139). Rhees links this with Wittgenstein's remark in *Investigations* I: 242: 'If language is to be a means of communication there must be agreement not only in definitions but also (queer as this may sound) in judgements. This seems to abolish logic, but does not do so.'

Appreciating the conclusions we have reached can qualify as a logical insight, since they do cast light on our linguistic and conceptual situation, and anything which, in this sense, is descriptive of our practice belongs to logic.

How are Our Conclusions Related to the Notions of a Form of Life or World-picture?

In many of our discussions to this point, the appeal to practice, in Wittgenstein's sense of that word, has been central. What if someone asks whether our practice agrees with reality, or tallies with the facts? The logical issues we have discussed return. Wittgenstein would say that these questions have been given no context of application.

One example Wittgenstein discusses is whether it makes sense to ask whether induction is true, or to assert that it is true. Rhees says that Wittgenstein's remarks about Lavoisier's methods are extremely important in this context: 'He has got hold of a definite world-picture – not of course one he invented: he learned it as a child. I say world-picture and not hypothesis, because it is the matter-of-course foundation of his research and goes unquestioned' (*OC:* 167). There is no point in discussing induction, as Hume does, as though it involved a justification of why we move from one set of facts to another set only associated by constant conjunction. That is not what we do. In fact, our inductive conclusions are not always justified. This may be pointed out. But when this happens, the error is investigated by the same inductive procedures. When someone asks of a specific conclusion, 'Why do you regard it as probable?' we wait to hear the details of the objection, and discuss it. But if members of a tribe without our procedures ask of our conclusions in general, 'Why do you call that probable?' we wouldn't know what to make of their question. We might be able to persuade them to adopt our ways. If so, that would be a matter of initiating them into new procedures and interests.

At this point, Wittgenstein is likely to be accused of relativism, as though he were saying that all world-views are equal, or that everyone is entitled to his own, or some such thing. Such matters are of no interest to Wittgenstein. His concern throughout is a logical one. That is why he wants to combat those who advance a voluntaristic view of world-pictures. He sees that it will not do to speak of our world-picture as our *presuppositions* about how things are. Rhees emphasizes that Lavoisier's world-picture is not the presupposition of the experiments he conducts. Rather, conducting the experiments in the way he does *is* his world-picture.

For similar reasons, it will not do to say, with Stroll, that facts about the age of the Earth are the presuppositions of history. He argues: 'History as a practice depends on the fact that the Earth has existed for many years. If this were not so, if the Earth had just come into existence five minutes ago or even 200 years ago, historical enquiries of the sorts many persons have engaged in would be incomprehensible.'[53] An interest in the age of the Earth is not the presupposition of an historical world-picture. Having such an interest is one expression of that world-picture.

Rhees says that such a world-picture shows, for example, what we accept as an explanation. We may ask why the belief in progress is not so influential as it was in the nineteenth century. Two world wars may be offered as part of the explanation. Someone may object and want to give greater emphasis to some other factor. We are still seeking the same kind of explanation. *'But'*, Rhees argues,

> *it would not mean much if someone asked WHY we regard something of this sort as an explanation* ... Or put it so: you understand *why* we speak in this way, why we regard this as an explanation ... when you yourself are able to speak in this way, to see it as an explanation (when you are convinced by the explanation of that form, or suggest a better one). The way to show someone why the calculations in arithmetic have the form that they do is to teach him to calculate. (p. 117)

Rhees applies his point more generally:

> Why did Spenser write *The Faerie Queene* in the stanzas that he did? Why did Shakespeare choose the sonnet form for his sonnets? Did he *choose* it? Certainly not: 'Shall I write in this way or that?' Why did Rembrandt paint in his style and not in the style of Michelangelo? Why do we think as we do, and why do the Azande think as they do? We can give histories of those societies, but that does not explain it. We aren't claiming that their histories *had* to go

169

that way – they did go that way, that's all. (p. 83)

One may be tempted to mark the difference between ourselves and others by saying that we employ different categories from those of people who consult oracles, but, Rhees says, the use of 'employ', here, is misleading:

> In procedures which physicists follow they may use different frames of reference – light-waves or particles. They may switch from one frame of reference to another. This is something they do *within* physics. This can't have any parallel when we talk of our trust in the results of physics, so the use of 'categories' or 'framework' here as an explanation or elucidation doesn't help. A physicist would say, 'I switched to that frame of reference because it was simpler, more convenient, because relations could be made more elegant'. But: 'Why do we rely on science?' No answer. (p. 83)

It may now be appreciated how radical Wittgenstein's conclusions are. Yet they are radical by being modest and realistic. Wittgenstein is not trying to *establish* anything. In that respect, his philosophy is very different, in its conception, from that of Moore who, from one point of view, can be seen as concerned with giving the right picture of the world. Rhees recalls that Moore

> used to say that in philosophy we try to give, not just '*an* analysis', but *the* analysis, or the *right* analysis of the propositions we consider. Although, apparently, he did not think that anyone had ever succeeded in doing so. And his work in philosophy is tentative, uncertain and probing in trying to get clear as to the right method of getting there (i.e. of completing the right analysis). (p. 116)

Wittgenstein, on the other hand, though concerned with the sureness in our language-games, does not speak of our world-picture as 'the right one'. But this is not because he is unsure of the matter, but because that notion means nothing. We may think that we can say that our scientific world-picture is right because the world is so constituted. But that adds nothing to saying that our inductive methods get the results that they do. We learn from nature, but nature does not dictate *how* we learn from it. For this reason, it cannot be said that our world-picture is adopted because of its success or high probability. What science tells us about reality is what scientists are interested in. But Wittgenstein says that it is a philosophical superstition to think that the world forces us to take a scientific interest in it. Rhees says it would be a hard task to show why our physical environment *must* give rise to the kind of reasoning we find in the physical sciences. People *do* reason in that way. Wittgenstein is opposing the view that they *must*. Hence his remarks on the tribe who have no physics, but who consult oracles. Wittgenstein, in this context, also imagines circumstances which, if they occurred, would annihilate all our yardsticks. But he says, importantly, 'But of course I do not intend this as prophecy' (*OC:* 492). Rhees comments: 'Here, as throughout *On Certainty*, Wittgenstein's concerns are logical. He is not concerned with asking, "What would happen if ...". In envisaging circumstances in which I'd say "I must be crazy", his interest is not in these circumstances, but with the *sureness* involved in the various ways in which we *do* judge and act' (p. 124).

How do Wittgenstein's Conclusions Differ from Some Classical and Contemporary Views of Our Relation to the World?

If we appreciate the questions in logic Wittgenstein has been wrestling with, we can see why we do not stand in any *epistemological* relation to our world-picture. It is not something we can be said to know, believe, presuppose, trust or take for granted. To use any of these terms would be to sublime them, metaphysically; to take them out of the context of their normal employment. This is partly why Wittgenstein says: 'Am I not getting closer and closer to saying that in the end logic cannot be described? You must look at the practice of language, then you will see it' (*OC:* 51). Wittgenstein is not looking for the principles of logic, something which could be captured in a logic book. Nevertheless, as a result of Wittgenstein's reflections, we do gain logical insight into what is meant by our being in the world. For example, we no longer respond to the sceptic's 'You don't know' with Moore's 'I do know', but get the sceptic to reflect on our being in the world in such a way that the sceptic no longer wants to advance a sceptical thesis.

As a result of Wittgenstein's reflections we can see how an argument such as Descartes's dream argument can be diffused. Descartes challenges us to show how we can know anything if we cannot know that we are not dreaming. It is said that no feature of our experience enables us to distinguish between dreams and waking life, since any feature we choose can simply be said to be part of a dream. If this argument is successful, Barry

Stroud argues, we lose the whole world.[54] But instead of asking, as Descartes does, how we *can* distinguish between dreams and waking life, Wittgenstein asks us to reflect on how we *do* distinguish between them. The moving last entry of *On Certainty* reads:

> 'But even in such cases I can't be mistaken, isn't it possible that I am drugged?' If I am and if the drug has taken away my consciousness, then I am not really talking and thinking. I cannot seriously suppose that I am at this moment dreaming. Someone who, dreaming, says, 'I am dreaming', even if he speaks audibly in doing so, is no more right than if he said in his dream 'it is raining', while it was in fact raining. Even if his dream were actually connected with the noise of the rain. (*OC:* 676)

Descartes invites us to take up an Archimedean point outside our language-games, whereas Wittgenstein shows why we should reject such an invitation. To attempt to occupy this 'higher' position is to seek a place which not even God could tell us anything about, since it is no place at all. Yet it was this Cartesian vantage-point which was supposed to give us grounds for saying that we *know* that we perceive a world independently of ourselves. Wittgenstein comments on this sublimed use of 'know':

> In its language-game it is not presumptuous. There, it has no higher position than, simply, the human language-game. For there it has restricted application.
>
> But as soon as I say this sentence outside its context, it appears in a false light. For then it is as if I wanted to insist that there are things I *know*. God himself can't say anything to me about them. (*OC:* 554)[55]

It is important to remember the *logical* import of these remarks. They are meant to expose logical confusion, not confess to any epistemological deficiency. It is a disaster, therefore, to align his remarks with the epistemological naturalism of Thomas Reid, which would have us believe that Wittgenstein is referring to an ineffable realm beyond the reach of our faculties which God could tell us of only if he had endowed us with different faculties. Such a view would be a complete anathema to Wittgenstein. He is not saying that because we do not know the correctness of our world-picture we have to believe in it, or that such a belief is the condition of what we do know. That would be to misunderstand the whole import of *On Certainty*. Thus I cannot concur with H. O. Mounce's remark that when William Hamilton says, 'belief is the primary condition of reason and not realism the ultimate ground of belief', these 'remarks of Hamilton's might have served as a motto for Wittgenstein's *On Certainty*.'[56]

Nicholas Wolterstorff makes the same mistake of seeking for another term to replace Wittgenstein's rejected, sublimed use of 'know'. His choice is another of Wittgenstein's rejected terms, namely, 'take for granted'. This leads him to the following epistemological misreading of *On Certainty*:

> An application of Wittgenstein's general point would be that in our everyday activities of gathering evidence, offering arguments, and so forth, we all take for granted the reliability of our perceptual faculties – the fifth of Reid's First Principles of Contingent Truths. It's true that what we actually take for granted in this regard is much more finely articulated than that; but we can let that pass.[57]

No, I'm afraid we can't let that pass. Wolterstorff's emphasis on us as evidence-gatherers takes us away from Wittgenstein's logical emphasis on the sureness in our language-games. Rhees, in chapter 4, discussed the complexity in the notion of 'seeing', and the hopelessness of the Positivists' conception of 'pure observation' by comparison. Equally hopeless would be the attempt to reduce it to a matter of 'the transitions from sensations caused by external objects to beliefs about those objects, that they exist as external'.[58] Wittgenstein's concerns with issues in logic are not even addressed by Reid's psychologism.[59]

That psychologism depends on a causal view of our relation to the world, a view Wittgenstein opposed from the outset. From our previous discussions, we ought to be able to see that whether we are thinking of our perception of red, or of our reaction to an expression on a person's face, these can never be derived from what Wolterstorff calls our 'hard-wiring', or from our alleged human constitution, any more than they could from the pre-linguistic, instinctive reactions Rhees discusses in chapter 15.

In chapter 16 Rhees discusses Russell's attempts to ground what we say in our causal relations to the world. He asks us to assume that something has a causal effect on us so that we say 'Cat'. So far, that is neither correct nor incorrect, but simply what that effect is. Rhees comments: '"All we know is what the senses tell us" – do they tell us anything? Even if they do provide pictures, they do not provide sentences in which the pictures appear. Only I say things. If they *did* say anything, we couldn't translate them' (p. 109). Rhees says that Russell might respond: 'But it doesn't work like that – people generally say the same thing'. Rhees replies: 'Perfectly true, but this doesn't need all this causal machinery. All you need to know is that most people would say the same if you asked them what a cat

173

is when they are confronted by one: "That's a cat"' (p. 108). But that agreement belongs to the lives they live together, an agreement which involves, as we have seen, not simply an agreement in definitions, but *an agreement in judgements*. It is in this context that what makes no sense is ruled out. A causal theory of meaning can give no account of this. Wittgenstein writes:

> When I say that the orders 'Bring me sugar' and 'Bring me milk' make sense, but not the combination 'Milk me sugar', that does not mean that the utterance of this combination of words has no effect. And if its effect is that the other person stares at me and gapes, I don't on that account call it the order to stare and gape, even if that was precisely the effect I wanted to produce.[60]

As we have seen in our discussions, Wittgenstein speaks of ways of talking which *do* not mean anything to us, not ways which *cannot* mean anything to us. Further, what is ruled out in certain ways of living, may not be ruled out in others. Yet, we have seen, also, that this does not lead to the conclusion that our ways of living are preferences or choices. It simply means that these differences are simply there, like the lives in which they are expressed. Rhees writes: '"But what is a foundation in one way of living needn't be that in another. And one might almost say that these foundation-walls are carried by the whole house" (*OC:* 248). There is no specific class of indubitable propositions, the foundations of all our language. Kant searched for the indubitable, but this is very different from what Wittgenstein was doing' (p. 109).

IV

Rhees's Development of Wittgenstein's Concerns

In this final section I am departing from the pattern of previous sections. There, I have been concerned with different aspects of Rhees's discussions of *On Certainty*. In this section I want to give some indication of what I take to be a development of Wittgenstein's concerns in Rhees's own work. I shall do so with reference to an open question about *On Certainty* which some commentators have raised.

In discussing what is meant by sureness in our language-games, in the previous section, I said I would return to Stroll's suggestion that what is held fast for us is something *other than* our language-games. Initially, that suggestion faced the difficulty that what is held fast, so far from being other than our language-games, is held fast by them; held fast by all that surrounds it. In our discussions, we saw that these surroundings are our ways of acting and judging, in which certain matters are not questioned, or do not even arise. Thus, Wittgenstein says, 'What I hold fast to is not one proposition, but a nest of propositions' (*OC:* 225). Rhees, too, says, 'a whole body of propositions determine the form of our language-game, or the game in which we make empirical judgements' (p. 45). But Rhees also says of Wittgenstein in this context: 'he does not say much about "the form of the language-game"' (p. 45).

It is in connection with references to 'a nest of propositions', 'a whole body of propositions', and his inversion of architectural foundationalism, where he talks of the foundation-walls being held together by the whole house, that Wittgenstein introduces his notions of a form of life, or world-picture. But he does not say much about these notions either. Rhees is not alone in thinking that more needs to be said. Henry Le Roy Finch asks of the systems within which things hold fast for us, 'What is the nature of these systems?' He says:

> Wittgenstein did not live to answer this question. He may well have been aware that there was a gap here. Toward the end of the book we find this entry under date of 4th April ...: 'Why is there no doubt that I am called L. W.? It does not seem at all like something that one could establish at once beyond doubt. One would not think that it is one of the indubitable truths' (*OC:* 470).

Finch continues:

> The next entry, on the following day, 5th April reads: '[Here there is still a big gap in my thinking. And I doubt that it will be filled now.]' If, as seems likely, the parenthetical remark refers to the immediately preceding entry, then the 'big gap' may well have had to do with the question of what kind of systems we have here.[61]

In relation to these systems, or forms of life, Leyvraz says: 'Now the question about the continuity between language-games arises – a topic Wittgenstein seldom mentions. Language-games do not have a common essence, but Wittgenstein maintains that there is a family resemblance between them.'[62]

Given this open question, we may rephrase the issue Stroll raises in terms of language-games and the community as follows: what is the relation of language-games to our world-picture? This will turn out to be a misleading question, but it is a good way to begin. Beginning with it helps us to work through certain tensions in *On Certainty*. For example, in relation to our testing of empirical hypotheses, Wittgenstein writes:

> All testing, all confirmation and disconfirmation of a hypothesis takes place already within a system. And this system is not a more or less arbitrary and doubtful point of departure for all our arguments; no, it belongs to the essence of what we call an argument. The system is not so much the point of departure, as the element in which arguments have their life. (*OC:* 105)

Winch points out that there are times when Wittgenstein makes it sound as though 'the system' *is* 'a point of departure', rather than 'the element in which arguments have their life'. For example, he speaks of Lavoisier's 'world-picture' as though it were an *explanation* of what he did: 'the matter-of-fact foundation for his research'. Again, in talking of world-pictures, Wittgenstein says, 'The propositions describing this world-picture might be a kind of mythology. And their role is like that of rules of a game; and the game can be learned purely practically, without learning any explicit rules' (*OC:* 95). The internal tension in these remarks is obvious: at first rules are spoken of as a point of departure, but, then, this is denied.

Winch says that he did not find his own way out of these difficulties until he realized that in Wittgenstein's main emphasis, procedures and world-picture go together. Whether we are referring to specific pictures, such as the picture of the Earth as a floating ball, or to world-pictures which are pervasive in our thoughts and actions, it is essential to note, as Winch does, that they cannot be the foundation of our procedures, 'since it is the procedures which make them the pictures they are'.[63]

'Procedures', however, as a term, is more at home in relation to the use of the specific picture of the Earth as a floating ball, than it is in relation to talk of world-pictures. In the latter context, it is more natural to say that our world-picture is not the foundation of the lives we lead, since it is the lives we lead which make our world-picture what it is. 'World-picture' and 'our life' go together. That is a central emphasis in Rhees's own work.

This should enable us to see what is wrong with our reformulation of Stroll's question. We asked: what is the relation of our form of life or world-picture to our language-games? It invites us to think of some kind of *transition* from the language-games to the world-picture, whereas, as we have seen, they go together. What Rhees has highlighted in his own work, however, is that it is precisely the analogy between language and games, an

176

analogy Wittgenstein retains to the end, that stands in the way of our understanding this. Our understanding of the sense in which our world-picture and our lives go together is advanced if we go beyond the analogy between language and games. Here, I give the briefest of indications why Rhees thinks this is so.

Four years after the publication of Wittgenstein's *Investigations*, Rhees began writing critical reflections on the masterpiece he had helped to edit, especially on Part One of that work. These reflections became *Wittgenstein and the Possibility of Discourse*. Much of his criticism had to do with the analogy between games and language. Rhees recognizes the usefulness of the analogy in emphasizing the different forms our discourse takes, but thinks it is misleading as an elucidation, of a general kind, of what it means to participate in discourse; of *what it means to say something*. Yet, this latter phrase, for Rhees, sums up Wittgenstein's concerns from first to last.

The disanalogy between language and games is obvious once stated: the games we play do not make up one big game, whereas the language-games we play occur within the *same* language. The question of what the *same* means here cannot be avoided. Wittgenstein had said in the *Investigations* that each language-game is complete, and that language itself is a collection or family of such games. To which Rhees responds by saying that if this were the case, we wouldn't be talking of language at all. In saying that every language-game is 'complete', Wittgenstein wanted to get away from the idea that language has the kind of unity that belongs to a calculus. In his desire to do so, however, Rhees argues that he threw out an important part of the analogy between language and a calculus, namely, the reference to an interlocking intelligibility. There is a great deal in *On Certainty* which, as we have seen, recognizes this point, only now, the 'interlocking', although sometimes called 'a system', is not of a formal kind, although of course, procedures of a more or less formal kind will be part of it.

Rhees points out that the analogy with games also obscures the deepest problems Wittgenstein was wrestling with, namely, confusions relating to questions concerning logic and reality, and language and reality. These problems cannot be dealt with in the same way as we deal with confusions about different forms of discourse, although recognizing these will be an important part of the enquiry. Where the latter confusions are concerned, Wittgenstein's method is to give perspicuous representations of the grammatical differences between them. But confusions about language itself cannot be dealt with in that way, for what would be a perspicuous representation of the whole language? Among the confusions which cannot be dealt with in that way is the analogy between language and games.

Games are relatively self-contained. What is said or done in one game need have little bearing on what is done in another. By contrast, Rhees argues, unless what we say in one context had a bearing on what is said in other contexts, it is difficult to see how anything would be being said at all. This important fact cannot be captured by the formality of games. If I dream of a brilliant move in a chess game, the move, as such, is just as brilliant, in my dream, as it is in an actual game. Whereas I haven't said anything if I say it in a dream, although matters change if the dream is given a significance in the wider contexts of a life.

Rhees emphasizes the dialogical character of discourse, hence his huge regard for Plato. That dialogical character is captured best if we concentrate on conversation. Not that Rhees thinks that all language is conversation, or that we are all engaged in one big conversation in which we all have a part. Yet, he thinks that conversation is important as a centre of comparison which throws light on those aspects of discourse which are not conversation.

Rhees's suggestion, then, is that the kind of unity discourse has can be understood best in the ways in which parts of a conversation are related to each other. Here, too, the analogy between language and games does not serve us well. After we have enjoyed a game, we may say, 'Let's play it again'. But does it make sense to say this of the conversation – 'Let's do it again' – the *same* conversation? It makes sense to speak of knowing one's way round a game, or of mastering it, but one would not speak of knowing one's way around a conversation, or of mastering it. This is partly why McGinn's comparison between mathematics as a system of *techniques*, and the moves we make within our language-games is unsatisfactory. Not only does it give too little recognition to the fact that, in *On Certainty*, it is emphasized that what we learn is not simply rules of grammar, but certain facts we do not question, but it also tries to capture what learning comes to within the narrow conception of a technique. McGinn writes:

> Coming to understand an expression means coming to have the practical ability to use the expression in a way that conforms to the ordinary practice of employing it. Just as we are to think of the meaning of a word in terms of a customary technique for employing it, so we are to think of understanding a word as a practical mastery of a technique. 'To understand a language means to be master of a technique' (*PI*: 199)[64]

Yet one has only to look at Rhees's discussion in chapter 4, especially in relation to Part Two, section xi of the *Investigations*, to see that Wittgenstein does not always concur with the general remark McGinn alludes to. He recognizes, clearly, that all forms of language and understanding could never be accounted for in terms of 'technique'. The problem is that there are times when his own analogies encourage one to think the opposite. Rhees thought this of the analogy between words and tools. I use the tools for a purpose, and there are circumstances where one can speak in this way about language – 'I used my words to good effect'. But one cannot speak of language generally in this way. In this context, one of Rhees's most important contributions is to point out that I do not *use* language. When I greet someone in the street, I do not use language to say 'Good morning'; it is not my technique for doing so. I greet the other in language. The comparison of language with techniques is closely connected with talk of language as a skill. This confusion may invade conceptions of human life in various ways. The Sophists would have been pleased with the popularity in our time of talk of social skills, interpersonal skills, and even life skills. What would it be like to be a master of them – a master of the skill of life?

For Rhees, our language and our lives go together. Referring to Wittgenstein's remark in *Investigations* I: 242 about the importance of 'agreement in judgements', Rhees says that in an earlier manuscript, in 1941 or 1942, Wittgenstein spoke of 'agreement in the lives of people'. This is an emphasis we find in Rhees again and again. He says that language makes sense if living makes sense. It is an emphasis which he thinks is closely connected with the notions of 'form of life' and 'world-picture'.

Some commentators on *On Certainty* have said that Wittgenstein's work gives us a new way of looking at the world. I think I know what they mean. They are referring to the way in which Wittgenstein rescues us from thinking of ourselves as externally related to our being in our world; the conception of being the 'knowers', 'believers', 'trusters', 'presupposers' or 'takers for granted' of this relation. We are rescued from this false transcendentalism, which we owe to the influence of Cartesianism and empiricism. On the other hand, Wittgenstein said that his problems were Plato's. He can be seen as restoring a contemplative relation between philosophy and the world, although he makes considerable advances in his work in what he shows us of that relation.

Yet old tendencies die hard. Even in the work of writers deeply influenced by Wittgenstein, there is a failure to be content with philosophical contemplation of our world. Philosophers want to find a lesson for it, a lesson underwritten by philosophy. For example, I have discussed an influential move, in the thought of Stanley Cavell, from the recognition that there is nothing outside our life-with-concepts which determines the form

179

it takes, to the claim that we, therefore, have a responsibility to maintain that form of life. This swiftly becomes a responsibility to maintain *desirable* forms of life. It is not difficult to see how such a concept of 'responsibility for maintenance' becomes sublimed, and how we stand, once again, in an external relation to the culture as 'minders' of it. Of course, there are expressions of concern within various movements when signs of decline are detected, but those concerns are expressions of the movements, not of a responsibility which transcends them. The desire for such transcendence in this context by philosophers reminds one of the unhelpful aspects of Wittgenstein's tool-box analogy to illustrate what we do with words – the desire to be technicians of the culture.

When the task of maintaining a form of life becomes more explicit in the writings of others, the sceptic's refusal to acknowledge that form of life is said to be an alienation from it. To accommodate the undeniable heterogeneity of human voices, we are said to be faced with the task of acknowledging them. This acknowledgement goes far beyond the *conceptual* acknowledgement Rhees has in mind, one which would include distances as well as proximities between people, dislike as well as liking, lack of respect as well as respect, the enigmatic as well as the familiar. Rather, the acknowledgement said to be underwritten by philosophy is said to be one that asks only for respect. This is because human voices are said to be made for each other, so much so that a failure to acknowledge a voice other than my own is said to be a repression by me of what I need to hear in it. The task of reading and being read by others is an endless one. Wittgenstein's philosophy, it is said, calls us to this romantic undertaking.

There is no such romanticism in Rhees's work. I think he would say that Wittgenstein would have found such a notion extremely distasteful. When Rhees says that language makes sense if living makes sense, he is not suggesting for one moment that a single account could be given of the sense to be found there. In *Wittgenstein and the Possibility of Discourse* Rhees emphasizes the hubbub of voices which confronts us. Here, a remark he makes at the outset of chapter 2 of the present work is extremely important: 'Plato in the *Sophist* speaks of the conditions for the possibility of discourse. He was concerned with the distinction between philosophy and sophistry, between genuine discourse and sham discourse. Not showing *how* the distinction is to be made, but *that* there is one to make' (p. 6). The 'romantic' adaptation of Wittgenstein, it seems to me, passes from the 'that' to the 'how'.[65]

But what happens when the ways sense is made of things are so different that people simply pass each other by? Wittgenstein asks us to imagine a people who have no physics, but who consult oracles. He asks whether it is wrong for them to do so. If we say it is, he asks, 'aren't we using our language-game as a base from which to *combat* theirs?' (*OC:* 609). Wittgenstein says further: 'I said I would "combat" the other man, – but wouldn't I give him *reasons?* Certainly; but how far do they go? At the end of reasons comes *persuasion.* (Think what happens when missionaries convert natives.)' (*OC:* 612).

Churchill sees a lapse in Wittgenstein's treatment of this conflict of fundamentals: 'We are plummeted into irrational persuasion only on the assumption that reason-giving must be the provision of foundations'.[66] Wittgenstein's remarks cover a number of cases, especially in the reference to how missionaries convert natives, which can range from conversion through condemnation, assimilation or suppression. Having recently seen a documentary on the conquistadores, it became so obvious why both Aztecs and Incas realized that what confronted them was nothing less than the destruction of their civilization. In the case of the Incas, the coming of knowledge of modern history destroyed for ever their world lived in sacred time. As one of them said, 'We thought we had the whole world. We knew of no other until the savage came.' Such examples aside, however, it is odd that Churchill sees a discontinuity between Wittgenstein's example and what he has said already about a world-view. Churchill recognizes the fundamental appeal Wittgenstein makes to our ways of acting and judging. Within these reasons are given for and against various courses of action. But if we ask why we accept these reasons as reasons, there is no answer. We proceed without reason. That is what Wittgenstein means by 'persuasion' – the way we take things. Even in the case of techniques, we have no technique for taking our techniques in one way rather than another. When, therefore, there is a fundamental disparity in the ways things *are* taken, why should it be odd that a change from one to the other would be more like an initiation than the correction of a mistake?

Further, Churchill's own suggestions about such a situation seem to me to lead him away from his previous insights into Wittgenstein's *On Certainty.* Churchill suggests that an advance on Wittgenstein's remarks could be made by seeking 'an extension of rationality into a discourse about human nature and human culture' in which one will achieve 'a reasoned comparison of competitive *practices* measured against the interests they serve … to discuss the interests that give shape to forms of human life'.[67] Churchill argues that damage has been done to Wittgenstein's later work by the lingering influence of the *Tractatus* in Wittgenstein's inability or unwillingness to make this extension in *On Certainty.*

Rhees, by contrast, would say that to understand the *Investigations* and *On Certainty* is to see why Wittgenstein would not accept the notion of the extension Churchill advocates. Wittgenstein said that the aim of many philosophers was to show us that what looks different is really the same, whereas his aim is to show us that what looks the same is, in fact, very different. He taught us differences. This is very much a feature of Rhees's work in philosophical logic, ethics, political philosophy and the philosophy of religion.[68]

The first thing Rhees would point out is that practices do not serve interests, but are an *expression* of them. Given that fact, what is to inform the comparison in the clash of fundamentals Wittgenstein has in mind? If the answer offered is in terms of certain interests, they will be the interests of some individual or movement. Obviously, they cannot be sublimed as the interests which shape the form of human life. On the other hand, if it is said that interests may emerge through dialogue, one is assuming that the differences are not irreconcilable after all, and that clearly cannot be assumed in all cases. Even if interests do emerge, *that* is the interests they are. To say 'they are the interests that shape the form of human life' adds nothing to their emergence.

Neither Wittgenstein nor Rhees is concerned to stop us making moral, political, aesthetic or religious judgements. Both were men of strong personal convictions. But in philosophy, their interest was different. They had a contemplative interest in doing conceptual justice to the world in all its variety. It is that interest which leads them from an emphasis on a conception of logic as that which determines what can and cannot be said, to an emphasis on a logic which shows itself in 'the agreements in people's lives'.

Winch finds the contemplative tradition of philosophy I am talking of in Plato (writing in dialogue form, especially in the early dialogues), in Kierkegaard's pseudonymous works, in Simone Weil's depiction in her essay on the *Iliad, The Poem of Force*, of a morality which is not her own, and in Wittgenstein's battle with his voices in the *Investigations*. That battle, as we have seen, continues in *On Certainty*. Speaking of this contemplative philosophy Winch says that it imposes 'a task of enormous difficulty, both at the technical level and also because of the moral demands it makes on the writer, who will of course him or herself have strong moral or religious commitments and will also be hostile to certain other possibilities'.[69]

I was privileged to have Winch and Rhees as my teachers. I believe that Winch, throughout his work and life, strove after this contemplative conception of philosophy with great passion. Yet, I know he would agree with me, that in *that* respect, no one associated with or influenced by Wittgenstein can be compared with Rush Rhees.

NOTES

1 *On Certainty*: A New Topic?

1 G. E. Moore, 'Proof of an External World', in Thomas Baldwin (ed.), *G. E. Moore: Selected Writings* (London: Routledge, 1993), pp. 165–6.
2 See appendix 1.
3 Editorial addition.

2 Saying and Describing

1 See Wittgenstein, 'Notes for Lectures on "Private Experience" and "Sense Data"' and 'The Language of Sense Data and Private Experience', notes by Rush Rhees, in Wittgenstein, *Philosophical Occasions 1912–1951*, ed. James Klagge and Alfred Nordmann (Indianapolis, IN and Cambridge: Hackett, 1993), pp. 200–367.
2 The previous three paragraphs are adapted from Rush Rhees's 'On Wittgenstein' edited by D. Z. Phillips, *Philosophical Investigations*, April 2001, pp. 154–5.

3 Concept-Formation

1 Ludwig Wittgenstein, *Remarks on the Foundations of Mathematics* (Oxford: Blackwell, 1956), pp. 172–3.

4 'SEEING' AND 'THINKING'

1 Ludwig Wittgenstein, *Philosophical Investigations* (Oxford: Blackwell, 1955), II: xi, p. 193.
2 *Investigations* II: xi, p. 200.
3 *Investigations* I: 81.
4 *Investigations* I: 520.
5 *Investigations* I: 654, 655.
6 *Investigations* II: xi, p. 227.
7 *Investigations* II: xi, p. 226.
8 *Investigations* II: xi, pp. 226–7.
9 *Investigations* II: xi, p. 208.
10 *Investigations* II: xi, pp. 213–14.
11 *Investigations* II: xi, p. 201.
12 *Investigations* II: xi, p. 202.
13 *Investigations* II: xi, p. 211.
14 *Investigations* II: xi, pp. 227–8.
15 'This is what might be called a soul truly in love.'
16 *Investigations* II: xi, p. 228.
17 *Investigations* II: xi, p. 227.
18 *Investigations* II: xi, p. 228.
19 *Investigations* II: xi, p. 227.
20 Rhees crossed out the comments within the brackets. I have retained them. (Ed.)
21 *Investigations* II: xi, p. 223.
22 *Investigations* II: xi, p. 222.
23 *Investigations* II: xi, p. 225.
24 *Investigations* II: xi, p. 227.
25 *Investigations* II: xi, p. 227.
26 *Investigations* II: xi, p. 222.

5 THOUGHT AND LANGUAGE

1 Ludwig Wittgenstein, *Philosophical Investigations* (Oxford: Blackwell, 1955), I: 574.
2 *Investigations* I: 693.
3 *Investigations* I: 571.
4 *Investigations* I: 559.
5 *Investigations* I: 664.
6 *Investigations* I: 650.
7 *Investigations* I: 545.
8 *Investigations* I: 544.

9 *Investigations* I: 509.
10 *Investigations* I: 511.
11 *Investigations* II: xi, p. 220.
12 *Investigations* II: xi, pp. 220–1.

6 PICTURING REALITY

1 In their 'Editors' Note' to the *Investigations*, G. E. M. Anscombe and Rush Rhees write: 'If Wittgenstein had published his work himself, he would have suppressed a good deal of what is said in the last thirty pages or so of Part I and worked what is in Part II, with further material, into its place' (p. iv). (Ed.)
2 Ludwig Wittgenstein, *Philosophical Investigations* (Oxford: Blackwell, 1955), I: 522.
3 *Investigations* I: 523.
4 *Investigations* I: 527.
5 *Investigations* II: xi, p. 214.
6 *Investigations*, pp. 214–15.
7 *Investigations* II: xi, p. 219.
8 *Investigations* I: 524.
9 *Investigations* II: xi, p. 218.
10 *Lectures and Conversations on Aesthetics, Psychology and Religious Belief*, ed. C. Barrett (Oxford: Blackwell, 1966), pp. 18–20.
11 *Investigations* II: xi, p. 223.

7 WHAT MAKES LANGUAGE LANGUAGE?

1 'Remarks on Frazer's *Golden Bough*', *The Human World*, no 3, May 1971, p. 31. Later published at Redford, England by Brynmill Press, 1979. For an alternative translation see *Ludwig Wittgenstein, Philosophical Occasions*, ed James Klagge and Alfred Nordmann (Indianapolis, IN and Cambridge: Hackett, 1993).
2 Ibid., p. 28.
3 Ibid., p. 29.
4 Ibid., pp. 32–3.
5 Ibid., p. 30.
6 Ibid.

8 THE LOGICAL AND THE EMPIRICAL

1   This and the next three sentences are taken from Rhees's 'On Wittgenstein', *Philosophical Investigations*, April 2001.
2   Ludwig Wittgenstein, *Philosophical Investigations* (Oxford: Blackwell, 1955), II: xi, p. 218.
3   *Investigations* II: xi, p. 214.

9 *ON CERTAINTY*: A WORK IN LOGIC

1   *Tractatus Logico-Philosophicus*, trans. D. F. Pears and B. F. McGuinness (London: Routledge 1988), 5.55.

11 PREFACE TO *ON CERTAINTY*

1   My emphasis.
2   My emphasis.
3   My emphasis.

14 WITTGENSTEIN'S PROPOSITIONS AND FOUNDATIONS

1   See Hans Reichenbach, *Wahrscheinlichkeitslehre* (Leiden: 1935); trans as *The Theory of Probability*, 2nd edn (Berkeley and Los Angeles: University of California Press, 1949).

15 LANGUAGE AS EMERGING FROM INSTINCTIVE BEHAVIOUR

1   Norman Malcolm's 'Wittgenstein: The Relation of Language to Instinctive Behaviour' was the J. R. Jones Memorial Lecture delivered at Swansea in May 1981. It was later published in *Philosophical Investigations* vol. 5, no. 1, January 1982. In a footnote to the paper Malcolm says that he is grateful to Bruce Goldberg and Rush Rhees for their criticisms of an earlier draft of his essay. Rhees's letter is the earlier criticism Malcolm is referring to. In the light of recent discussions, e.g. Lars Hertzberg, 'Primitive Reactions – Logic or Anthropology?' *Midwest Studies in Philosophy* vol. 17: 'The Wittgenstein Legacy'; and Elizabeth Wolgast, 'Primitive Reactions', *Philosophical Investigations* vol. 17, no. 4, October 1994, Rhees's remarks are of interest in themselves. They have appeared in *Philosophical Investigations* vol. 20, no. 1, January 1997. We

gratefully acknowledge permission to reprint the material here. (Ed.)

2 *Ursache und Wirkung: Intuitives Erfassen*, edited by Rush Rhees. *Cause and Effect: Intuitive Awareness*, trans. Peter Winch, *Philosophia* vol. 6, nos. 3–4, September–December 1976 (Ed.).

3 'Notes for Lectures on "Private Experience" and "Sense Data"' edited by Rush Rhees in *Ludwig Wittgenstein: Philosophical Occasions 1912–1951*, ed. James Klagge and Alfred Nordmann (Indianapolis, IN: Hackett, 1993), p. 245. (Ed.).

4 '... and write with confidence "In the beginning was the deed"' (cf. Goethe, *Faust* I).

16 Words and Things

1 Ernest Gellner advanced the same view in *Words and Things*.

2 Bertrand Russell, 'The Limits of Empiricism', *Proceedings of the Aristotelian Society*, 1935.

3 For paragraphs in *On Certainty* relating to this whole discussion see appendix 2.

17 Not Worth Mentioning?

1 *Äußerung* (editors of *On Certainty*).

18 Certainty and Madness

1 *Merry Tales of the Mad Men of Gotham* is a collection of twenty stories. They have to do with the wise men of Gotham, a village in Nottinghamshire, six miles from Nottingham. Their exploits are also mentioned in books and plays of the fifteenth and sixteenth centuries. They are said to have performed the most foolish actions, such as building a hedge around a cuckoo to imprison the bird. (Ed.)

Afterword

1 Rush Rhees, 'On Wittgenstein', *Philosophical Investigations*, vol. 24, no. 2, April 2001, p. 153.

2 'Wittgenstein's Builders', *Proceedings of the Aristotelian Society* 1959–60, reprinted in *Discussions of Wittgenstein* (London: Routledge, 1970). For Rhees's wider explorations see his *Wittgenstein and the Possibility of Discourse*, ed.

D. Z. Phillips (Cambridge: Cambridge University Press, 1998).

3 'Love' in Rush Rhees, *Discussions of Simone Weil* (New York: State University of New York Press, 1999), p. 114.

4 For an important discussion of the difference between questions concerning logic and language, and questions concerning language and reality, see Rhees's *Wittgenstein and the Possibility of Discourse*.

5 This must not be taken to mean that Wittgenstein was defending all rituals in an *a priori* fashion. Rhees told me that at the time he wrote his remarks on Frazer, Wittgenstein thought that most rituals probably contained some confusion, but that this was more akin to metaphysical confusion than to a scientific mistake. See Rush Rhees, 'Wittgenstein on Language and Ritual' in Rush Rhees, *On Religion and Philosophy*, ed. D. Z. Phillips (Cambridge: Cambridge University Press, 1997).

6 Ludwig Wittgenstein, *Philosophical Investigations* (Oxford: Blackwell, 1955), II: xi, p. 221.

7 Jerry H. Gill, 'Saying and Showing: Radical Themes in Wittgenstein's *On Certainty*', *Religious Studies*, vol. 10, pp. 281–2.

8 Peter Winch, 'Judgement: Propositions and Practices', *Philosophical Investigations*, vol. 21, no. 3, July 1998, p. 192.

9 Jean-Pierre Leyvraz, 'Logic and Experience in Wittgenstein's Later Work: "On Certainty"', *Man World*, vol. 2, 1978, p. 263.

10 Avrum Stroll, *Moore and Wittgenstein on Certainty* (Oxford: Oxford University Press, 1994), p. 157.

11 Marie McGinn, *Sense and Certainty* (Oxford: Blackwell, 1989,) p. 104.

12 Frederick Stoutland, 'Wittgenstein: On Certainty and Truth', *Philosophical Investigations*, vol. 21, no. 3, July 1998, p. 204.

13 McGinn, *Sense and Certainty*, p. 85.

14 James Conant, 'Wittgenstein on Meaning and Use', *Philosophical Investigations*, vol. 21, no. 3, July 1998, p. 226. The discussion of McGinn by Conant is in terms of the proposition, 'I know that a sick man is lying there', said while sitting at his bedside. This does not affect the point.

15 Ibid., p. 242.

16 Ibid., p. 242.

17 Elizabeth Wolgast, 'Whether Certainty is a Form of Life', *Philosophical Quarterly*, vol. 37, no. 147, p. 164.

18 Ibid., p. 162.

19 Ibid., p. 163.

20 It ought to be said that in his paper Conant is not exploring 'either Moore's avowals or the skeptic's disavowals of knowledge' ('Wittgenstein on Meaning and Use', p. 222). His aim is solely with Wittgenstein's charge of 'Nonsense!' with respect to them.

21 McGinn, *Sense and Certainty*, pp. 102–3.

22 Ibid., p. 103.

23 John Churchill, 'Wittgenstein: The Certainty of Worldpictures', *Philosophical Investigations*, vol. 2, no. 1, January 1988, pp. 33–4.
24 John Cook, 'The Metaphysics of Wittgenstein's *On Certainty*', *Philosophical Investigations*, vol. 8, no. 2, April 1985, p. 85.
25 Ilham Dilman, 'On Wittgenstein's Last Notes (1950–51)', *Philosophy*, vol. 46, 1971, p. 163.
26 Lance Ashdown, 'On Reading *On Certainty*', *Philosophical Investigations*, vol. 23, no. 4, October 2001.
27 McGinn, *Sense and Certainty*, pp. 113–14; Stoutland, 'Wittgenstein: On Certainty and Truth', p. 205; Stroll, *Moore and Wittgenstein on Certainty*, p. 150.
28 As well as Stroll's book already cited, see his 'Foundationalism and Common Sense' in *Philosophical Investigations*, vol. 10, no. 4, October 1987.
29 Cook, 'The Metaphysics of Wittgenstein's *On Certainty*', p. 89.
30 Winch, 'Judgement: Propositions and Practices', p. 198.
31 Ibid., p. 198.
32 Cook, 'The Metaphysics of Wittgenstein's *On Certainty*', p. 87.
33 Ibid., pp. 81–2.
34 Ibid., p. 99.
35 See Norman Malcolm, 'Wittgenstein's "Scepticism" in *On Certainty*', *Inquiry*, vol. 31 (appendix devoted to Cook); Deborah Jane Orr, 'Did Wittgenstein Have a Theory of Hinge Propositions?', *Philosophical Investigations*, vol. 12, no. 2, April 1989; Jon Dorbolo, 'What Turns On Hinges?', *Philosophical Investigations*, vol. 11, no. 2, April 1988.
36 Cook, 'The Metaphysics of Wittgenstein's *On Certainty*', p. 82.
37 Ibid., p. 82.
38 John Levett, 'Discussion: Wittgenstein and the Metaphysics of Propositions', *Philosophical Investigations*, vol. 16, no. 2, April 1993, p. 154.
39 Ibid., p. 162.
40 Wolgast, 'Whether Certainty is a Form of Life', p. 163.
41 Orr, 'Did Wittgenstein Have a Theory of Hinge Propositions?', p. 140.
42 Ibid., p. 141.
43 See Norman Malcolm, 'Wittgenstein: The Relation of Language to Instinctive Behaviour', *Philosophical Investigations*, vol. 5, no. 1, January 1982.
44 Stroll, *Moore and Wittgenstein on Certainty*, p. 170.
45 Ibid., p. 171.
46 Ibid.
47 Ibid., p. 142.
48 Churchill, 'Wittgenstein: The Certainty of Worldpictures', pp. 32–3.
49 See Peter Winch, 'True or False', *Inquiry*, vol. 31, pp. 272–3.
50 Stoutland, 'Wittgenstein: On Certainty and Truth', p. 212.
51 Winch, 'Judgement: Propositions and Practices', p. 198.
52 Ibid., p. 200.
53 Stroll, *Moore and Wittgenstein on Certainty*, p. 151.

54   See Barry Stroud, *The Significance of Philosophical Scepticism* (Oxford: Clarendon Press, 1991). The absence of Wittgenstein from Stroud's essay is surprising given its theme.

55   I have discussed these issues in greater detail in 'Epistemic Practices: The Retreat from Reality' in *Religious Concepts* (Basingstoke and New York: Macmillan and St Martin's Press, 2000); in 'What God Himself Cannot Tell Us', *Faith and Philosophy*, October 2001; and in 'Wittgensteinianism: Logic, God and Reality' in the *Oxford Handbook for Philosophy of Religion*, ed. William Wainwright (Oxford: Oxford University Press, forthcoming).

56   H. O. Mounce, *Hume's Naturalism* (London: Routledge, 1999), p. 139, n. 2.

57   Nicholas Wolterstorff, *Thomas Reid and the Story of Epistemology* (Cambridge: Cambridge University Press, 2001), p. 243.

58   Ibid., p. 242.

59   See Peter Winch, 'The Role of Suggestion in Thomas Reid's Theory of Perception', *Philosophical Quarterly*, 1953, for related criticisms.

60   *Investigations* I: 498.

61   Henry Le Roy Finch, 'Wittgenstein's Last Word: Ordinary Certainty', *International Philosophical Quarterly*, vol. 15, 1975, pp. 394–5.

62   Leyvraz, 'Logic and Experience in Wittgenstein's Later Work', p. 267.

63   Winch, 'Judgement: Propositions and Practices', p. 195.

64   McGinn, *Sense and Certainty*, p. 141.

65   I cannot do justice, in the present context, to either the arguments of those I see as espousing a kind of romanticism, or to my criticisms of them in relation to Wittgenstein's and Rhees's work. For my criticisms of Stanley Cavell's *The Claim of Reason* (Oxford: Oxford University Press, 1979), see 'Cavell and the Limits of Acknowledgement' in my *Philosophy's Cool Place* (Ithaca, NY: Cornell University Press, 1999). Cavell's influence takes various forms. See Cora Diamond, 'Losing Your Concepts' in *Ethics*, January, 1988. For my criticisms see 'Philosophy and the Heterogeneity of the Human' in *Interventions in Ethics* (Basingstoke and New York: Macmillan and State University of New York Press, 1992); Richard Fleming, *The State of Philosophy* (Lewisburg, PA: Bucknell University Press). For my review see *Philosophical Investigations*, vol. 17, no. 2, 1994; Stephen Mulhall and Stanley Cavell, *Philosophy's Recounting of the Ordinary* (Oxford: Clarendon Press, 1994). For my review see *Philosophical Investigations*, vol. 19, no. 1, 1996; Timothy Gould, *Hearing Things* (Chicago: University of Chicago Press, 1998). For my review see *Philosophical Investigations*, vol. 22, no. 4, 1999); Richard Eldridge, *Leading a Human Life: Wittgenstein, Intentionality and Romanticism* (Chicago: University of Chicago Press, 1997). For my criticism see 'Winch and Romanticism', *Philosophy*, vol. 77, 2002.

66   Churchill, 'Wittgenstein: The Certainty of Worldpictures', p. 47.

67   Ibid, pp. 47–8.

68 Apart from *Wittgenstein and the Possibility of Discourse* and *On Religion and Philosophy*, see Rhees's *Moral Questions*, ed. D. Z. Phillips (Basingstoke and New York: Macmillan and St Martin's Press, 1999) and Rhees's political and social essays in *Without Answers* (London: Routledge, 1970).
69 Peter Winch, 'Doing Justice or Giving the Devil his Due' in *Can Religion Be Explained Away?*, ed. D. Z. Phillips (Basingstoke and New York: Macmillan and St Martin's Press, 1996), p. 173.

INDEX

INDEX